D1031838

Gunman's Territory

Also by the author:

Poems of a High School Student
Jack Staton's Christmas
Anchors of Gold and Other Poems
The Law of the Primitive

Gunman's Territory

by Elmer LeRoy Baker

The Naylor Company
Book Publishers of the Southwest
San Antonio, Texas

Dedication

In memory of Cassie Virginia Burris-Hutchins and John Andrew Hutchins; and Maud Mitchell McCallie-Baker and Thomas Kelly Baker — pioneers of the Chickasaw Nation and Southern Oklahoma — who were aware of many of the events in this book as they occurred.

To them, this book is dedicated; also, with reverence to the memory of James Robert (Bob) Hutchins, whose outstanding career as a frontier officer inspired it all.

Contents

List of Illustrations   ix
Acknowledgements   xi
Introduction   xiii

Red-Topped Boots and Silver Spurs   1
A Bear, a Snake, and a Gunfight   8
The Handy Stranger   15
Code of the Colt   18
A Real Stampede   22
Bob Hutchins Leaves the Spur   28
Home Again and Gone   33
Little Crow—the Spy   38
The Case of Dead Man's Cave   48
The BoB H Brand   60
Fired   64
A Gunfight and a New Resolve   71
Riding Posseman   76
The "Hanging" Judge and His Court   83
The Prince of Hangmen   92
Robin Hood of the Boston Mountains   100
Belle Starr—Friend of Friend and Foe   108
The Courtship   116
Belle Starr's Avenger   123
The Dalton Boys Come Calling   138
The Chicken Peddler   143
He is Dead Over There   148
The Big Fight   156
Handcuffs and Code of Honor   171
Al Jennings—the Outlaw Imitator   174
An Ivory-Handled Mountain Belle   185
Triangle Trap at Hell Hole   193

Stand Off at Buckhorn   201
The Checker Checked   212
Honor Versus Honest Men   220
Bert Casey—As Tough as Any Outlaw   225
Mill Creek Melody   233
The Nickel Hill Old Settlers Picnic   239
The Keystone Becomes the Capstone   242
Novel Schemes and Schemers   248
Dealers: Past and Present   261
The Little Blue Goose   265
Close to the Limit   270
Hutchins Takes a Tip   273
State Seal Larceny   278
Hell in Ardmore   288
The Three Sleuths   296
Six-Shooter Man   300
The Bold Evasion   311
Guard on the Border   322
Trail's End   327
The Fifty Years Record   334
Bibliography   336

Illustrations

Picture section between pages xvi and 1

Page 1   James Robert (Bob) Hutchins, about thirty years of age.

Page 2   Bob Hutchins while serving as a guard on the Mexican border.

Bob Hutchins under the Pecos High Bridge on the Mexican border.

Page 3   Belle Starr (Myra Belle Shirley) about eighteen years old. This is the earliest known photograph of her.

Lou Bowers, the outlaw woman who put a bullet in Bob Hutchins' hip. He carried it to his grave.

Page 4   The main cabin room of Belle Starr's home in Younger's Bend.

The homestead of Belle Starr in Younger's Bend in 1888.

Page 5   The bone-handled "Belle Starr" six-shooter and five cartridges. Bob Hutchins' 1910 census badge.

The .45 Belle Starr was wearing when killed. Hutchins' boots, holster, hat, and census badge.

Page 6   Belle Starr's tomb in the old yard, now overgrown with brush and weeds where her cabin once stood.

Bob Hutchins, chief of police of Ardmore, and officers destroying a shipment of whiskey in November, 1916.

Page 7   Buck Garrett, right, and Bud Ballew, left, famous officers of Southern Oklahoma after 1900.

Grave of James Robert (Bob) Hutchins in Rose Hill Cemetery on south edge of Ardmore.

Page 8   James Robert (Bob) Hutchins, age seventy-nine, taken in 1950.

Acknowledgements

The author wishes to take this space to enumerate and publicly thank the following persons who contributed assistance in some way; with facts, references, the loan of photographs, and other favors helpful in the writing of this biographical history.

Mr. Ben F. Earnheart, photographer, Hugo, Oklahoma.

Mrs. Pearl Hutchins-Eaves, deceased, Ardmore, Oklahoma.

Mr. Arthur Hutchins, Gene Autry, Oklahoma.

Mrs. Essa Hutchins-Smith, deceased, Los Angeles, California.

Mr. George Norris, retired reporter for *The Daily Ardmoreite* and author, now deceased, Ardmore, Oklahoma.

Mrs. Ethel Rockett, Staff Writer, *The Daily Ardmoreite*, Ardmore, Oklahoma.

Mr. Floyd Randolph, former Sheriff of Carter County, Ardmore, Oklahoma.

Mr. Cecil Crosby, former Deputy Sheriff of Carter County, Gene Autry, Oklahoma.

Mr. J. B. Ponder, Proprietor of The Westward Motel, Ardmore, Oklahoma.

Mr. Ancel Graham, Carter County Court Clerk, Ardmore, Oklahoma.

Mr. Shelby E. Priddy, retired pioneer merchant, Ardmore, Oklahoma.

Mrs. Blanch Priddy-Lee and Mr. Guy Lee, Ardmore, Oklahoma.

Mrs. Ross Pendergraft, Manager of Southwestern Newspapers, Ft. Smith, Arkansas.

Miss Muriel H. Wright, Editor of *The Chronicles of Oklahoma*, Oklahoma City, Oklahoma.

Mrs. C. E. Cook, Curator of Oklahoma Historical Society, Oklahoma City, Oklahoma.

Professor Foster-Harris, Oklahoma University, Norman, Oklahoma.

Dr. Walter Stanley Campbell, deceased, Oklahoma University, Norman, Oklahoma.

Mr. Fadjo Cravens, Fort Smith, Arkansas.

Professor Robert W. Frazier, History, Southeastern State College, Durant, Oklahoma, retired.

Professor Minnie Mitchell Baker, Professor of Art and Department Director, Southeastern State College, Durant, Oklahoma, retired.

Mr. Hugh H. Collum, Pottawatomie County Attorney, Shawnee, Oklahoma.

Mr. James B. Rhoads, Chief of Diplomatic, Legal and Fiscal Branch, General Services Administration, Washington, D.C.

Mrs. Lois Longino, Ardmore, Oklahoma.

Introduction

James Robert Hutchins' fifty year career as a frontier United States Deputy Marshal of the Indian Territory and a peace officer in various capacities in Oklahoma and the Southwest took place during a critical period in American history — the westward advancement of the white men and the defeat of the last great efforts of the native Indians.

Driven by the white men's greed and United States government policies, the Indians known as the Five Civilized Tribes sought to set up a civilization around which the land-hungry hordes of migrating white settlers might swarm past, leaving them in a sort of *bayou* — a Choctaw Indian word that means backwater from an onrushing stream.

But this was not to be the destiny of the Americans, who were totally absorbed and vanquished by the white race in less than five hundred years.

Bob Hutchins began writing early in his career about his own and his fellow officers' experiences with the outlaws and other miscreants against whom they struggled. Most of his exploits occurred in the exact order in which they are here described, except for a few which have been fitted into place as accurately as possible.

The dialogue in these chapters is often reproduced exactly as he set down the spoken words still vivid in his mind. In other cases, they are conjecture in an attempt to convey the thoughts and facts, according to the individual situations and the personalities involved.

In many instances, pages of his manuscript have been followed with little or no editing.

I have been fortunate in my endeavors to have not only the actual written memoirs of Mr. Hutchins, but also the privilege of knowing him personally from the time I was a young newsboy in Ardmore, Oklahoma, and he was chief of police of my native town. We planned this book together four years before Mr. Hutchins died, and tentatively outlined fifty chapters. Then I expanded the material to sixty-five chapters, but for reasons of expedient economy, some chapters and much out of print and unpublished history of early Oklahoma had to be deleted. The chapters left out, incidentally, were those in which Mr. Htuchins figured little.

I have not only affidavits to certain aspects of this book, but an affidavit, signed by Mr. Hutchins and notarized, attesting to this book, completed as we planned. We made every effort to ascertain that these chronicles would be historically correct. The first fourteen chapters were produced and approved by him. Eight short, published stories were also approved by him. Some of them were published before and some after his death.

For a few years after that, this work lay dormant while I pursued my own career of teaching school, and served three years and seven months as undersheriff of Carter County, Oklahoma. The Hutchins biography, however, was dormant only in the actual completion of this book, itself. At various intervals, I turned out short stories from Hutchins' manuscripts and my interviews with him. These have been incorporated as chapters in this book.

During the last twenty years of Mr. Hutchins' career, he was employed by railroad companies and the United States government to enforce the law on the Mexican border. The final seventeen years of his career were spent as inspector and guard on the international high bridge across the mouth of the Pecos River. He was employed by the Southern Pacific Railroad Company, in cooperation with the federal government. His responsibility was to make constant daily inspections of the bridge and to discourage smugglers, *wetbacks*, and other criminals between the two countries on both sides of the border. During his leisure hours not spent in fishing, Mr. Hutchins pecked out unrecorded earlier events of his career on an old portable typewriter, and wrote others by hand. Some of the pages of his handwritten manuscripts are yellow with age.

I have checked the Hutchins manuscripts against every source of information available. I have gone to considerable trouble to investigate some of the subjects, and to find photographs. In most cases, what Mr. Hutchins had written was accurate. In some instances, I have made his versions correspond with what I found to be historical facts and dates. But in a few important cases, it was simply a matter of choosing between his narrative and that of another human being. After considering the conflicting material carefully, I chose Mr. Hutchins' version; for this is *his* biography.

But the primary reason for my decision in these rare cases was the consideration that *Mr. Hutchins was the last of the great frontier deputy marshals of Oklahoma to die.* He outlived all the men with whom he rode and, also, the outlaws they arrested who served their sentences in the penitentiary and died natural deaths.

Mr. Hutchins knew he had but a few more years to live. He knew there was nothing to gain by disguising the truth, or apologizing for it. I knew Mr. Hutchins well as a friend. He was honest and morally good. He endeavored always to do good, even for those few who hated him. He was fearless and stubborn with the truth.

He had penetrating insight into a man's character and dependability. He had steel-grey eyes that arrested your attention and held you in focus about a controversy — just as his unwavering six-shooter held many outlaws and other types of lawless men, and discouraged them from their rash activities.

I am humbly grateful and proud to have been chosen and trusted by him as his biographer. My deepest regret is that circumstances prevented completion and publication of this book before his death, April 29, 1951.

Elmer LeRoy Baker

James Robert (Bob) Hutchins, about thirty years of age.

Bob Hutchins under the Pecos High Bridge on the Mexican Border.

Bob Hutchins while serving as a guard on the Mexican Border.

Lou Bowers, the outlaw woman who put a bullet in Bob Hutchins' hip. He carried it to his grave.

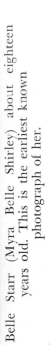

Belle Starr (Myra Belle Shirley) about eighteen years old. This is the earliest known photograph of her.

The main room of Belle Starr's home in Younger's Bend.

The homestead of Belle Starr in Younger's Bend in 1888.

The bone-handled "Belle Starr" six-shooter and five cartridges. Bob Hutchins' 1910 census badge.

The .45 Belle Starr was wearing when killed. Hutchins' boots, holster, hat, and census badge.

Belle Starr's tomb in the old yard, now overgrown with brush and weeds, where her cabin once stood.

Bob Hutchins, chief of police of Ardmore, and officers destroying a shipment of whiskey in November, 1916.

Buck Garrett, right, and Bud Ballew, left, famous officers of Southern
Oklahoma after 1900.

Grave of James Robert (Bob) Hutchins in Rose Hill Cemetery on south
edge of Ardmore.

James Robert (Bob) Hutchins, age seventy-nine, taken in 1950.

Red-Topped Boots
and Silver Spurs

The small boy, hardly seven years old, listened with round eyes to the glowing tales John R. Hall was spinning about the Spur Ranch in West Texas.

"You ought to go home with me, Kid," the big man said persuasively: "That's where your pa used to ride and rope and shoot before he met your ma. He was a good hand, too!"

The Spur boss smiled down into the boy's grey eyes. "But you'll make a better hand, I'll bet!"

The cowman looked off into space as the boy waited breathlessly for his next words. Young James Robert Hutchins had been captivated for two days by the tales told by his father's big-hearted friend.

The far-away look went out of Hall's eyes now, as they returned to rest kindly on the lad again.

"Yep!" he boomed, "you'll be tall and slim — taller than your pa, for he's a little man. I reckon you'll get your tallness from your ma's Injun blood. You'll be tough and wiry as a cactus, like your pa.

1

"I'll teach you to ride and rope and shoot with the best of them! You ought to make the best cowpoke in all of Texas!"

"John Hall!" Cassie Hutchins chided. She stood erect in the bedroom doorway, confronting him. Her chin was poised and her grey eyes flashed. "Will you stop talking to this child? He's too young to go dilly-dallying away from home with you!"

"Why, Cassie!" Hall was crestfallen as he turned his blue eyes pleadingly on her.

She glared at him steadily and his hair appeared to grow redder and his six-foot frame seemed to shrink a little under her gaze. Cassie's one-eighth Chickasaw Indian blood was just enough to control her Irish spirit and regulate her temper. She was a handsome woman.

"It's just what the kid needs, Cassie," Hall insisted. "Good, clean outdoor living and cattle savvy. It'll make a real man out of him."

He turned to John A. Hutchins for support. "It'll make a real Texan out him, won't it John A.?"

Hutchins cleared his throat and glanced briefly at his wife. "Don't know as it will harm him none," he said, uncomfortably aware of Cassie's unwavering gaze. "I reckon he'll be in good hands. I was."

"There, Cassie!" John Hall exclaimed triumphantly. "That kid is your eldest at seven. You have three more under foot around here. I'll do right by the boy, Ma'am. I'm powerful lonesome out there."

Cassie Virginia Ann Hutchins did not like the idea of her fledgling leaving the nest this early. She knew John Hall would be devoted to her young son. But that was another thing. He was a single man — a bachelor. There would be no woman at the Spur Ranch. Just a lot of rough cowboys! Only her knowledge of Hall's good, moral sense and conduct could relieve her fears on that point.

Would Bob ever really know her the way a son should always remember his mother? In these seven short years, how much had she schooled into him to be of lasting value to his life and his memory? And the boy's father? He did not seem to realize James Robert might return a stranger with no real attachment to his family and their home!

2

What did men know about such things? Growing up was so important to her — and it seemed a matter so minor to him! Men like John Hall and John A. suddenly wanted a boy to jump into a man's boots and be competent to rough it out with grown men.

John Hall would teach Sonny Boy good things, she knew, but he would also spoil him unbearably .

Little Bob Hutchins was closely watching the expressions on their faces. He seemed to sense what his mother was thinking. He loved her and he was reluctant to leave her; but that was where he stopped thinking logically. John Hall had fired his imagination. Bob saw himself booted and spurred, riding like the wind across the range on a fine-spirited horse, on a silver mounted saddle. He was dressed flashily, as he had once seen cowboys dressed at a rodeo, and his horse was a fine, red sorrel.

"Shucks, Mom!" he said stoutly. "I'll come ridin' back here on a good hoss, with red-topped boots, silver spurs and a silver mounted saddle!"

John A. and John Hall laughed at the earnest expression on the boy's face; and Cassie's worried look turned into a fond smile.

"I'll be the best cowboy in Texas!" he assured her, encouraged by her smile. "You'll be awful proud you let me go, Mom!"

"Sure she will!" John Hall echoed.

But the aspiring boy had a practical as well as an imaginative mind. He was not overlooking any bets. If this red-headed bene-factor wanted to take him on so badly, he ought to be willing to stake him to a few things he had to have for the new life.

"Can I have some red-topped boots and silver spurs, Uncle John?" he asked eagerly.

"The best we can find in Austin!" John Hall promptly agreed.

"Oh, Mom!" Bob cried out his joy and looked at her with wonder. "Let me go. I wanta go!"

Eagerly, he caught her cold hand in his own hands, which were warm and impulsive with anticipation. "I'll be back!" Then, to reassure her, he added, "I'll be good, too, Mom!"

Out of the corner of his eye, he saw his father nod gravely, and his mother said in a forced, gay voice, "All right, Sonny

Boy! But please — please — " Her voice faltered. "Come back to us soon, Sonny Boy! Don't stay away too long!"

Bob laughed with delight. But only John Hall and his father laughed with him. The two men hustled him off to town, where his red-topped, brass-toed boots were waiting at the boot shop. They searched for silver-plated spurs to fit him, and John Hall found him a little Stetson and threw it in for good measure.

"I've already got a saddle and pony waitin' for you at the Spur," John Hall told him laughingly. "Just fit you to a T!"

The Spur boss had come to Austin to visit Dr. Waters, his uncle. Hall was a good persuader. He talked his cousin, Clay Waters, into giving up his little ranch in Travis County to come along with him as a range boss for the Spur Ranch, which was owned by the Espuela Cattle Company, whose main office was in Fort Worth.

After talking Clay Waters into selling him his four hundred head of prime heifers and taking the range boss job, they went to Fort Worth to cinch the deal. There John Hall did some more persuading with C. R. Brittain, the manager. Knowing his Spur boss to be honest and a shrewd judge of cattle and men, Brittain unhesitatingly okayed the deal. Hall found himself with a new range boss, four hundred head of prime cattle and a small boy to move west over the long trail.

He bought a covered wagon, a span of mules, a camping outfit, and hired a Negro cook nicknamed Rabbit. He had tried to hire John A. Hutchins to help drive the herd to the Spur, for in his opinion a better cowpoke than Hutchins never saddled a horse or threw a rope on a steer. When he failed to hire Hutchins, the Spur boss offered to move Cassie and the kids to the Spur, if John A. would accept the job as foreman, but she would not agree to either offer. This made Hall more surprised when she finally consented for young Bob to go.

It was a proud, young cowboy who said good-bye to his mother and father. He put on the boots, spurs, Stetson and .41 calibre six-shooter with a belt and scabbard and climbed into the wagon beside Rabbit.

"Be a good boy, Sonny Boy," his father told him quietly, but farewell was not that easy for Cassie Hutchins. She managed to control herself from open sentimental weeping. She

4

wanted to send her son away with a smile. But her eyes were dark and troubled as she held him close.

"God bless you, Sonny Boy!" she said in a voice that almost broke. She held him away from her then and looked into his clear, grey eyes. "Don't forget us at home, Sonny Boy — and — and come back soon to your mother!"

The sadness of the parting was soon forgotten as they began the first stage of their long journey westward.

"It will be a long old trip, Kid!" the cowman said, "But we are on our way. I'll give you a chance to see how big Texas is! There will be lots to see, and the farther west we go, the bigger the feeling will grow on you. Just like the country — big and free!"

"Will we see Injuns, Uncle John?"

"Can't tell, but if we do, I sure hope they're friendly ones. I'd guess that they are all back in the Indian Territory right now."

"Shucks!" Bob declared indignantly. "I wanta see Injuns in their war paint and feathers. I ain't scared of 'em!"

"Well now, that's right brave of you, Kid. But always remember never to underestimate an Injun. And don't go 'round pullin' blazers on 'em. We got them about tamed enough to accept us white folks in their country. Ever' time a little trouble flares up, the soldiers or the rangers find out that some fool white man has done somethin' to rouse them!"

"I thought Injuns try to scalp all white people, Uncle John," Bob said frankly.

"I know," Hall replied. "That's because you've heard too much of the white man's side and not enough of the red man's, I reckon. An Injun is generally a good friend, if he likes you, and they'll all usually like you if you treat 'em fair."

"Do you have any Injun friends, Uncle John?"

A smile spread over the cowman's face. "I have you, Kid!"

"Shucks! I ain't but a little part Injun! Besides, the Chickasaws have been livin' like white people for a long, long time, Mom says. She learned me how to speak some Chickasaw!"

"Well, pardner, I have got a few Injun friends, I reckon,"

5

Hall admitted. "I wish I had a couple I know at the Spur with me now. I could use 'em for trackin'."

"Trackin'?"

"Yep," the cowman said sharply. "Trackin' or trailin'! I could use 'em when cattle stray into the badlands, and other times to track down cow thieves and hoss thieves. You can't beat an Injun for that. They see ever' little thing. They savvy signs in trackin' just like you know the buttons on your shirt."

"Gee!" Bob exclaimed. "I'd like to learn to trail like that."

"You will," Hall nodded. "You'll learn that and a lot more. You won't get much book-learnin' on the Spur, Kid, but you'll learn range country and cowpoke chores pretty smart. And what's more important, you'll learn to be a man — *an honest-to-God man!*"

His big hand dropped affectionately on the boy's shoulder. "I'm puttin' a lot of store in you, boy," he said gravely. John Hall looked gently into the boy's eyes now and reassured himself. He sighed. "You're like your pa, Kid. You got guts and self-control. You got the sense and good graces of your ma. I hope you'll always do the right thing by everybody."

The boy frowned and considered this. "Why shouldn't I, Uncle John?" he asked. "I don't want no trouble with anybody. I want to be friends with people and treat them like I want them to treat me!"

John Hall smiled. "That's Cassie's teachin' — God bless her — straight from the Bible!" he announced. "Your mother is a good woman, Kid. They don't live any better. Don't you ever forget that. It was pretty selfish of me to get your pa to help me lure you away from her like I did. Your father and me talked it over, and we thought —"

He broke off with a half-uttered oath, deciding he was talking too much. His hand gripped Bob's shoulder till it hurt, but he said nothing. He pressed his lips together tightly and endured the pain.

The Spur boss suddenly realized the power in his grip and relaxed his fingers. He smiled at Bob's stoic self-control. "I'm sorry, Kid!"

A smile spread over his broad, rugged features. "We'll make it up to her some day, won't we?"

The boy looked up into the face of his benefactor with open frankness. "I'll always love my mother," he said solemnly. "I'll always do right by her. Some day, I want to do something real nice for her!" His grey eyes were glowing proudly now.

Hall's blue eyes misted slightly. "Sure you do," he agreed gently, "and I want to help you, too."

A Bear, a Snake
and a Gunfight

Days passed and the smell of spring was in the Texas air. The strong winds uprooted the sunburned grass and tumbleweeds and sent them rolling in flurries over the undulating plains. Then came the spring rains, hard and drenching. At night, Bob loved to poke his head out from under the wagon cover and watch the slickered cowboys keep the herd milling in a circle to avoid a stampede. Often, lightning cut a beautiful, but terrifying zigzag across a bramble of longhorns.

Bob saw all this with open wonder. Everything exciting fascinated him. When these quick storms had ended and the moon was shining again, he could hear the night riders singing their plaintive trail songs over the drowsy lowing of the cattle. From a lone butte or hilltop, a coyote's sharp, staccato cry would often pierce the dense night air. Bob slept in the wagon, warm and dry in his bed, and wondering what the next morning would bring.

The herd progressed slowly and tortuously at an average rate of fifteen miles each day. All the cowboys took an interest in "the Kid." After joking and bantering with him, they would spend serious hours telling him stories and earnestly showing him tricks with a six-gun, a rope and a horse. Watching him imitate their tricks with rope and six-gun, they realized he had sharp, quick eyes and swift, steady hands. They laughed and bragged about him, and the boy worked harder than ever to please them.

They crossed several small creeks and the San Saba River without mishap. They were swinging in a northwestern course that would bring them back to the Colorado again. This had been the wild, untamed land of the Comanche raids only a few short years before, where Mackenzie's Fourth Cavalry had been hard pressed to protect the sparsely settled white families.

Through this region, outlaws still threaded their ways between Dodge City and San Antonio. Judge Six-gun Colt was about all the law there was, since the soldiers had gone. Bob Hutchins heard the cowpokes talk about it often, but despite hardships and annoyances, he loved every mile of the journey thus far.

Itinerant riders sometimes fell in with them for a night or two or three days. John Hall made them welcome in the established Texas fashion. They were glad of the chance to eat Jim Tate's chow. They willingly rode herd for their board and keep as did the regular hands.

Bob Hutchins was quick to pick up cowpoke lingo. He was the most popular, most pampered member of the lash-up. At their bidding, he rode in the saddle with first one and then another of the men. Each day, he learned more about the lariat, the six-shooter and the cowhorse.

One night, a bear prowled the camp and wreaked havoc with the grub supplies before the alarm was out. She fled from the assault of angry six-guns. The next morning, Lem Cates set off on her trail. Three hours later, he rode into camp, grinning broadly.

"I got that she-critter all roped and hog-tied fancy," he declared.

"Where?" John Hall asked.

"Down the crick, in a cedar brake." Cates pointed at a dense thicket within sight of the camp. "She's stubborn as hell! Some of the boys better come and help me drive her in."

J. D. Stallcup, Jim Irkson and Slim Woods rode off with Cates.

An hour later, they came into camp driving and dragging the harassed and weary marauder. Two of them had their lariats on her, and they tied each of these to a cottonwood tree. The bear gave up fighting the ropes and settled back on her haunches, growling angrily. Her little, bloodshot eyes darted from one to another of her two-legged tormentors.

She was the first bear Bob had ever seen. He walked around her and looked her over with avid interest. Dick Fowler suddenly got the idea of wrestling with the bear, and boldly suggested that they draw straws for the privilege.

Nine men, including Jim Tate, the Negro cook nicknamed Rabbit, took part in three drawings and six of them were soon eliminated. The three who had drawn the short straws in the first drawings now competed for the last time. Rabbit drew the unlucky straw. The others laughed at his stricken expression. Rabbit was a husky, burly fellow, about twenty-five years old. John Hall loaned him his chaps and he wore a heavy buckskin coat for further protection. One of the lariats was flipped off the bear to allow freedom for wrestling as Rabbit advanced warily upon her. Taunting the bear with scathing insults, Rabbit circled her cautiously.

"Jest stay right dere, you ole grub-robber," he warned. He decided that the bear was afraid of him when she tried to escape, until she discovered one lariat still held fast to a tree.

"Dat's right," Rabbit boasted. "Run, you she-debil. When I gits hold of you, yore fur am sho' gwine ter fly!"

"Yes, suh!" Johnny DeWitt aped him. "You sho' goin' ter lose all yore hide, Missus Bear! Rabbit sho' is hankerin' after it!" He laughed fitfully. "Wait jest a minute, Missus Bear. Don't you go and run off!"

This set up a barrage of taunts and jeers. Some cheered for the Negro and some for the bear.

Rabbit grew bolder when the bear kept retreating in a circle. He closed in cautiously and the bear suddenly realized something sinister was going on. Whirling, she flung herself at Rabbit so quickly that he let out a screech as they went down in a tussle.

They rolled and boxed and bit and scratched and growled

10

and yelped. Rabbit fought only to get loose from the bear's tight hug.

"Lord! Lord!" he moaned. "Help me turn this b'ar loose!"

"Git 'er hide, Rabbit!" Johnny DeWitt cried out. "Git out yore old Bowie knife and scalp her good!"

The cowboys did not recognize any immediate danger. They laughed and whooped their encouragements. Little Bob Hutchins looked on, tense and fearful.

When Rabbit's buckskin jacket ripped under the bear's teeth and claws, he cried out, "She's killin' our cook, Uncle John. That old bear's eat our grub and now she's killin' our cook!"

Clay Waters rushed in then and viciously kicked at the bear's head. When this failed to deter the snarling beast, he raked her brutally with boot and spur. This made her roar and attack Rabbit even more furiously. Now it was clear to all that the poor Negro was in a desperate fix. Clay's hand streaked to his holster and his gun roared twice. The bear slumped with two bullets in her great head. Rabbit rolled free and scampered to his feet, breathing hard. His mouth was twitching and his eyes rolled till the whites gleamed in the morning sun. He was too stunned to utter a single word; but now he began moaning at the thrashing and jerking bear in her last death agonies.

"We will have to skin that bear," Hall said. "It's about all the meat we'll have until we decide to kill another steer. She sure played the devil with our rations."

Colorado City was about ninety miles away, and Abilene was even farther. Neither was on the trail to the Spur Ranch. John Hall decided to send Dick Fowler and Slim Woods to Colorado City to bring back a new supply of provisions in the wagon.

"Make it steady and fast," Hall told them, "but don't crowd them mules too much. You better pick up some oats, too, if you can. They will be needin' them for these extra miles."

The camp settled down for a week's wait. It would give cattle and horses a chance to rest and catch up on their grazing. An extra wagon sheet was thrown over a pole frame for shelter from spring rains. Rabbit cooked bear steaks until they all grew tired of them. To break the monotony, some of the men caught some fish and killed some ducks.

11

The cattle and horses fattened in the brakes, and the men lounged around with little to do but play cards and joke. Someone got careless with his talk and Rabbit found out that he had been framed to fight the bear. He dropped his happy-go-lucky attitude and grew sullen and morose. He did not share the fun and enthusiasm of their jokes anymore. Bob Hutchins noticed he even grew short with him.

Rabbit got careless with his cooking after that, and spent more time sleeping every day. The men began to quarrel among themselves. On the fifth day, it led to a tragic end.

John Hall took Bob out for a jaunt about the camp. Jogging along aimlessly, his horse skittered and jumped. Something slithered in the grass and halted with a rattling hiss. Hall dismounted and lifted Bob to the ground beside him.

"There he is," said the Spur boss. "He's a whopper of a rattler! See?"

"Gee, yes!" Bob exclaimed as he watched the big rattlesnake writhe his coils and weave his head in a fascinating rhythm. "I'll shoot his old head off, Uncle John!"

The boy brought out the .41 calibre Colt the Spur boss had given him. Hall watched with mingled feelings of amusement and amazement as Bob thumbed back the hammer with both thumbs.

"Easy now, Kid!" he coached softly. "Hold her steady in both hands. Swing her slowly down. When that sidewinder's head pops into yore sights, pull the trigger."

Bob took a deep breath and followed instructions carefully. The Colt roared and Hall gasped his astonishment. The snake lay thrashing, with its head shot off entirely.

"Kid, you shore do learn fast," he declared. "I never thought you could've done it!"

Hall insisted on taking the snake into camp to show the rest of the fellows, but his horse shied nervously away and refused to carry the rattlesnake.

"It's just a little way to camp," Hall said. "Here, Kid, up you go in the saddle! I'll walk with it. I wouldn't miss showin' this snake to the boys for anything!"

When they arrived in camp with Hall dragging the snake, the men quit their card game and gathered around.

"You shore shot his head off smooth!" Clay Waters declared.

12

"I didn't shoot it," Hall told them, grinning broadly. "We got a new gunman amongst us!"

"I'll be damned!" Lem Cates said.

Ed Raines and Jim Irkson were counting the rattlers.

"Thirteen!" Ed exclaimed. "That's shore unlucky!"

"Unlucky for the snake, anyhow!" Jim Irkson laughed.

John Hall spotted Rabbit fast asleep on his bedroll under a tree. A mischievous look came into his blue eyes. The other men winked knowingly and grinned broadly. Striding over, the Spur boss laid the six-foot snake down beside the Negro cook. All the men sat down to their cards again as they waited.

After awhile, Rabbit opened his eyes, saw the huge snake, snorted, yelled and took off like a crazed steer. The loud guffaws from the men stopped him short. He came back and cautiously inspected the snake. When he saw the head had been blown away, he turned with a scowl and demanded, "Who done dis tuh Rabbit?"

Nobody answered.

"Dat's th' last straw!" he declared. "Fust a b'ar. Now a rattlesnake!" He glared at John Hall. "You all hire yo'self a new cook, Mistah Hall. I wants my pay. I'm through with dis crazy outfit!"

"Now hold on, Rabbit!" Hall argued. "I put that snake there. It was all in fun."

"Ah don't lak that kind o' fun," Rabbit declared. "Ah's tired o' all dis open country we're comin' to, nohow. Ah's gwine back to Austin."

"You're just mad now, Rabbit," Hall said gently. "You stay on with us. I'll see no more pranks are pulled on you. You're a good cook when you want to be. We'll need you at the Spur."

But Rabbit stubbornly insisted on his wages, and the more Hall tried to reason with him the more determined he grew. Hall was willing to give him his wages and even a bonus, but he argued that he had no horse and saddle to spare Rabbit for loan or money to ride back to Austin. Hall tried to explain to the Negro the odds against setting out on foot.

Rabbit lost his head completely. He began cursing and raving at John Hall and everyone else who tried to placate him. Not until now did they realize how seriously Rabbit had

13

nursed his grudge about the bear deal. His fear of snakes had heaped fuel on his flaming fury.

Finally, Clay Waters said, "That's enough from you, Rabbit!" His voice was sharp-edged with warning.

But Rabbit was determined to have the last word. He called Clay *no good white trash,* which even then, several years after the Civil War, were "fighting words."

"Now get over there to the fire and start supper," Clay ordered. He advanced upon Rabbit as he spoke. "You will get over this, when you've had time to think it over. Then we won't have any more trouble."

The Negro cook stopped backing up, thrust his hand under his coat and pulled out a six-gun. Clay Waters stopped short, stiffened and drew. His hand came away from his holster with blurring speed, and even though Rabbit's gun was trained on him, Clay fired the first shot.

Rabbit staggered and rocked on his heels. His face worked convulsively while blood spread through his fingers clutching at his stomach. Then his Colt roared once and Clay's blazed twice again in sharp, quick succession. Rabbit's face was instantly transformed into a bloody blotch as he lurched forward and slapped flat on his chest with an awful thud.

Clay Waters clutched at his arm where blood was oozing through his fingers and dripping slowly to the ground. He stared silently at the crazed black man he had really liked, but had been forced to kill. The camp was deathly quiet.

Little Bob Hutchins stared in awe as the realization came over him. It ran up his back and spread through his body, making goose pimples stand out on his sensitive skin. Now he knew the real death-dealing power of a Colt. It had been quick, sharp and terrible.

Rabbit, who had told him funny stories and laughed so joyously himself, lay sprawled on the ground, a thing of dead clay, while the gleaming pool of his life's blood spread out wider around him.

"Better get the kid away, John," Clay Waters said quietly, "till we get this mess cleaned up!"

14

The Handy Stranger

The next day, the wagon returned from Colorado City. They left Rabbit buried at the foot of a big cottonwood tree, with a plain *gyp* rock as a tombstone. The lazy, fattened herd was reluctant to move on, but after some hard riding and quick hazing their sudden rebellion was quelled and the cowboys got them going on the trail again.

The horses followed, with the covered wagon bringing up the rear, temporarily driven by John Hall. He had thrown his saddle and blanket into the wagon and turned his horse loose with the remuda.

Cooking became a major problem. Rabbit's services were sorely needed. But nobody made any comments. The men took turns at cooking, and John Hall announced that the first man who complained about the chow would cook for a solid week.

On the third day, north of the Colorado, a young fellow rode into camp just after they had chosen the camping site for the night. He rode a fine, spirited horse and asked to be put up.

"We buried our cook three days back," Hall explained. "You're welcome, if you can put up with our chow."

"I can fix that," the man said pleasantly. "My name is Sam," he announced loud enough for everyone to hear. "I guess I can help you folks out a few days. Cook is my second handle."

The men all greeted this information eagerly. They assured him they didn't care what his name was, or whether he had one, if he could cook a good meal for them.

Sam not only cooked well, but he rode herd part of the time. The men admired his bay and never doubted his word that the animal was a racehorse. He looked like a thoroughbred with his long, sleek legs and tireless gait. Not a horse in their remuda could compete with him.

Sam spotted another fine looking colt in the remuda and took an instant fancy to it. "He's got racehorse blood in him or I miss my guess," Sam declared. "Where did you get him, Mr. Hall?"

"I picked him up from Clay," Hall said.

"He sure looks like something out of Indiana or Kentucky," Sam said admiringly. Every evening, he spent time petting and pampering the colt, whom he named Ben.

"Sam, I believe you are gettin' to be a fool about that colt," Hall said, "and it's plain to see he's gettin' to be a fool about you."

"Sure thing, Mr. Hall," Sam admitted. "I want to trade you out of him when our trails fork. I could make a racehorse out of him."

"Well, I won't be stubborn about it," Hall said agreeably, "seein' how you two like each other. We've got plenty more at the Spur."

Sam proved to be very handy, and popular with everyone. He showed them tricks with cards that opened their eyes wide. His horse was what the men called "educated," for Sam had taught him numerous tricks. Clay Waters would not believe Sam's horse was faster than Buckskin until they raced them for a half mile one evening.

But the stunts that really made them perk up were the things Sam could do with a six-shooter. He was, John Hall declared, the quickest and most accurate man he had ever seen in all this Judge Colt country.

Sam took a liking to Bob and spent long hours telling and

showing him things. It amazed Bob to see him pull his gun from leather.

"For quick action, Kid," he said, "always shoot from the hip in close-up fighting. Pull your Colt out smoking."

He demonstrated with a blur, a flash and a roar.

"Some gents use swivel holsters." He grinned. "Not a bad idea!"

Code of the Colt

One night, Bob sat up later than usual with John Hall and they talked about everything that struck their fancy. The others had already turned in to bed. Bob liked these quiet, private talks with John Hall. The range boss had a good enough understanding of boys to treat nothing that the boy asked indifferently.

Hall could see that the boy was maturing swiftly for a boy of his age. He had learned the whole routine of the cattle trail. His days had been spent learning about cattle, horses, six-guns and the vital tricks in handling all of them. With this basic knowledge, he had already begun to reason things out for himself. He had never once shown a single symptom of homesickness.

Hall considered this to be remarkable. The boy had braved the cold, the rain and storms without complaint. Hall decided young Bob had more of the traits of his mother's Indian heritage in him than his blood heritage indicated. Bob had seen men laugh indifferently while Jim Tate was being mauled by the fierce bear. He had, himself, shot the head off of a huge rattlesnake without flinching. He had seen Clay Waters shoot

18

poor Rabbit down in a gunfight without betraying his own fright or pity. Hall was well aware that these experiences had imprinted themselves in the lad's mind.

"Uncle John," Bob said to the big cowman tonight. "I wonder how it feels to kill a man?"

The question was so unexpected it nearly threw and hog-tied the Spur boss. It was not a question to answer lightly, he knew. The last thing Hall wanted to do was to encourage the boy to kill; but he most certainly wanted him to be prepared to defend his own life, if ever it became necessary.

"Well, Kid," he said slowly, "a good man always feels bad about killin'. Some can hardly get over it. But a bad man has no heart and no conscience. He is a ruthless killer. I never saw such a man that didn't die with his boots on. But the bad thing about some of them is they don't die soon enough. They kill too many people before they cash in their chips."

"Was Clay a wicked killer?" There was anxiety in Bob's voice. John Hall knew Bob was fond of Clay Waters and that Clay was fond of the kid. He knew, too, that despite Jim Tate's surliness, the boy had grown to like Rabbit.

Hall cleared his throat and measured his words. Here was something he hoped he could make the boy understand.

"Listen carefully, Kid," he said slowly, "and don't get any wrong ideas. Poor Rabbit's death — just like others I know about — grew out of harmless fun. None of us knew what it would lead to. We never counted on Rabbit takin' it so mad like he did."

"Then Clay didn't kill Rabbit because he was a nigger?"

"No, Kid. Clay may be a little mean, but not as bad as that. He liked Rabbit until that argument came up. I reckon Clay bein' a white man and quick with his six-shooter made Rabbit afraid of him. When poor Rabbit got scared and angry, Clay walkin' up on him got him excited. We were all surprised when Rabbit reached inside his coat for a gun. Wasn't you?"

"I sure was, Uncle John! I didn't even know he had a gun."

"I reckon none of the rest of us knew it either. Bein' a lone Negro amongst all us white folks, I guess he figgered he needed one. But Clay had only a second to act when Rabbit hauled out that hoglaig. Quick as Clay is, he got hit in his arm. He shot to save his life, Kid. He would have done the same to any man — black, white or red! You remember how Clay killed the bear to save Rabbit's life, don't you?"

"Yes, Uncle John."

There was a long silence while Hall let the boy think about it. Then Bob remarked, "Sam says when in trouble to draw your gun out smokin' and shoot snap shots from the hip."

"That's good advice," Hall admitted, "if you shoot straight. Never trust a dangerous or suspicious man, Kid, nor a liar!"

After a pause, Hall added, "I hope you never have to do it, Kid, but if the time ever comes when you are in a bad spot, don't hesitate to kill any man who is gunnin' for you. If Clay had tried to talk any more, he would have got killed! It's always too late to argue with a man whose six-shooter is already talkin'!"

They sat for a while longer, and then wordlessly went off to bed. Slim Woods' sweet, tenor voice sounded clear as a silver bell on the still night air:

> "Buffalo gals, won't yuh come out tonight?
> Come out tonight? Come out tonight?
> Buffalo gals, won't yuh come out tonight
> And dance by the light of the moon?"

Bob listened drowsily to the cowboy's song until sleep claimed his senses.

The shrill cry of a horse brought him awake with a start. Bulls were bellowing and cows and calves bawling excitedly. Hooves beat the ground in an ever increasing rumble that grew into a thunder of sound. As he groped in the dark for his boots, Bob knew it was growing into a stampede.

Men were cursing and calling to each other as they ran for their horses to join the night watchers. Bob heard their horses snort as saddles were slapped on their backs. They grunted as cinches were jerked tight recklessly. The men rode out of camp after the thundering herd at a dead run, and Bob was left alone in camp.

Soon he heard the herd circling as the pounding hooves slowed down. Then three shots barked out and the men cursed as the herd tried to break loose again. After a while, all was quiet and the men rode back into camp — all but Johnny DeWitt and Slim Woods, who still had the watch.

They were cursing whoever fired the shots that nearly started the stampede all over again.

"Who fired them shots?" John Hall demanded.

Sam rode up just as Hall spoke.

"I did," he confessed. "I just killed the mountain lion who started the stampede. He killed Ben, the colt, and was eatin' him when I found him and let him have it!"

"That was the hoss scream we heard!" John Hall exclaimed.

"His death scream," Sam said. "Come on and I'll show you the biggest mountain lion you ever saw!"

They returned directly, dragging the Mexican lion. He was a big beast, all right. Nearly as big as Ben.

Sam lamented Ben's loss. "I would have made a racehorse out of that colt for sure," he declared.

"Let's skin this customer while he's still warm and cure his hide along with the bear's," John Hall said. "Stallcup, give me a hand. We oughta have quite a collection of throw rugs by the time we reach the Spur!"

By lantern light, they skinned the lion. Soon the camp was dark, except for the moonlight filtering through the leaves of the cottonwood and sycamore trees. The last Bob Hutchins heard was Slim Wood's voice, taking up his song again:

> "Won't yuh, won't yuh, won't yuh,
> Won't yuh come out tonight?
> Come out tonight? Come out tonight?
> Won't yuh, won't yuh, won't yuh,
> Won't yuh come out tonight
> And dance by the light of the moon?"

21

A Real Stampede

Storm clouds gathered, low and threatening, as they reached the Double Mountain Fork of the Brazos.

"We'll camp on this side and cross over in the morning," John Hall decided. "Clay, you better put out a double watch to close-herd dogies and horses tonight. It shore looks like it's goin' to blow. I hope it don't turn into a tornado. I don't like the looks of them clouds."

Darkness came early because of the overcast skies. Sharp streaks of lightning split the dark heavens, lighting up the boiling, twisting clouds. Never before had Bob heard such awful crashes of thunder as the lightning played in skipping, freakish streaks from longhorn to longhorn of the herd.

Horses neighed nervously. Bulls bellowed and calves and cows bawled loudly as they milled about, restless and uneasy.

The men refused to turn in for the night, even though they had the extra tarp to cover their pallets.

"No use tryin' to sleep with a hard storm brewin'," Clay Waters said. "It's shore goin' to hit or miss us darn soon!"

The men dragged on their cigarettes and said very little.

22

Bob could see the glow of their cigarettes and their tense faces sharply profiled in the lightning flashes.

"Scared, Kid?" John Hall asked softly.

"Shucks, not yet!"

"Well, don't lose your grit," the Spur boss told him. "Stick tight to the wagon and don't lose your head!"

"All right, Uncle John."

Bob had seen the men saddle fresh horses before turning the remuda loose to graze. They were now standing by for instant action.

The wind had been rustling the leaves of the cottonwoods and mesquite for a long time. Now they began to rustle louder and the limbs creaked and groaned as the wind grew in force.

Sam came riding into camp at a gallop, yelping the alarm. "It's coming, men," he said. "She's a hard twister and she's coming like hell!"

They could hear the roar now and see the dark, spinning funnel shape bearing down upon them with a noise like the thundering of ten thousand stampeded cattle.

Clay Waters bounded into his saddle. "It's hell among the yearlings tonight!" he shouted shrilly as he spurred his horse at breakneck speed for the herd. Other men were riding off, too.

"Stay here, Kid, and sit tight in the wagon!" John Hall cried out. "If you're not safe here, you're not safe anywhere!"

For the first time, the boy detected a note of excitement in his voice. Then the Spur boss was astride his horse and gone hell-for-leather after the other riders.

Already the herd was running. The riders were yelling and shooting as they raced to head them. They charged first for the river. There at a bluff, a six-gun cracked and a man screamed. Something in that scream chilled Bob into a paralyzed silence.

The cattle and horses swerved, running together in a mixed herd. Bob got glimpses of them and two riders as they swept by, skirting the little hill and the mesquite thicket sheltering the wagon.

The wagon stood resolute, but bounced as they thundered by. The wind clutched at the canvas, which billowed and popped like a shotgun, but held. Swiftly, the funnel-shaped

23

cloud disappeared, but the rain came down in gushes. Six-shooters vainly blasted away, and even Bob knew the cattle and horses were in full stampede.

One long, shrill, agonizing cry rose above everything. Then Bob heard a voice shout, "Good God!" After a while, the loud thundering diminished to a rumbling that faded out slowly.

After a while, the flurry of rain ended and the night was dark and still. Bob waited, straining his ears for the sound of hoofbeats returning.

John Hall was the first to come back. He rode straight to the wagon. "You all right, Kid?"

"Shucks, yes," Bob replied calmly.

"I'm glad of that. The herd is scattered. It would have been worse if that tornado had hit us. Didn't miss us very much as it was. No tellin' how long it will take to round them up again. Can't tell about the losses yet, nor if all the boys are safe." The Spur boss lighted the lanterns.

"They sure did run, didn't they, Uncle John?"

"They shore did. I reckon you will remember this night a long time, Kid. You've seen a real stampede!"

One by one, the disgruntled riders straggled back. Gruffly, they swore and lamented the night's misfortunes. Finally, they had all returned but four. Then came Lem Cates slogging through the mud, leading his limping horse.

"Slim Woods is dead," he announced grimly.

"Are you shore?" John Hall asked anxiously.

"Sartin' shore!" Cates said. "Both of us hit a gully at the same time and both our hosses went down. Slim got crushed under his hoss and was dead when I crawled over to him. His hoss broke a laig. I shot him. I reckon Hardrock will be all right. He just got a bad sprain."

Bob took the news dry-eyed and silent with the rest of them. But he thought of Slim's sweet, tenor voice and knew how much the cheerful young cowboy would be missed.

They started the fire to going again, heated coffee and waited another anxious hour for Dick Fowler and Johnny De-Witt to show up. When they didn't, John Hall said, "We better look around. If they are dead, we can't do them no good, but if they're hurt or on foot, we can. Each man try to recollect

24

where you saw them last and which way they're headin'." He turned to Lem Cates. "Lem, you feel like ridin'?"

"I'm all right."

"Think you can make your way back to where Slim is?"

"I reckon," Cates said dryly, "but I can't ride this hoss, and the remuda is stampeded."

"Take mine," Hall said. "I'll stay here with the kid."

They came back at dawn, bearing two still forms face down across saddles. Clay Waters was riding behind one and Lem Cates the other.

One man groaned as they lifted him down. When the lantern light fell upon his pale face, Bob recognized Johnny DeWitt.

"He's pretty bad hurt," Clay Waters whispered huskily to John Hall. They fixed him a warm, dry pallet near the fire, against the cottonwood trunk. DeWitt lapsed into a deep coma, and they could do nothing but wait for him to regain his senses. He had been trampled by the herd and was hurt internally.

"We found him in a wash," Lem Cates remarked. "Don't know what happened to his hoss."

They laid Slim Woods out straight and folded his arms and closed his eyes and mouth for the death-set of rigor mortis. The next morning, they dug a grave on the hill above the mesquite thicket and laid him to rest.

They found where Dick Fowler and his horse had been crowded off the bluff into quicksand below. The signs were unmistakable. Some among them remembered seeing him riding at breakneck speed toward this point to turn the herd. He had not realized the bluff was there until it had been too late. They had heard him shoot and scream and shoot in a sudden blinding glare of lightning. Now, not a single trace of the rider could be seen. Both horse and rider had been completely swallowed in the treacherous sands below.

Johnny DeWitt lingered four days. John Hall and Bob watched over him while the rest of the men rounded up the scattered cattle and horses. When the search ended, twenty dogies and three horses were missing, and they knew positively that one horse and two yearlings had been killed.

Johnny DeWitt regained consciousness toward the last. He spoke of his dear old mother back in sunny Tennessee and a girl named Mary he had planned to go home to and marry. He asked John Hall to write to them.

Then he asked for Slim Woods. "I want Slim to sing me a song," he said with a wistful smile. They had to tell him what had happened to Slim.

Spotting Bob standing quietly by, DeWitt said, "Hello, Kid!"

"Hello, Johnny!" Bob's voice was husky as a lump rose in his throat.

"Sing for me, Kid — a — song — like Slim Woods taught you —" His breath was jerky now and he closed his eyes, as if waiting. Then he opened them and looked up at the boy, full of pleading. Bob's eyes blurred and he looked at John Hall uncertainly. The Spur boss nodded and Bob managed to control himself. Wetting his dry lips, he began to sing.

The words came hard at first, but when he saw the happy look in Johnny's eyes, he realized it was the last thing he could do for his friend. The boy sang softly and clearly a trail song he knew Johnny DeWitt loved.

When he finished, Johnny opened his eyes and stared straight into Bob's eyes. He opened his mouth to speak, but Bob could not make out the words. Yet he knew by the cowboy's smile that he had tried to thank him.

The sun was setting as they buried Johnny DeWitt beside Slim Woods on the low hill. On a ridge across the Brazos, a coyote howled mournfully. For a moment the boy, Bob Hutchins, saw the dark figure against the glow of western light before he was gone.

The next day, they made the crossing of Double Mountain Fork without mishap. With caution born of experience, they picked a shallow, rocky spot free of quicksand, and the herd snaked out again on the trail.

The very next morning, Sam rose and cooked breakfast, as usual. When they broke camp, he saddled his horse and lazily rolled a quirley. "Well, gents," he announced, "I'm leavin' yuh. My business lays yonder." He waved his hand toward the southeast.

The men expressed their regret openly.

"Mighty sorry to lose you, Sam," Hall told him. "You've really made us a good hand. Two hands — both cook and herder!

26

I had sort of hoped you would go on to the Spur and ride for the Espuela awhile."

"I've thought about it," Sam said, "but I have to meet some friends in Fort Worth in a few days. I've got just about time enough to get there."

"A man ought to know his own mind," Hall said. "We shore are goin' to miss you. We wish you the best of luck, Sam —"

There was a note of question in John Hall's voice. He had meant to say more, but he stopped short because he did not know the rest of the young man's name.

"The last name is Bass, Mr. Hall. Sam Bass — that's me!" Smiling at the stunned look of astonishment on everyone's faces, he vaulted into his saddle. "I've had more fun and peace with you folks than I've had in a long time!"

He asked Clay Waters to go with him, but Clay politely declined. He looked down then into Bob Hutchins' upturned face. "Kid," he said, "you'll make your mark some day. I hope it will be a proud one. So long!"

They stood watching him as he grew smaller in the distance. From a rise, he paused, twisted around and waved back. Then he was gone.

"I'll be damned!" John Hall ejaculated. "I might of guessed who he was by the tricks he pulled. But he ain't such a bad fellow after all!"

It was the only time Bob Hutchins ever saw Sam Bass, the notorious Texas outlaw. The few days he spent with them, they found out later, he had been on the dodge from rangers and other officers for hold-ups of stagecoaches, banks and railroad trains. In less than three months, he was killed at Round Rock on his twenty-seventh birthday, July 21, 1878, and was buried in the graveyard there.

Within a year, cowpunchers on the Spur were singing the ballad of Sam Bass. Bob Hutchins sang it too, with kind memories of the gay, young fellow who had showed him tricks with a six-shooter.

27

Bob Hutchins
Leaves the Spur

They crossed the Salt Fork of the Brazos the next day without any trouble. They stopped for the last time at Soldier's Mound where, just three years earlier, an army camp had been maintained under the command of Colonel Ronald Slidell Mackenzie. These temporary fortifications had been called Anderson's Fort, and had been maintained as a precaution against marauding Indians who had strayed from their reservations over in the Indian Territory.

At the western edge of the Staked Plains, the Cap Rock rose to an elevation of 2,464 feet. The tallest mountain to the north had been named Mackenzie Peak after the colonel.

Riders from the Spur Ranch met them there and, with twice the number of cowboys, they hustled the herd over the last few miles of Mackenzie Trail to the home ranch. The next week, the Spur brand was added to that of Clay Waters and the cattle and horses were turned loose on the range.

The big, rambling bunkhouse and kitchen had been built out of rough cottonwood lumber. The Spur range consisted of

28

some 500,000 acres of grazing land for nearly 100,000 head of cattle and hundreds of horses. To perform the work of this giant ranching business, some half-hundred cowpunchers, range riders and maverick branders were employed.

For several years, young Bob Hutchins stayed at the Spur. He rode the range and with the chuck wagon, and slowly became a seasoned roundup hand. Throughout this time, John Hall, Clay Waters, Lem Cates, J. D. Stallcup and the other cowboys kept a watchful eye on the boy.

John Hall saw to it that Bob kept up his lessons in reading, writing and arithmetic. He had not been at the Spur many months before he was corresponding regularly with his mother. The mail was slow, and letters from Cassie Hutchins were long intervals apart, but they kept his mother alive for him, and the boy answered every one faithfully.

Bob handled the mail for the Spur Ranch. He always liked to ride over to Doakum's Ranch to listen to range talk. But, more important, he listened to the conversations of strangers who were coming and going across the country.

Doakum's Ranch was just a store built from rough cottonwood boards. In addition to the main room of the store itself, there was a side room for storage and a back room which was Doakum's living quarters. The storekeeper was a big, six-foot, flat-footed Dutchman who weighed about two hundred pounds and talked through his nose. He was very friendly and hospitable to young Hutchins.

Doakum hauled all his supplies himself from Colorado City in Mitchell County, about ninety miles away. He owned his own huge freight wagon and three spans of mules for this purpose. He went as often as he needed to and simply locked up the store when a trip was necessary. In a few days, he returned with a new load of merchandise and business would boom again.

When a mail route was secured for this area, the Dutchman was named postmaster. At first, the mail carrier came in a cart with the mail from Colorado City every six weeks. Then he exchanged this for a two-seated hack, in order to be able to take passengers.

Every mail run usually brought a leter or two from Bob's mother, and he generally sent a few back to her. His letters from Cassie Hutchins were full of home news and love and

29

motherly advice. When a letter would fail to come on occasions, his father would write to apologize for Cassie, because she was not feeling quite up to par at the time. John A. encouraged the boy to work hard and to be a good hand for John Hall. The next letter from Cassie Hutchins would announce another member of the family, and young Bob Hutchins would breathe easily again, knowing his mother was all right, and then he would begin to wonder what his new brother or sister was like.

One day, news came that the Espuela Land and Cattle Company would soon sell out, possibly to English buyers. At this time, there were a great many travelers passing through on their way to Indian Territory. People were now able to settle there without trouble from the government or the Indians. Young Bob Hutchins heard these people talk as they stopped to replenish their supplies of tobacco, sugar, coffee, salt, or groceries in general. Sometimes, they purchased a little stock feed when it was available.

Bob also talked to men who had been in the Indian Territory, looked over the lay of things and were returning to get their families. He became convinced that it was an area he'd like to see.

In the meantime, he had received a letter from his mother that John A. had gotten itching feet again and the family was moving to Lamar County, near Paris, Texas. Rather than stay on here to take his chances with the new and foreign management, Bob decided to saddle up and ride to Lamar County and then drift over across Red River into the Choctaw Nation.

The hardest thing Bob had ever had to face was telling John Hall that he was leaving. The Spur boss was over fifty now, and troubles weighed heavily on his shoulders. With the sure knowledge that the Spur was changing ownership, the riders who had been there so many years were none too happy about it.

Hall said the real trouble was being experienced by the cowmen who had thrown in their small herds and taken stock with the Espuela Land and Cattle Company when it had first been organized by A. M. Britton and S. W. Lomax. Britton had represented the Spur as embracing 120,000 head of cattle.

Hall had tried to convince him that this figure was exaggerated. The count might have been taken at the peak of production, but severe winters, management losses, rustlings, inflated assets and accidents common to all ranges had eaten away at this figure. Just how much, he did not know. But it was obvious the buyers would insist on an actual count.

A good man had been selected. He was John Farrington, foreman for Charles Goodnight, a very popular rancher with extensive holdings north of the Spur. Farrington was plainspoken, honest and knowledgeable about the cattle business. Hall knew many of the small stockholders had put everything they owned into the Spur when it had been organized.

These were the ones he knew would come out short in the settlement; and some of these cactus-tough, honest, range-bred customers were not going to be at all happy about it.

Bob Hutchins hated to leave the Spur boss in this state; but what could he do to help even if he stayed? The problem was too big for both of them. They were only employees.

Hall was more important, of course, but it meant the end of his job as boss for the Spur. He had done as well as anyone could have done. Such shortages in big cattle operations happened often and were expected. Perhaps the Espuela had elected to sell at a bad time.

As a going away present, Hall gave the boy the big, fine red sorrel he had been riding and a red, high-backed Applehorn saddle and bridle to match. Hutchins had named the horse Star Face.

Strapping on his roll and checking his saddlebags, Hutchins turned to the redheaded Spur boss with a grin. "I came here with red-topped boots and silver spurs," he said. "Now I'm leaving with the finest red horse in the country. You've sure been a godfather to me, Uncle John. I won't ever forget you, if I live to be a hundred!"

During the past years, John Hall had poured into this boy his own virtues; generosity, honesty and strength. He had taught him not only cowboy lore, but things such as how to read and write and play the violin with fiddling skill.

Hall brushed aside his tears and the lump in Bob's throat subsided as the cowman's blue eyes twinkled. He was looking Hutchins over carefully, taking careful note of the changes that the years at the Spur had made in the lad. He was in that un-

31

gainly, awkward stage of swift growth, during which boys seem to shoot up like bean sprouts.

Bob Hutchins was now going on his thirteenth year. He was almost six feet tall and weighed only ninety-nine pounds, but already he was hard and tough and fast.

The Spur boss chuckled. "Well, Kid," he said, "you've growed sort of tall in the saddle. You're cactus bred! I reckon you'll pass. Tell Cassie I've kept my word. You're comin' home clean. God bless her!"

"Thanks, Uncle John. I'll stow that away with all the other good things you've said and done for me. If you ever come to Indian Territory, look me up. I'll be there, rememberin' you and tryin' to do something to make you right proud of all you've done for me." Bob could hardly keep the emotion from his voice.

x "If you ever need me, Uncle John, just send word. I'll come on a dead run!"

"I know you will, son! I hope I won't ever be needin' help, but I shore hope to see you again soon. Good luck!"

He thrust out his hand and Hutchins grasped it firmly. Then Clay Waters and the other boys came up to wish him well.

Smiling, Hutchins turned, vaulted into the saddle and rode off at a fast clip. Once he turned and waved back and saw a crowd of hands and hats wigwagging a last farewell.

32

Home Again
and Gone

Bob Hutchins rode leisurely to
Paris, Texas, letting Star Face
pick his own pace, for he knew he had a good horse, and intended to keep him that way.

He met other Texans on their way across Red River into
Indian Territory. "Texas seems to be spreading north," he
thought wryly, "as if it isn't big enough as it is!"

Hutchins was tempted to cross over now to look over this
Indian country, but he restrained himself because of his obliga-
tion to go home first. It had been a long time. Only his father
and mother would he know. The house would be full of brothers
and sisters who were strangers to him.

He asked around in the small town of Paris and finally found
the general store where his father traded. He learned the family
was farming about twenty-two miles southeast from there. He
bought a nice gift for his mother, candy for his unknown brothers
and sisters and rode out of town.

He arrived at the Hutchins farm around sundown, as the family was sitting down to supper. Riding into the yard, he called out loudly, "Hello!"

His father and mother came to the door. The children crowded around them. One small one clung bashfully to his mother's skirt.

"Git down, stranger!" John A. invited politely. Bob knew he had used the word "stranger" with complete sincerity. He wanted to laugh, but he felt oddly disappointed. No one recognized him.

Swinging down, he unfastened his saddlebags and faced them. He looked straight into his mother's eyes and asked gently, "Don't you know me, Cassie?"

Cassie Hutchins shrieked joyfully and ran forward to welcome her firstborn. Her Indian reserve melted away instantly.

"Sonny Boy!" she sobbed. She clutched at him hungrily, smothering his mouth with kisses, as she strained on tiptoe and pulled him down to her.

She drew back then, facing him with happy, tearful eyes. John A. gripped his hand. They were hard, rough hands, with steely toughness that Bob remembered. His father was smiling broadly, but retained the same self-control that never left him.

The children, who had heard so much about their older brother, plied him with a barrage of eager questions. Bob stopped them by handing over the sackful of candy.

Bob Hutchins stayed only three weeks with his family, working with his father in the fields. But like all cowboys, he revered the saddle and scorned the plow.

"This is not for me, Pa," he told his father. "I'm headin' for the Territory. I wish you'd pull up stakes and come along."

Bob knew that his father's cowboy instincts were against farming, but there were Cassie and the children to feed and clothe. "I've got to stay here, son, and finish this crop," he declared. "You go on ahead and if you find a likely place where I can farm and raise a few head of cattle and hosses, let me know. According to talk in Congress, Cassie ought to get a land grant from the government in the Chickasaw Nation. I think she'd like it better on that side of Red River, from the way she talks."

Cassie Hutchins hated to see Bob leave home again, but she

34

did not try to restrain him. Bob eased the parting by telling her he would not be very far off this time. "Pa promised to bring the family along when I can find a good location," he told her.

Cassie's eyes brightened. "Did he really?"

"He sure did."

"Then he's beginning to agree with me!" There was a note of triumph in her voice. "There is plenty of land there, Sonny Boy. Good land! Even if I can't prove up my Indian rights, we can buy what we need. It will be cheap. It is a fine country."

Bob Hutchins ate one more of his mother's delicious breakfasts just before sunup. Mid-morning marked his passage through the slumbering little town of Paris as he headed toward Red River. He fell in with other horsemen and listened to their talk. By the time they reached Raymond, a little settlement of mixed Choctaws and white people — now Hugo — Bob had heard so many glowing tales about the Chickasaw Nation, he was positive he should push on up there. Four days later, he rode up to the old 700 Ranch house.

Bill Washington was sitting in the yard, enjoying the cool breeze and sawing on an old fiddle. He had a brown jug near his stool, which kept him content. Supper was over and a few of the cowboys sprawled lazily on the grass as they listened to the boss make music.

Washington was playing "Horny Deer" lustily when Bob rode up and sat on his horse in silence. Nobody rose to greet him, but they were aware of his presence, he knew. When he finished the tune, Bill Washington pushed his dirty, gray hat back on his thick mop of dark hair, shrugged his broad shoulders and squinted up at Hutchins.

"Howdy, Kid!" he drawled. "Where you headed?"

"Looking for a job," Bob answered tersely.

Washington considered this for a while, as he sized the boy carefully. Finally he said, "How'd you like to have a job with me?"

"What doing?" Bob asked warily.

"Peeling mavericks."

"What's that?" Bob asked boldly, exposing his ignorance.

Washington snorted, took a drink from his jug and wiped his

35

mouth with the back of his hand before explaining patiently, "Brandin' them. This here whole country is open range clear past the Arbuckles."

"Why didn't you say so?" Hutchins laughed. "I wasn't sure if you were talkin' about a *cow* crop or a *peach* crop!"

The cowboys, who had sat up to listen, laughed and gave the two their intent attention. Washington eyed him indignantly. Hutchins knew he was endangering his chance of a job, but he did not care.

"You own this ranch house?" he asked curiously. He knew that no white man owned any land yet in this Nation. It was all owned by the Chickasaws, who still held it communally. White men who rented from them owned only the improvements on the land.

"Nope!" Bill Washington admitted. "It b'longs to the Roff brothers, but they ain't needin' it right now. I *am* sort of temporary. Possession is nine points in law, so I've been told, and the law is a helluva long way from here!"

"I brought mine along with me," Hutchins said meaningfully. "I come from a Judge Colt country like this one 'pears to be!"

Hutchins glanced at the thin, doubtful smiles on the cowboys' faces which watched Bill Washington's smile.

"Where's that?" Washington asked.

"The Spur Ranch out West Texas way."

Washington nodded as he appraised the boy again. Hutchins still packed the Colt John Hall had given him, and he carried it slung low on his thigh.

"I've heard of the Spur," acknowledged the cowman. "Out near the Panhandle, ain't it?"

"That's right. South of the Goodnight range."

"Did you just come here from there?"

"Nope."

"Where 'n hell have you been?"

"None of your business," Hutchins said and stared him straight in the eyes for a moment. "But I don't mind telling you. I come by way of Paris to see my folks who live there."

Bill Washington grunted his approval and looked blandly up at him as he asked, "What's yore handle?"

"Bob Hutchins."

He scrutinized Bob closely and asked bluntly, "You're part Injun, ain't you?"

"A little."

Washington considered the situation as though he were trying to find some good trait on which to make his decision. He looked at the fiddle in his hand and grinned slyly. "Kid, if you can play this fiddle," he announced, "I'll hire you on!"

Hutchins left the saddle in one leap and strode forward. "Let me have it."

He sawed the bow awkwardly across the strings and the fiddle gave out a terrible screech. Bill Washington roared and rocked, nearly falling off his stool. The cowboys joined in thunderously.

Bob grinned wryly. "Why don't you ever tune it?" he drawled. He fumbled with his hat, rubbed his nose and pretended to be plagued by his predicament. Then he skillfully struck up a local favorite called "Hell Among the Yearlings."

He watched amazement replace the grins on their faces. Then as the catchy tune roused their emotions, some of the cowboys sprang to their feet, whooping and dancing. Washington leaped up, jerked off his old Stetson, slapped it against his thigh and yelled like a Rebel.

When Hutchins finished and handed back the fiddle and bow, Washington asked him soberly, "What tribe do you belong to, Kid?"

"Chickasaw."

"Hell, this is the Chickasaw Nation. You'll be gettin' a head-right before long. You're hired. Twenty and feed. Unsaddle yore hoss and turn him loose. He'll be safe. Go tell the cook to rustle you up some grub."

As Bob Hutchins unbuckled the cinch strap on Star Face's belly, he heard Washington snort again and saw him set down his jug. He went around to the cook-wagon, as his boss settled back on his stool and struck up "Snow Bird in the Ashes."

37

Little Crow — the Spy

That night, Bob Hutchins fell in with Washington's cowboys easily. To their delight, he raked off several lively tunes on Bill Washington's fiddle before they all turned in for the night.

They bunked out under the jack-oaks. The log house, with its open porch, called a breezeway, between the two rooms, was too small and too warm for sleeping. It was summertime, but at night the south breeze blew cool and soft.

While Bob was feeding his horse before grub the next morning, a squat, good-natured cowboy came up to him.

"The boss is sendin' yuh up to the Cross O L today in the Arbuckles, ain't he?"

"I don't know yet," Hutchins replied. "He hasn't told me." He eyed the friendly cowpoke speculatively, wondering at the man's strange, secretive behavior. It was clear Squatty did not want to be overheard.

"I think that's what Bill's got in mind."

"Which spread he wants me to work on doesn't make much difference, I reckon," Hutchins grinned. "All this country is new to me. Do you know the way?"

"Sure. You take the Whiskey Trail almost to the cedar log cabin about a mile this side of Whiskey Mound."

"I don't get this Whiskey Trail and Whiskey Mound talk. Why all the fancy names?"

"They ain't fancy," Squatty said. "Just plain and simple. Whiskey Trail is the way from Red River north through the Arbuckles. It's called that because whiskey runners from Texas bring it here to sell and trade to white men and Injuns alike. This country is *dry* to protect the Injuns. It's a penitentiary offense to sell or give Injuns liquor. Didn't you know that?"

"Nope!" Hutchins replied indifferently. "What's Whiskey Mound?"

"Just a big, bald hill in the Arbuckles, like the rest of 'em 'cept there's a big oak growin' there. Sort of a meetin' place for whiskey runners and peddlers."

"Thanks."

"That ain't what I want to tell you."

"What then?"

Squatty looked around carefully. "There's a little, old nigger up there named Little Crow," he whispered hoarsely. "Better watch him. He's a mean little hombre. Killed two other niggers and a white man. He's a spy for the boss. Runs all kinds of errands and tells the boss ever' damned thing he sees and hears!"

"I'll keep it in mind," Hutchins said gratefully. Squatty had seriously wanted to warn him about Little Crow. "I'll keep an eye on the nigger. Much obliged."

Just then the cook sounded the gong for chow and they went around to the cook-shack and stood in line for breakfast.

Bill Washington called Bob aside and told him, "Kid, I've picked you to go up into the Arbuckles north of here to find and brand every unbranded critter you can. The brandin' iron is in the little line-shack up there. There's everything you'll need up there now. I'll keep supplies coming up from time to time. We use the Cross O L brand on both sides of Red River, which is the boundary between Texas and the Territory. The cook is sendin' along a fresh supply of grub. You'll take what you need on a pack mule. Little Crow will do the cookin' while he's there. When he's gone, you'll have to shift for yourself. He comes and goes."

39

"Who's Little Crow?" Hutchins inquired innocently, feigning surprise.

"Why, I forgot to tell you. He's a nigger who works for me, too. I use him a lot as a messenger to keep the boys posted about things. I need him here with me. That's why I'm hiring you to take his place up there. He's just a temporary hand up there anyhow. The last 'poke I had there got so damned lonesome he quit."

Hutchins singled out one remark and asked, "What things must you be posted about? Am I supposed to look out for them, too?"

"Well, it's like this," Washington explained patiently. "We Washingtons are running cattle from three locations. Kind of scattered about, I'll admit. My brother Jerry stays down closer to the river most of the time. My pa is over across the river near Gainesville. I've got to have some way of sending word at times. I use Little Crow for this quite a bit. He's a smart little nigger and he's loyal and dependable, too."

"How far to the shack in the Arbuckles?"

"About twenty miles."

"How far to Jerry's camp?"

"Right about the same distance south, I reckon. Gainesville is across Red River twenty, twenty-five miles."

Hutchins nodded. "Where do you want me to do the branding? How much range do I cover?"

"The Arbuckles are free!" Washington grinned. "Anything goes. Anything else you want to know?"

"Yes," Hutchins said bluntly. "Who does the bossin' up there? Me or the nigger?"

Washington reddened, then stammered, "Why — why — you, of course!" Then he asked a bit tersely, "You got any objections to shackin' up there with Little Crow?"

"I'll know later," Hutchins declared frankly, "after I get to know him. Niggers are just like white men to me. Some I get along with. Some I don't."

"Well, Little Crow is all right," Washington assured. "You'll like the little cuss. I'll be up in a few days to see how you're doin'." He paused, searched Bob's face for approval and then added with a grin, "Might bring my fiddle along and let you make it talk some more!"

Hutchins grinned back. "I'll be looking for you. Someday, I'm going to buy me a fiddle. That's one thing Uncle John Hall didn't think to give me. His was a family treasure."

He loaded his mule, mounted Star Face and led the mule away. He was in no hurry. He urged neither mule nor horse faster than an easy gait. He was on the payroll now. Up in the Arbuckles, he would be lonesome most of the time. Maybe all the time. It would depend on how Little Crow received him and how often he would be there.

Smoke was pouring out of the chimney against the setting sun when he reached the line-shack. He found Little Crow cooking supper. Bob sized him up as he came to the door to stare out at him. He was a little man, all right; jockey-sized, slender and wiry. Bob guessed he was about forty, for his kinky hair was already turning grey. He could undoubtedly stick to a horse like a leech. Two long-legged, long-barreled chestnuts stood in the corral; sleek and trim and ready for instant use. They were racehorses or Bob was a poor judge. He remembered the qualities of good horses that Sam Bass and the others had taught him.

"Put more in the frying pan," he announced to the little Negro. "You got a star boarder movin' in."

"Who sent you?" Little Crow asked sullenly.

Hutchins swung down and faced him. He saw the Negro's eyes widen as he caught a glimpse of his low-slung Colt. Hutchins, at the same time, made a mental note that Little Crow was also packing a six-shooter.

"Now who else would have sent me here but Bill Washington?" he asked testily. "Ain't he the same boss who sent you here?" He didn't wait for an answer, but announced, "My name is *Mister* Hutchins. Why do folks call you Little Crow?" Lightly, he added, "You may be black, but you ain't got wings!"

This amused the little Negro. "No, suh!" he agreed. "I can ride like the wind, but I cain't fly. The Injuns done named me Little Crow."

He helped Hutchins unpack the mule and carry the luggage inside. Hutchins unsaddled Star Face, hobbled him and the mule to make certain they would stay around until they

41

got used to their new range. He carried his saddle inside and put it against the wall. There was a bunkroom with four bunks and a smaller kitchen with a box-iron stove for both heating and cooking, some pots, pans and tins, and a crudely handmade table and four chairs.

This, Hutchins thought as he surveyed the frugal layout, would be his home for a while. For how long he did not know and did not even want to guess. Twenty dollars per month and feed was a slow way to get rich, but he had to have some money before he could even begin to make any plans for the future.

He turned suddenly and startled the Negro who was silently appraising him. "You sleep outside when it doesn't rain, don't you?"

"Yas, suh, and it sho' do git cold 'fore mawnin', too! A suggan feels good!"

Hutchins decided Little Crow was going to accept him easily enough. They'd get along all right. When they sat down to supper, there was one thing about which he was certain. Little Crow was a real cook. The thick steak was tender enough to be cut with his fork.

The next morning after breakfast, Bob saddled Star Face and asked Little Crow for the branding iron. He brought it out from behind the stove, then saddled one of the chestnuts and rode along with Bob.

Riding in and out of the draws, around worn, rock-round, balding hills of the ancient Arbuckles, Bob was able to learn several things that first day. Deer were plentiful. Rattlesnakes, too. And it was easy to get lost in those mountains. Too many of the draws and the little valleys, cedar brakes, and persimmon and sumac thickets looked exactly alike.

They found and branded three mavericks. Hutchins shot the heads off of two snakes and learned Little Crow could shoot straight enough to clip the head off another. Late that evening, Bob killed a deer with his Winchester rifle. It was a difficult shot, which drew praise from Little Crow. The little Negro was obviously impressed at his skill with firearms. And the deer steaks he cooked for supper were delicious.

During the meal, Hutchins asked him about relief horses to ride. "I don't want to put too much work on my own

42

horse," he told Little Crow. "He ain't used to these rocky hills, and since I'm ridin' for the Cross O L, the outfit ought to furnish horses to ride."

"There's some around," Little Crow assured him quickly. "Take yo' pick of any critter with the Cross O L brand."

"Well," Hutchins declared with deliberate devilment, "I like the looks of them two in the corral out there. Now the one I like the best is —"

Alarm shot into the Negro's eyes. "Not them, Mistah Hutch!" he protested. "The boss would skin me alive for sho' if I let you ride them. They is for special use!"

Hutchins faked disappointment. The horses were clearly a very touchy subject with Little Crow. "I sure could get over the range with one of them racehorses," he said sadly, shaking his head. "I'll bet they could run all day, without anyways near playing out. I sure would like to fork one of them. I could cover more ground and find a lot more mavericks."

Two days later, Hutchins rode in at sundown and discovered Little Crow had gone. Both horses were gone, too. But the signs indicated that Little Crow had ridden one of the chestnuts and had led the other.

It was a week before the little darkey showed up again. Bill Washington was with him, riding the other racehorse.

"How's it goin', Kid?" Bill Washington's voice was casual and friendly.

"All right. I've found and branded thirty head. I can't hardly believe it!"

"What?" Washington asked, looking at him closely.

"So many loose, wild cattle! I ain't seen one single rider from any other outfit. Yesterday, I found a young cow and calf, both unbranded, and I threw the Cross O L on both of them."

"Good!" Washington settled back on his heels with a smile of satisfaction. "Make hay while the sun shines, Kid! When them other cattlemen find I'm working this range, you'll see some more riders. There's gonna be competition!"

Hutchins nodded. "Got a smoke?"

"You out of tobacco?"

"Sure thing."

"Figgered you might be," Washington said pompously. "I

43

brought some along. Whenever you run short of anything, ride over to Bywater's Store."

"Where's that?"

"Southwest ten or twelve miles."

"Just a store?"

"A store and a blacksmith shop, but it's a growin' community. Families movin' in around there regular. Be a good-sized settlement there first thing we know."

Little Crow took the bucket and went down under the hill to get fresh, spring water. Washington said suddenly: "About hosses for you to ride —"

"I've rounded up four head," Hutchins cut in.

"Good! There ought to be a dozen around here with the Cross O L on them. Take yore pick or ride 'em all if you can." Washington cleared his throat. "Don't use the racehorses. They're strictly for Little Crow. He's foolish about them chestnuts."

"Show me a cowpoke that ain't foolish about horses," Hutchins said.

"They're mine," Washington explained, "but I assigned them to him special." Washington's eyes grew mildly accusing. "I wouldn't tease Little Crow about them hosses, if I were you."

Hutchins laughed. "You ain't me, Bill," he said gently, "but don't fret none about Little Crow. I don't aim to ride his horses and I ain't hurt him yet, but he's a nigger that will bear watching if he can't take a little funnin'."

Washington's eyes searched Hutchins' face sharply. As if he had reached a decision on the spur of the moment, he said, "Little Crow won't be around much anymore — now that you're here. I need him to run errands for me."

"Suits me," Hutchins said indifferently. "Be a little lonesome at times, I guess, and I will miss the little darkey's cookin', but I ain't no hand for crowds, anyhow."

The next morning, Washington and Little Crow left and Hutchins went his lonely way, doing his routine duties.

As he grew to know the country better, he ranged wider and farther. To the north, he rode beyond the Washita River to a rough, wild, lonely region of the Arbuckle Mountains; with small draws, ravines, and washes choked with scrub cedar, persimmon, plum, and sumac thickets and dwarfed thorn and prickly-pear cactus. Some of these scraggled up the rocky peaks and were hardy and sturdy enough to put down roots in between the rocks and survive.

Along the creeks and the river, there were giant cottonwoods, sycamores, elms, oaks and black-jacks. But in the mountains, it was some of the worst country to ride that Bob Hutchins had ever seen. Sometimes he took his horses to Bywater to get them shod, sometimes to Dresden, and once over to a little place north along the Washita, which he had come across on the Whiskey Trail, known as Dougherty.

Occasionally, Bob met whiskey runners, roving cowboys, and a few road agents along the trail. But none of these ever gave him any trouble. They swapped news with him from places as far down in Texas as the Brazos. Hutchins always got the bargain, for local news was scarce with him. He was often able to offer a weary rider a bear or deer steak, which made up for the uneven exchange of news.

Once Hutchins spent a day exploring the lay of the land to the east. He became acquainted with Eastman James, who remained his staunch friend for years to come. Like all fullblood Indians, Eastman contributed only a few monosyllables to a conversation, until Hutchins learned enough Chickasaw to talk to him. Eastman lived in a one-room log cabin with his two squaws at the head of Oil Creek. But Eastman James was not the harem man that Josiah Lewis was. That venerable old buck lived many miles farther east on Blue River, with eleven squaws.

This discovery amazed Hutchins, but didn't interfere with their friendship. Josiah Lewis also became quite friendly with Bob Hutchins. When Eastman and Josiah learned that Hutchins, himself, had a strain of Chickasaw blood in his veins, the young cowboy became a cousin to them; for all Chickasaw Indians thought of each other as cousins. Josiah Lewis generously offered Bob the pick of his youngest squaws, but Bob politely declined; though he thought her charming enough.

Westward, he explored the timbered mountains of the Arbuckles, and found Henry House Creek beyond Honey Creek. Both streams had fine, big shade trees along their banks that made the clear, blue water look darker. He followed Honey Creek to a pleasant waterfall and swam in the cold, deep-blue hole beneath. It was a fishing paradise, and Bob frequently changed his diet from deer, raccoon and bear to fish.

The falls on Honey Creek had already begun to be called Turner Falls after Mezeppa Turner, who lived nearby. He, too, was part Indian. Every time Bob could, he rode over to take a swim in Blue Hole, catch a fish or two and talk to Mezeppa Turner. When Mezeppa learned that Bob was looking for a place for his father's family to settle, he was interested. "Why don't you ride over to Oil Springs and talk to Tom Boyd," Mezeppa urged. "His wife is Chickasaw. They have several hundred acres of land under headrights. One hundred acres is in cultivation now, but they need someone to farm and graze the rest."

Bob Hutchins thought it was a good idea; and a few weeks later, he rode over to Oil Springs to talk to Tom Boyd. He was willing to do business whenever Bob's father could come and talk to him.

A few weeks later, Little Crow showed up. Hutchins left him to look after the cattle, and he rode all the way back home, beyond Paris, to tell his parents of his discovery.

Bob enjoyed being with his family again, but his mission was not successful. His mother still wanted to move, but his father hated to leave the region where he had lived most of his life. There would be property to sell and many other decisions to make. John Andrew Hutchins knew that if they moved over into Indian Territory, they would be pulling up stakes in Texas for the future. He didn't see his way clear now to do that in a hop, skip and a jump; but he promised Cassie and Bob that as soon as he could, he would do it.

Bob Hutchins cut through the open country from Raymond, in the Choctaw Nation, avoided Bill Washington's Cross O L headquarters at the 700 Ranch house, and followed the beaten trails into the Arbuckles, back toward the line-shack. He learned from travelers what was going on among the Indian and white settlers of the sparsely settled region. There was a Deputy United States Marshal out of "Hanging" Judge Isaac Charles Parker's court at Fort Smith, Arkansas, who was "resting his saddle for a spell in Dresden." Folks figured he was investigating something, but what it was all about was still a mystery.

Hutchins rode into Dresden and found the marshal, Colonel

J. H. Mershon. He had a posseman with him who was a young, stocky Pennsylvania Dutchman named John Spencer. Boldly, Hutchins told Colonel Mershon that he would like to be a posseman in whatever case he was investigating.

Realizing the kid was in dead earnest, Colonel Mershon repressed a grin as he surveyed the tall, lanky young fellow before him. Then he noticed the young cowboy's six-shooter swung low on his right thigh, worn with a poise that suggested the gear had been a part of his attire for most of his life.

"How old are you, Kid?" Colonel Mershon asked.

"Old enough to be your posseman," Hutchins said evasively, but easily. He grinned as he spoke.

"Well, it doesn't matter," the colonel replied, not wanting the embarrassment by pressing him for his correct age. He had already seen that Hutchins was wise and experienced beyond his years. "You are still a button, but you've got nerve. Where do you live?"

"Over west a few miles. In Bill Washington's line-shack. I'm brandin' mavericks for him."

Colonel Mershon knew about Bill Washington. "Are you *branding* them for Bill, Kid, or *stealing* them?" he asked, grinning.

"Meanin' what?" Hutchins stiffened, alertly.

"No offense. Bill Washington is known to take cattle wherever he finds them."

"That's right," Hutchins agreed. "The ones I'm brandin' are runnin' wild."

"You know these Arbuckle Mountains very well?"

"Been ridin' around in them for three or four months now," Hutchins replied.

"Kid, I can't hire you on as a posseman," Colonel Mershon declared, "but I don't mind your stringing along. I'd be obliged for your help. You'll have to get a little more age on you before you can be a posseman. You really hankering to become a lawman?"

"That's right."

"What about your job with Washington?"

"It will keep for a while yet. I left a little nigger holdin' down the shack till I get back."

47

The Case of
Dead Man's Cave

People in the Arbuckles first suspected something was wrong at Bud Stephens' ranch when they saw his corral fence down and all his stock gone. Nobody could be found at the ranch cabin; and neither he nor Mrs. Stephens had been seen for several months.

The truth about it began to come out when a Negro freedman's daughter, who had been courted by Henry Loftus, came to Uncle Charley Henderson's store in Dresden and told him that she had not seen Henry Loftus for about a year. Henry's brother, William Loftus, and his aged parents came with her. They were all law-abiding citizens in the community, but Henry Loftus had been considered a wild and reckless character.

"He told me if he was found dead," the girl said in agitated tones, "to tell the Laws to arrest Bully July. He said he and Bully was gonna help Mistah and Missus Stephens drive all their cattle and hosses to Louisiana, and that they was sellin' out and movin' back to Texas. He told me about the yaller

48

gals, red likker and good times he and Bully was goin' to hav' in New Orleans."

"Didn't I see Bully the other day?" Uncle Charley Henderson asked.

"Yas, suh, he's back now!" exclaimed William Loftus in a trembling voice. "Befo' they take away the cows and hosses, Henry git drunk and he tell me he and Bully kill Mistah Bud and Missus Stephens and dump 'em in a cave somewheah over in dem mount'ins 't other side of Mistah Bud's cab'n. Now Bully show up ag'in alone. We iz all scared somethin' done happen to Henry!"

Bully July was a Chickasaw Negro freedman, several years older than Henry Loftus and his local sweetheart. He had been a small boy when his folks had been emancipated by their Chickasaw masters.

Uncle Charley Henderson sent word to United States Marshal Thomas Boles at Fort Smith to send Deputy Marshal J. H. Mershon out to investigate the case and solve the mystery of three apparent murders.

Colonel Mershon and his posseman, John Spencer, quietly organized a search party to scour the Arbuckles. They finally found Henry Loftus' skeleton staring vacantly up at the sky from the center of a sumac and persimmon thicket in a lonely little valley.

The colonel and Spencer returned to Fort Smith late at night, and the next morning Mershon strode into United States District Attorney William H. H. Clayton's office, dropped a grain sack on the floor and, above the clattering noise, announced, "Here's one of the four horse thieves!"

Attorney Clayton was accustomed to such brusque remarks from the deputy marshals about gruesome crimes. He had prosecuted most of the murderers and cutthroats hanged by Judge Parker's court. He was at that moment absorbed in preparing prosecution of two other murder cases. Glancing up abstractedly, he asked, "What horse thieves?"

Colonel Mershon snorted indignantly. "This is one of the niggers from the east end of the Arbuckles over in the Chickasaw Nation. He worked for Bud Stephens and his kid-wife!"

"Oh, *that* case!" Clayton exclaimed. "They are coming so fast now I can hardly keep up with all of them." He sat stiffly now at his desk and looked at the sack. "Have you located the missing couple yet and brought in the murderer?"

"I know who it is, but he wasn't around to arrest. I'm going to bait a trap for him," Colonel Mershon declared, grinning, "with the best trap bait for a man in the world."

Then he told Clayton about finding the skeleton of Henry Loftus and the deep, well-like cave, in which the bodies of the Stephenses were thought to be.

"Who do you think the murderer is?"

"He's a nigger freedman. He goes by the aliases of Bully July and Bully Joseph."

"You ought to find what's left of those other two victims, too, so we can get the murderer's confession and use them for evidence. They will make a better case for hanging Mr. Bully than the dead nigger you've got there," Clayton said matter-of-factly.

"Great God!" Mershon exclaimed. "That hole is full of rattlesnakes!"

He grinned again wryly. "We'll get them for you if you want them. John Spencer, my Dutch posseman, wanted to go down in that deep, dark hole on a rope, but I didn't think it was necessary. If you want the bones of the white couple, we'll get them."

During his investigation, Colonel Mershon had learned about the rivalry between Bully July and Henry Loftus over the squatter's daughter. He rightly assumed Bully July — feeling safe now — would come courting again. The investigation had been carried on quietly and only a few of the most reliable men knew about it. He grinned as he joked with posseman Spencer and young Bob Hutchins: "Where the honey is, the bee is bound to return."

They would set the trap and bide their time, for they didn't want any gossip to scare the murderer away. The colonel instructed the Negro girl to make a date with Bully July when he asked her. Bully had a weakness for women, but like most men of his kind, wine and song were also a part of it. Except for whiskey smuggled into the mountains or some that was occasionally distilled in the mountains near some remote spring, Indian Territory was dry. Yet despite the federal government's attempts to enforce prohibition, there was plenty of liquor to be had ordinarily. But when federal officers came around, it was "as scarce as hen's teeth."

Colonel Mershon sent Bob Hutchins clear across Red River to Dexter, Texas, and the closest legal saloon, to bring back some whiskey to bait Bully July. Arriving in Dexter, Hutchins conceived an imaginative idea to improve on ordinary whiskey in trapping the Negro murderer. He met James Chancellor, a Texas officer and an old friend of his father's. He told him his mission in Dexter.

"Uncle Jimmie, do you know anything about doping whiskey?" he asked.

"I'm not an expert," Chancellor replied, "but I've got a bartender friend down the street who is."

In Riley Deaton's saloon, Green Thompson mixed up a quart concoction of alcohol, gin, whiskey and blackberry wine. Hutchins sampled it. "That's good enough to drink, myself," he declared.

"You better go easy on it," Thompson warned. "That's slow-acting dynamite. Tastes good, easy to drink, but after two or three swigs, you don't know what hit you."

On second thought, Hutchins bought a gallon of straight bourbon whiskey for the posse and rode out of Dexter at sundown.

At sunup the next morning, he arrived in Dresden (later named Berwyn and now Gene Autry) and delivered the mixture to Colonel Mershon and John Spencer at Uncle Charley Henderson's ranch. They made up a posse to search for the cave, including Wilson Fryback, White Frost and Charley Henderson.

One of them discovered the red scarf, which Uncle Charley identified as one he had sold to Dora Stephens. They were hot on the trail now, so they spread out and soon found the cave.

The next problem was to find the bodies at the bottom of the dark pit and bring them up. Nobody was eager to go down; but the young Pennsylvania Dutch posseman, true to his earlier promise, volunteered.

They dropped stones into the cave and calculated the depth at fifty or sixty feet. It was too dark down below to tell whether the bottom was dry or muddy.

Enough rope was joined together from saddle lariats, and

51

the Dutchman went over the edge. He had not gone far when he signaled, by jerking on the rope, that he wanted to be hauled up.

"There are snakes down there as big as a man's leg!" he ejaculated. "I struck a match and they stuck their tongues out at me from a hundred places!"

"That makes a more difficult situation," Colonel Mershon declared. "We might have to try to grapple for the bodies."

"Just give me a six-shooter and a lantern," Dutch Spencer said resolutely, "and I'll go clear to the bottom."

A lantern was brought. The marshal handed him his belt and guns. Strapping them on and carrying the lantern gingerly in one hand, the young man went cautiously below again. He was nearly at the bottom when he fired the six-shooter, putting his lantern dark. He signaled to be pulled up again.

"I just killed a rattlesnake as big around as I am!" he exclaimed. "The bottom is pretty dry and I think I saw the bones."

Lighting the lantern again, he went down a third time, sent up the huge, dead snake first, then an improvised canvas hamper was lowered and he sent up the skeletons. They had been picked almost clean by varmints, and barely hung together by their rotted clothes. More than one man present was able to identify the remains of Bud and Dora Stephens.

That night, the squatter's daughter met Bully July out at the horse lot. She took out the quart of liquor and said, "Bully, here is some mighty good stuff of Pa's I found. I knew you'd want a drink, so I fetched it."

Bully July was superstitious and nervous. He sniffed the bottle suspiciously. "It's got a funny smell to it," he declared. "'Tain't whiskey!"

"Of course not, nigger!" the squatter's daughter retorted indignantly. "That's Pa's special drink. There ain't no whiskey good as that!"

"Uh-huh!" Bully July grunted. "If it's so good, I reckon you want a snort fust!"

"You didn't think I's gwine t' let you drink it all, did you? You hog!" she ridiculed disdainfully. Without another word, she lifted the bottle and appeared to drink a long swig. In the dark, Bully July could only hear the gurgling, but he didn't know how full the bottle had been. Colonel Mershon had wisely poured out some of it. The marshal had coached the girl in her part, and she was playing it perfectly.

They sat down on a log and Bully July held the open bottle as he waited to see what effect the liquor would have on the girl. When she moved closer to him with seemingly growing affection, Bully laughed and tossed caution aside. "Well," he remarked. "I reckon it ain't pizened or doped!"

Raising the bottle, he took a liberal swig, then smacked his lips and exclaimed about the surprisingly good taste. He took another, longer drink.

"Yo' pa sho' knows his likker!" he gasped. "It's the best stuff I evah had, and I sho' am thirsty!"

Now he became generous and amorous and insisted that she drink freely, too. She responded to his passion, but she cheated each time she lifted the bottle.

Bully July drank the potent liquid like a starved shoat. He became talkative and aggressive, and the girl pretended to be sleepy as she persuaded him to put her to bed.

There in her bedroom, Bully July was easy to arrest, for he was limp and helpless. On their way to Fort Smith, Colonel Mershon told the prisoner he had been arrested for the possession of liquor. The Negro knew that it was an offense for which he could draw two years in a federal penitentiary, but said nothing. When he was placed in a cell in Murderers' Row, he demonstrated that he was quite disturbed.

Colonel Mershon bought a tool chest and placed the skeletons of Bud and Dora Stephens inside it. Then he put the padlocked chest into Bully July's cell, with no explanation at all. The next morning, he took Attorney Clayton with him and they went to Bully July's cell.

"How did you sleep last night, Bully?" the marshal asked.

"Jest tolerable," the Negro replied, unsuspectingly.

"That's fine!" Colonel Mershon declared. "I knew you wouldn't mind Bud and Dora Stephens sharing your cell."

"Mistah Bud and —" His voice broke off. His face blanched and his eyes rolled in terror. "Heah?" he choked. "Wheah?"

His eyes went straight to the chest.

"They are in there, all right," Colonel Mershon said grimly. "Both of them. They'll haunt you tonight, Bully."

It was too much for the Negro's worried mind and his long-suffering conscience. He did exactly what the marshal had expected. Hysterically, he begged and pleaded with them to take the chest out. "Git 'em outa heah!" he screamed, and he fell on his knees, dazed and exhausted.

"When you tell us how you murdered them," Colonel Mershon promised gravely, "I'll have the chest removed."

Bully July regained his senses and became sullen and stubborn. The jailer unlocked his cell door and Colonel Mershon walked over to the chest, unlocked it, raised the lid, and reached down to bring up the end of the woman's long, thick tresses of hair.

As he saw the mute, lustrous evidence, Bully July fell to raving and pleading again.

"Now tell us your story," Attorney Clayton told him. "Tell it in the presence of the man and woman you killed, or their ghosts will haunt you for want of a decent burial!"

Bully July stared blankly, and the whites of his eyes rolled in his head as he tried to keep from looking at the chest.

"We found Henry Loftus dead in the thicket where you left him," Colonel Mershon said impassively. "We've got his skeleton here, too. God have mercy on your miserable soul if you don't come clean about these three murders!"

Blubbering and agitated, Bully July broke down and told them his story, which is included here in the following chronicle:

In a town in Texas, across Red River from the Indian Territory, there lived a beautiful, accomplished girl who will be referred to here as Dora Delton. Her parents were not wealthy, but they were respectable citizens. They were fond of Dora and, perhaps, spoiled her a bit. Dora never wanted for anything they could buy for her.

At a Fourth of July rodeo, she met a handsome, dashing cowboy. He was thirty-five years old, and she was only sixteen, but it was love at first sight for both of them. Dora's beauty drew Bud Stephens to her like a magnet, and his polished manners captivated her.

Bud Stephens' character, though colorful, was not too commendable. Dora Delton's parents learned about his reputation when it became known the two were regularly seeing each other. The Deltons were firm enough to forbid Dora to see him anymore. When Dora declared her intention of marrying him, Mr. Delton made strict plans to keep them apart.

About this time, Bud Stephens tangled with the Law over a stolen horse. He dodged about the country and met Dora on secret trysts, whenever he could.

"I've got to leave, Dora," he told her passionately, "but I can't go without you."

"You must, Bud," she pleaded. "When you send me word, I'll come to you, wherever you are."

He smothered her lips with kisses, and Dora's fascination for this man swept away her senses. She believed she could never again be happy without him. In her anguish and desperation, she made her fatal decision.

"I'll go, Bud," she promised. "Have a horse ready for me tomorrow night."

They eloped across Red River into Indian Territory, and were married by a circuit rider. Bud and Dora Stephens dropped out of existence to their relatives and friends as completely as if they had been swallowed by the yawning earth.

They went to Bywater's Store, south of Desperado Springs and Fort Arbuckle. It was a wild and woolly country, sparsely settled by people with the reputation of minding their own business. Some of the settlers had come to the Indian Territory because of something in their pasts. Some had even changed their names to new ones that suited their fancy.

Bud and Dora Stephens came into this country and went far back into the mountains and built a log cabin. Soon they had a fine collection of horses and a small herd of cattle. Bud bought and sold and traded in stock. They thought they were getting along fine. Both of them were experts with horses and good shots with pistols. They went off together at times and came back with a new herd of horses.

Bud Stephens found it necessary to hire a hand to take care of his increasing interests while they were away on trips. He ran across Bully Jully in Dresden and hired him. The business of trading grew and expanded, and he hired Henry Loftus and took him down into Texas where he had been getting horses. He was enough impressed at the young Negro's skill that he made him his wrangler when they returned.

Horses in those days sold for good prices, because horses were the chief means of travel. In Texas, Bud and Dora, and sometimes one or both of their Negro cowhands, would ride out on the range and round up their choice of horses. They quickly improvised a corral by stretching ropes from tree to tree, assembled their herd and drove them across Red River into the Arbuckles.

There the horses were loose-herded for a few weeks until other rustlers showed up with similar herds from Kansas, Missouri, Arkansas and West Texas. Two or three days of trading went on until each ramrod was in possession of strange horses which he could sell in his own neighborhood without arousing any suspicion.

A little later on, a bold robbery was committed in Grayson County, Texas. Bud Stephens was believed to be guilty, and Bill Everheart, the sheriff, organized a posse, invaded the Indian Territory and went into the Arbuckles to search for Stephens.

With the help of local nesters, they found where he had holed up in an old cabin at Sorghum Flat, north of what is now Dougherty. In the gun battle which followed, Stephens killed and wounded some of the posse and then escaped under cover of darkness. Later, he was captured, but he shot the deputy who was taking him to Texas and got away again. He made his way back into the Arbuckles, where a man could safely hide from the Law.

He found a cave which he made his chief hiding place. Dora Stephens made regular trips to Dresden for supplies, cooked his meals in the ranch cabin and carried them to him. Throughout all this, Bully July and Henry Loftus looked after the cattle and horses.

One day, Dora Stephens rode into Dresden to buy groceries at Uncle Charley Henderson's general store. Taking a fancy to a large, red scarf, she bought it and rode away on her sorrel.

Bully July confessed his share in the horse rustling and told of the many trips they made into Louisiana and Arkansas to sell horses and cattle.

"Henry was always talkin' 'bout how good lookin' Missus Bud Stephens was," Bully declared.

One day, as they were herding horses in the mountains, he and Loftus found a big cave, so deep they could not see the bottom. It was a yawning pit, which they came upon suddenly in the bushes, without the slightest realization it was there.

"This sho' is a good place to hide th' daid!" Henry Loftus exclaimed. "Let's kill the boss and throw him in theah and take Miss Dora. When we're tired of her, we can throw her in theah, too!"

As Bully July hesitated, he added, "Then we can take the hosses and cows into Louisiana and sell 'em. We can hav' all kinds of good times with 'em yaller gals in New Orleans and we can buy all the fancy likker we wants. If anybody evah find Bud and Miss Dora, they won't know who they is. They'll think we all done lef' this country. Nobody gwine ter come foolin' 'round down in dat ole hole."

While they were talking, Bud Stephens rode up. "Boys," he said, "tomorrow is Sunday. My wife has gone to the post office. If she gets a certain letter, we're all heading for Texas tomorrow. We'll have a good old trip!"

Unsuspecting of treachery, Bud rode along the foot of the ridge to a spring, lay down in the shade and went to sleep. Bully July and Henry Loftus shot Stephens in the head. Bully left Henry with the dead man and rode down to the ranch house. As he arrived, Dora Stephens rode in from town.

"You sho' do look purty, Missus Stephens!" he exclaimed, smiling boldly at her.

Dressed in Levi's, with the red scarf tied around her head, Dora was trim, supple and winsome as she climbed down from her sorrel. She flashed the Negro a pleasant smile.

Bully took off his hat and stood there awkwardly, turning his hat in his hands and staring at her. Sensing something was wrong, Dora halted as she swung the sack of groceries from her saddle.

"What's wrong, Bully?" she asked, anxiously. "You wouldn't be here this hour of day if something wasn't wrong!" A note of alarm crept into her voice.

"Well, Ma'am," the Negro began haltingly, "it's Mistah Bud."

"Something wrong?"

"He done fell down by the spring and break his laig," Bully lied. "He wants you to come."

Dora moved quickly. "As soon as I get these groceries in the house," she called back over her shoulder, "I'll be right with you!"

"Yas 'um! I'll jest throw yore saddle off and unbridle yo' hoss. You can ride behind me like you do Mistah Bud."

Dora paused at the door and frowned, but said nothing. When she returned, she climbed up behind the colored man and trustingly rode to her death.

Bully July rode with her straight to the edge of the big cave. There he raped Dora Stephens before Henry Loftus came up. Loftus did the same. Then they showed her her husband's dead body and dumped it unceremoniously into the yawning cavern.

Brutalized and hysterical, Dora Stephens begged the killers to murder her and cast her body into the cave with her husband's.

They laughed contemptuously at her pleas and satisfied their fiendish lusts. Nearby was a smaller cave in the mountainside where they kept her captive. For three days and nights, they assaulted her with inhuman cruelty.

"When we tol' her we wuz goin' tuh kill 'er," the Negro freedman confessed, "she quit cryin' and looked awful purty ag'in. After we killed her, she still looked purty. We pitched her in dat big hole with Mistah Bud. Then we made an oath that we wouldn't tell anybody, and if one of us did, the othah would kill him, too!"

When Bully July learned Henry Loftus was "sweet on that nigger squatter's daughter," he grew afraid of Loftus' talk and then he learned that Henry intended to marry the girl.

"They wuz gettin' so thick, I jest knowed that fool nigger was goin' ter let somethin' slip 'bout Mistah Bud and Missus Dora, so I fixed his clock fer him!"

Bully July had murdered Henry Loftus on his way to a tryst with the Negro squatter's daughter on a moonlit night. The United States Attorney got all the testimony.

The bodies of the victims rested in their caskets in a conspicuous place at the trial, but Bully July did not see them when he was ushered into court. When Judge Parker told him to stand up and plead to his guilt or innocence, he hesitated. Attorney Clayton picked up Bud Stephens' skull, identified it by a gold tooth, and held it aloft for Bully July and all the spectators to see.

The Negro broke down again and wept bitterly. "Take me back to jail," he pleaded. "Do anything yuh want with me! Only git them bones out of heah, and I'll do what you say!"

The skeletons were removed from the courtroom and, once more, Bully July confessed to his brutal and fiendish crimes. Before he was hanged, the Negro freedman claimed repentance and composed a religious song about his belief he was going to Heaven. He revealed his real name was Martin Joseph, and it is so recorded in the records of the old Fort Smith court.

Bob Hutchins' part in this case was minor, but he had found a friend in Colonel Mershon; and he made up his mind to become a United States Deputy Marshal.

The BoB H Brand

Bob did some more thinking on his way back across the Arbuckles to the line-shack where Little Crow was impatiently waiting for him. He realized that at the rate of twenty dollars each month, working, sweating, riding hard to acquire cattle for a man who didn't own them in the first place, he was just a chump, getting rich entirely too slowly. It was fine for Bill Washington. Every second one, Bob decided, should be branded for himself.

If Washington had really been running a herd of cattle up here in this free range, it would have been a different matter; but he knew Washington had taken advantage of him, thinking he was only a green kid, and as he reviewed the situation, he didn't like it. He realized now he should have thrown himself up a shack, or occupied the vacant Stephens place, and gone into the cattle business for himself. There were still plenty of cattle left for the taking, so that was exactly what he intended to do — just share the take with Bill Washington.

Cattle were still dodging about and hiding in the thickets, wild as deer, but he had gone in and branded them before, and he could do it again, with an extra branding iron.

60

He rode over to Bywater's Store south of Desperado Springs one day and had the blacksmith make him a branding iron that branded BoB H, intead of Cross O L (+OL). There he met Jackie Akers, a winsome young widow, who was the prettiest creature Bob had seen in a long time. He had been to the store before, but hadn't met Jackie. She had been going to school at Whitesboro Normal, in Texas, and had stayed on with her in-laws after her husband's death.

Bob took Jackie to some of the dances and was the envy of the other boys in that growing community, which would later be named Woodford. Bob had grown huskier now. He weighed about 130 pounds. He had started growing a black mustache that a few years later he could tie behind his neck. It was his proud achievement and the object of envy and some ridicule among the young men.

There was one young bully named Jed Biggers, who harbored cordial dislike for Hutchins. To Hutchins he was just a drifting tumbleweed who rode for another outfit. He took a few digs at Hutchins, but none of them were direct, and Bob ignored them.

When he had ridden for the Cross O L for a year, he realized he had acquired a pretty good spread for himself. He had branded his mark on mavericks, which had grown up and borne calves. So many of his cattle were around that it began to be talked of as a popular brand. But maverick "peeling" had ceased to be so free and easy. True to Bill Washington's prediction, the other outfits had caught on. More riders rode the range every day. An unbranded calf was growing hard to find. Bob sighed like a prospector whose gold diggings had run out too soon.

One evening, he found footprints where someone had been watching him do some branding. The tracks were familiar and he was not at all surprised when he reached the cabin and found Little Crow there cooking supper. The Negro handed Hutchins his monthly salary, as he did every month.

He told Hutchins the general news of what was going on south of the Arbuckles, but Hutchins knew Little Crow told only what he wanted him to know. He had already heard most of it from the other riders on the range.

The next morning after breakfast, Little Crow went to

the corral and began saddling his horse. Hutchins went out to groom Star Face.

Little Crow looked at him, grinning slyly, and asked in a sarcastic voice, "How many do you reckon to throw dat BoB H brand on today, Mistah Hutch?"

A wave of anger sped through Hutchins on the heels of the moment of surprise. "Every other one, as usual," he answered defiantly. "What's it to you?"

"Nothin' to me, Hutch," Little Crow declared scornfully, "but Mistah Washington sho' gwine ter be mad when he heah about it."

"Let him be," Hutchins retorted.

"I'm gwine ter tell him how you rustle dem yearlin's from him, Mistah Hutch!"

"They're not his cattle. This is open range. Go on back and report, you little spy!"

"You can't fool me, Mistah Hutch. You is a cow thief!"

Hutchins' hand fell to his side and he realized, with a shock, that he had left his gun and belt in the cabin.

He whirled and bolted for the cabin door. Just as he plunged through the open door, a bullet splintered the door facing. It had missed him so narrowly that the splinters stung his face. This fanned Bob's anger to a blazing fire. He jumped to the side as another bullet crashed into the back wall. By the time he had grabbed up his gun, belt and hat, Little Crow had taken off like a jockey at the starting post.

Rapidly, Hutchins saddled Star Face and rode after him, but Little Crow's racehorse was too fast for Star Face to overtake. Hutchins got close enough to take a couple of quick shots. But Little Crow stretched out low on the chestnut's neck and raced ahead.

Bob chased the Negro all the way to the ranch near Red River. As he rode up close to the bunkhouse, the cowboys warned him to stay back or they would shoot to kill. Hutchins pulled his horse up short and vented his anger on Little Crow and his protectors. He dared any two of them to come out with Little Crow and face him.

A cowboy detached himself from the group and strode forward. "Don't shoot, Hutch!" he yelled. Bob recognized Squatty.

62

"Go drag that little spy out here and let him take his medicine," Hutchins demanded loudly. "The little black devil is pretty good at shootin' at people's backs and high-tailin' it!"

"It's no use, Hutch," Squatty said. "He won't come out and if you go any closer, you'll get killed. The boys all know what the trouble is. They think it's a good joke on Washington, but they've got to protect the nigger. Bill will fire any man who doesn't."

"Where is Washington? I'll talk to him."

"He's been gone somewhere most all day with Jerry. You better stay healthy and go on back, Hutch. Bill will probably come up soon and fire you."

"Whatever he does," Hutchins said fiercely, "I'll brand every unsinged animal I can find for my own. I'll throw me up a cabin and go into the business right. He won't even get half!"

Hutchins rode into town to look for Bill Washington, but the boss had been there and gone. A couple of merchants were complaining about his riding his horse into their stores. It was a favorite trick of the cattleman, when he was drinking. Once he rode into the bank, wrote out a check on his saddle horn, cashed it and rode out, without ever leaving his saddle.

Hutchins bought himself a few items he needed and rode back to the Arbuckles. Calmly, he went about his routine work. When Washington came, he thought doggedly, they would have it out any way the boss wanted.

Fired

Hutchins was just saddling up Star Face when Bill Washington came a few days later. Bob had been hoping he would bring Little Crow, but he came alone.

"Mornin', Hutch!" The cowman's greeting was calm and pleasant.

"Hello, Bill!" Hutchins returned his greeting.

Washington swung down and strode forward. He was not a tall man, but he was heavy-set, strong and aggressive.

"How's everything goin', Hutch?"

"Same as usual."

"Who owns this BoB H brand that's got to be so popular lately?" Washington looked straight into Bob's eyes.

Hutchins looked back just as steadily and said bluntly, "I do."

Washington snorted. "You're damned plain about admittin' it!"

"As plain as my brand," Bob declared. "Quit stalling, Bill! Little Crow told you all there is to know."

"Except the count," Washington corrected. "Little Crow

64

didn't find out how many you branded for me and how many for yourself."

Hutchins grinned. "We've done all right, Bill," he assured, "gettin' a head start on the other cowmen like we did. But you got the most. I throwed your brand on a couple of hundred head before I got it into my thick skull what a bonanza this was!"

Washington scowled and scuffed one boot impatiently. "You don't have to rub it in, Kid." There was a trace of bitterness in his voice. "What *is* the count?"

"Your count is about six hundred head," Bob answered abruptly. "Mine, about four hundred."

Washington's face darkened. "I thought you were workin' for me, Hutch." His voice was now accusing and disdainful.

"I have been," Hutchins insisted stubbornly, "and for myself, too — when I found out you tricked me and how free this range is. There were a few things you didn't tell me, Bill. I didn't find but a few of them mavericks associatin' with Cross O L cows. Fact is, the lack of Cross O L cows in these mountains struck me as a mighty odd discovery."

"Why, you insolent —" Washington's hand sped to his six-shooter. The next instant, he froze and blinked into the muzzle of Bob's Colt.

Hutchins' voice was low and even. "I still say this is free country. Why, most of them cows strayed over here from the Chisholm Trail! I've seen brands from outfits way down on the Brazos. You've done all right for yourself, Bill, and you ain't lost nothing on me. Maybe I ain't the dumb young 'poke you thought you hired!"

The cowman laughed. "All right, Kid, you win. I'll buy you out."

The gun in Bob's hand never wavered as he thought it over.

"Sure enough!" Washington insisted, as he eyed the gun trained steadily on him with growing uneasiness. "I'll give you five bucks a head and no hard feelings." He managed to grin. "I reckon I'd have done the same as you, anyhow!"

Slowly, Hutchins leathered his six-shooter. "You've bought yourself some cattle, Mister Washington!"

The cowman took out a roll of bills big enough to strangle

a calf and peeled off two thousand dollars. Hutchins knew then he had come intending either to bluff or to buy.

Bob Hutchins took the money unhestitatingly. He was aware of the pains, the hard work and the long days of riding and sweating in the rough ravines and flesh-tearing thorn thickets to find those mavericks. He had gone farther and done more than any ordinary range rider. He had earned every dollar Bill Washington was paying him.

He took the money ungrudgingly and watched the cowman fork his horse again. Washington reined his horse around and faced Hutchins then. His jaws tightened and his voice turned hard and cold. "Pack up and get out — and don't waste any time!"

Hutchins laughed softly as his former boss rode abruptly away.

That day, Bob rode over to Bywater's Store, which was now owned by "Onion" Akers; a tall, lanky, slightly stooped man above his middle years.

"Howdy, Hutch!" Onion greeted. "Comin' to the dance tonight?"

"You throwin' one?"

"Yep! Jackie talked me into it. She's goin' back to school in a few days."

Hutchins bought some tobacco. "I thought it must be sudden. Jackie didn't mention it the last time I saw her." He added, as he rolled himself a quirley, "Much obliged. I've got lots of time on my hands. I'll be here."

Just then Jackie came in. Hutchins beamed as he saw her. "Hello, Jackie!" he said. "Onion was just telling me you're giving a dance tonight. You sure look pretty. Will you be my partner?"

"Well — I — I'm sorry, Bob, but I've promised already. You see —"

Onion Akers cut in. "Jed Biggers has done beat your time, Hutch. She promised him!"

Jackie was plainly confused. "I'm sorry, Bob," she apologized. "I haven't seen you in over two weeks, and I wasn't sure you would be here."

"That's all right." Hutchins smiled; but to himself, he

wished it had been anyone besides Jed Biggers. "You won't mind saving just one dance for me, will you, Jackie?"

"I don't see why I shouldn't." She flashed him a smile. "Maybe more than one!" She laughed.

"I'll sure be grateful," Bob assured her, his heart warming up inside him.

When she left, Onion Akers turned to Hutchins seriously. "I think I ought to warn you, Bob, that Bill Washington was by here three or four hours ago and did some talking. Several fellows were here and heard him. Jed Biggers seemed pretty much amused over what Washington said."

Hutchins stared into Onion's searching eyes. "What did he say?" he asked calmly.

Onion cleared his throat and looked sidewise at Hutchins. He seemed reluctant to say more.

"Go ahead," Hutchins encouraged him. "Tell me exactly what he said. I'll own up to it all, if it's true."

"Well, he said he had hired you to look out for his interests. Said you had been branding cattle for yourself that ought to have been his, and he fired you."

"That all?" Hutchins watched Onion's ruddy face closely. He knew the old man would spare him all unpleasantness that he could.

"That's about it, I reckon," Onion concluded lamely.

"He didn't make any threats?"

Onion Akers shook his head. "Nope, but he said you did."

"He didn't call me a cow thief?"

"Not in plain words, but everyone around got the drift."

Bob Hutchins laughed. "I just beat Bill to the draw," he explained. "He came to bluff or buy me out. I sold."

"Sold?" Onion's clear eyes grew wide.

"That's right. That ought to prove I had some rights to a free range." Hutchins pulled out the money Washington had paid him. "A man don't get two thousand bucks for stealing mavericks from their owner, does he, Onion?"

Onion Akers grinned. "No wonder Bill's sore!"

Hutchins nodded. "I came up here to brand mavericks for Bill Washington." He laughed scornfully. "He told me this was his range and that he had cattle up here thick as wild buffalo!" Bob broke off laughing again. "Twenty and feed!" he exclaimed. "Why, Onion, it didn't dawn on me at first how much of a bonanza Bill Washington had latched on to. Cattle were just running wild back over there in those hills. I found grown cows unbranded! I went into draws and hollers back in those thorn and cedar brakes that I had to go in on foot to get to! Bill Washington didn't have any cattle in there. I branded yearlings that God alone knows who owned. Some of those calves were running with cows carrying some brands I've heard of way down on the Brazos. Get it? Strayed cows from the Chisholm Trail! Every yearling I found running with a Cross O L cow — which were damned few! — I threw the Cross O L on it."

Hutchins paused and smiled at the understanding look on Onion's face. "I'm telling you, Onion, Cross O L cows were mighty scarce. When I realized this, I started my own spread!"

Hutchins saw the relieved look on Onion's face now. "Only a wooden-headed cowpoke would have branded all those mavericks for twenty and feed!" he went on. "After the first couple of hundred, I branded half of them for myself. Shucks! I could have quit Bill long ago and gone all out for myself. He got six hundred for not more than a dollar-a-head cost. He got the other four hundred for only five bucks apiece. That makes a thousand head for twenty-six hundred!" Hutchins looked at his friend squarely. "Fair enough, ain't it?"

"Fair enough!" Onion Akers agreed. "You could have quit him and gone into it yourself. Most ambitious young fellers would have."

Jed Biggers rode up to the store porch, jumped from his saddle and clumped in, spurs jingling. Hutchins tensed expectantly. Jed was a husky young fellow, dark and swarthy, with a sharp tongue and an imposing swagger. He was taller than Hutchins, nearly twice as big, and apparently aware of it.

"Gimme a couple of sacks of Bull Durham, Onion," Jed said, "and some papers."

Hutchins watched him silently as he poured tobacco into a paper and expertly rolled a quirley. As he wet the edge of the paper with his tongue, his eyes fastened on Hutchins. "Uh!" he grunted, as if noticing him for the first time. "Hello, Hutch! Still workin'?"

Hutchins fixed him with a baleful stare, intended to inform

Jed that if it was trouble he wanted, he could get it. "Meanin' what?" Bob asked. There was a purposeful, vibrant challenge in his voice.

Jed Biggers grinned. "Just what I said." His lips curled mockingly. He struck a match on his duckings and sucked on his quirley importantly. "Yuh been ridin' for Bill Washington, ain't yuh?"

"I have been — yes!"

Biggers chuckled. "Still ridin'?"

Hutchins decided to put an end to it. "You heard Bill Washington say I wasn't, didn't you?"

Biggers flashed a look at Onion Akers. "That's what he said this mawnin'. What's yore story?"

Hutchins' first impulse was to tell him it was none of his damned business. But then he decided to see how far Jed Biggers would go to goad him.

"I sold out to Bill Washington this morning," he announced.

Jed's eyebrows arched and his cheeks sucked in with a show of disbelief. "Didn't know you and Bill was pardners," he declared with false surprise.

"It seems Bill was a bit confused about the deal, too," Hutchins retorted dryly, "but he bought me out just the same." Then he rasped out sharply, "You got any different ideas about it?"

Biggers stiffened. "I might have —"

"Hold on!" Onion's voice cut in authoritatively. "There ain't goin' to be no shootin' in my store. Folks don't want to come trackin' 'round on a bloody floor!"

Jed Biggers looked from one to the other. "So that's the way it is!" He sneered and his mouth twisted scornfully. "I'll see yuh later, Hutch!"

"Any time," Hutchins promised cooly. "Whenever you feel game, Jed!"

They could tell by the way Jed jerked his horse around and dug in his spurs that this meeting had turned out quite differently from the one he had planned.

"I ain't no fortune teller," Onion Akers remarked ruefully, "but it looks to me like a dark complected man is cloudin' up your future, Hutch!"

"He's been workin' up to it for a long time," Bob agreed, grinning.

"It seemed he was a bit touchy about somethin' he didn't talk about. What's eatin' him, Hutch? Do you know?"

"We both like the same girl."

"Here, now!" Onion exclaimed. "I don't want Jackie's name dragged into a gunfight. Jackie's a good girl!"

"You damned right she is!" Hutchins agreed strongly.

But Onion was flustered. "He'll be with her tonight at the dance, Hutch, and —"

"Jed's not fool enough to start trouble over Jackie."

"No?"

"Ten to one he tries to make me out a cow thief," Hutchins said. "Onion, I'm apologizin' now for myself if Jed Biggers forces a showdown at your house tonight!"

A Gunfight and
a New Resolve

True to her promise, Jackie danced a set with Bob that night. From far and near, the young men and the old, the belles and the middle-aged women had gathered for the dance.

Hutchins chinned the belles with gay chivalry. He could hold his own with any man in the neighborhood. He danced in one set with Jed Biggers, saw the glitter in the bully's eyes, and smelled whiskey on his breath. Some uninvited whiskey runner was at the dance and Hutchins knew Jed Biggers was one of his customers.

Biggers was spoiling for trouble and was waiting for a chance to start it. It came when he and Hutchins arrived in front of Jackie Akers to ask for a dance at the same time.

Jeb grabbed the young lady's arm with rough possessiveness. He fixed Hutchins with a fierce glare.

"Go ride the range, you shitepoke," he growled. "Jackie don't want to dance with a cow thief." He looked down at her and grinned.

Jackie Akers shook herself loose from Biggers and offered

her arm to Hutchins. Indignantly, she declared, "I'll dance with whom I please, Jed Biggers. And Bob is no cow thief!"

Hutchins flashed Jed a look of triumph. He could have kissed Jackie at this moment.

Jed towered over them. His face grew as dark as a storm cloud. He wheeled away viciously and stalked out the door. Hutchins and Jackie went ahead; and as they danced across the floor, Hutchins saw Onion Akers had been watching. He nodded his head with a tight smile.

But Jed Biggers was not the kind to let the matter drop there. In the middle of the dance, a six-shooter roared. Biggers had come back in and fired a shot into the ceiling. For a moment, the room was deathly still. Then men and women fell back with frightened exclamations on all sides of the room.

Jed Biggers saw Hutchins where he and Jackie had stopped dancing, almost in the middle of the room. Glowering, he announced loudly, "There's a cow thief in this room I'm fed up on. I aim to salivate him!" He crouched like a panther and roared, "Try yore luck, Hutch!"

With his left hand, Bob Hutchins shoved Jackie out of the line of fire. All that he had been taught about a quick draw in close-up fighting flashed through his mind. Hundreds of times, he had practiced it, but never before on a live man. It was not in his heart to kill Jed Biggers, but he meant to defend his own life.

Hutchin's hand slapped against the handle of his Colt and the barrel flipped up when Jed's gun was only half drawn. With unerring instinct, he trained his gun on the bully's holster. His Colt roared once and Jed Biggers cried out in pain. His hand dropped to his side, limp and crippled.

A feeling of relief flowed through Bob Hutchins. He had done what he had always been sure he could do. Some of the men led Biggers away, while others gathered around Hutchins to congratulate and praise him.

Everyone knew he could have killed Jed Biggers more easily than he had winged him. In the moral phrasing of that time, Jed Biggers would have been "paid for." They all knew Biggers had forced the fight on Hutchins.

That night after the dance, he had a talk with Jackie Akers which greatly changed his future. She had heard about the trouble between him and Washington, and she pleaded with him to go to Whitesboro, Texas, and go to school.

"I aim to be an officer for the United States government," he declared doggedly.

"That's wonderful," Jackie encouraged him, "but get an education and be a good one!"

Somehow the words struck deeply into Bob's mind. The lamp light streamed through the front door, forming a kind of aurora around Jackie's nut-brown hair. Hutchins gazed at the young widow admiringly.

"By jacks! You've talked me into it, Jackie," he told her eagerly. "I believe I will!"

Pleased, she stood on tiptoe and kissed him lightly on the cheek. Then she turned and fled into the house.

"You're an angel, Jackie!" he called after her in an awed voice. He strode to Star Face, unhitched him and swung into the saddle, and Jackie called gaily from the doorway, "Good night, Bob!"

It was a moonlit night, and the breeze blew cool as he climbed into the mountains and took the short cut to Bill Washington's line-shack. The grass was like a silvery sea, rustling softly as Star Face waded through it. Scrub cedar stood out darkly on the steeps. The strange rows of ragged rocks were sharply etched against the sky. Hutchins thought of a story he had once read about a Greek named Jason who had planted dragons' teeth which instantly grew an army of soldiers. The rock formations of the Arbuckles had always impressed him with a mystery he never really understood. There was something constant and enduring about them, and they seemed oddly significant.

The next morning, he packed up and left the line-shack for the last time. He made his way to Lamar County, Texas, a week later.

"Cassie," he told his mother, soon after he arrived home, "I've decided to get me an education."

Cassie Hutchins' face brightened. "I'm glad, Sonny Boy. I always hoped you would make something of yourself. Will you go to school in Paris?"

"I've picked another place. The normal school at Whites-

73

boro, east of Gainesville. I think I can finish in three years or less."

Cassie nodded approvingly. "You've got a good mind, son. You read fast, figure quick and remember well." Now her eyes searched his face for more. "Then what do you plan to do, son?"

"Work for Uncle Sam."

"Uncle Sam?" Her eyebrows lifted and her inquiring eyes remained fixed on his countenance.

"Yes, Cassie," he explained gently. "I want to be a federal marshal, and the best kind there is! I want to do my best to make our country a much better one in which people can live."

She was not surprised. "You like six-shooters and guns and horses, and you like to be outdoors. Don't you, Sonny Boy?"

He nodded. "I can't stand confinement, Ma." He grinned. "That's why I want to be on the law's side."

Cassie sighed. "He who lives by the sword shall die by the sword," she quoted softly. "I hope it will never be that way with you, Sonny Boy. I am glad you have chosen the law. I can imagine the heartbreak of the mothers of such boys turned outlaws as the Jameses and Youngers and Sam Bass. These twenty years since the Rebellion have been rough times for us people in Texas, the same as in other southern states."

"I promise to be careful, Ma," Bob assured her gently. "I won't be foolhardy."

Cassie smiled. "I'll always want you to do your duty, Sonny Boy," she said bravely. "Just temper your courage with common sense. I don't want my boys to become killers, even for the law."

His father had been listening and saying little, as usual. Now he declared with a smile, "Your ma thinks the whole world is going to hell in a handbasket. You get your education, son, then use it for the best, and always do what you think is right."

Bob was in no great hurry to leave for Whitesboro. There would be a few days yet before the fall term of school began. For the first time in his life, he really came to know his own family. He worked with his father and brothers — John, Andy and Sam — in the field. There were four other children then.

Oddly enough, there were only two girls in the family. Bob had pampered his two sisters, Melissa Dellah and Sallie Ethel, since they were small. It seemed to him, during these brief days,

74

he had never before really known what a home was like. Big families were great fun. The children soon learned to be unselfish, and learned early how to give and take.

When they were not working in the fields, Bob hunted with John, Andy and Sam. The boys went fishing and swimming in the clear, cool water holes of a nearby creek. He took them all for boat rides on Hutchins Lake, named after their grandfather.

Before he left, Bob offered his mother a thousand dollars to spend as she pleased.

"I don't need it, Sonny Boy," she protested. It was true. They were doing all right with the farm. They had raised plenty of vegetables and fruit. His mother had canned enough for the winter, and the harvest was good that year. There would be ample feed for the stock, and the grass was still green and water plentiful. But he still was sure his father could do better in the virgin country across Red River.

"You can put this money up for me then, Ma, for safekeeping. I don't want to take it all with me. Just spend it, if you need it."

Luxuries were barely conceivable in the last quarter of the nineteenth century. Every man aspired to own a gold watch, and every woman wanted a closed-case, gold model to pin on her blouse. Engagement rings with diamonds and decorations were rare, but nearly every wife wore a plain gold wedding band.

When people on both sides of Red River did spend money, after having gathered and sold their crops and cut out their steers for market, they spent it in large amounts, from one hundred to a thousand dollars, for clothes, staple groceries, and for any items they needed that they did not produce or manufacture on their farms. Good horses, saddles, buggies, wagons and mules sold for high prices, but the money was well invested.

Cassie was a frugal woman. If she spent any of it, the fourteen hundred dollars, he knew, would be well spent for a good cause. If not, it would be waiting for him on his return.

He rode to Paris where he spent a day and night buying clothes to wear to school and a few other items he might need. Then the young cowboy headed Star Face westward toward Whitesboro and an education.

75

Riding Posseman

J. M. Carlyle, superintendent of
the Whitesboro Normal School,
was pleased to accept Bob Hutchins as a student. There was no
exacting requirement for entering the school. Most of the stu-
dents had never gone to any kind of school before. They had
been tutored by relatives or friends, or were self-taught. A few
of them could barely write and read successfully. The tutoring
John Hall had given Hutchins put him in a better starting
position, for he was ahead of these. Carlyle and his teachers
worked with them at all levels of study.

Carlyle was hardly six feet tall, but weighed over two hundred pounds. He had, soft, grey eyes, a prominent nose and a
fair complexion.

"I'd have been a big man for sure," Carlyle often said, "if
the Good Lord hadn't turned down so much of me!"

The first requirement for a good student is for him to get
along with his teachers. Hutchins liked Carlyle from the beginning. He was a versatile man and a good instructor. He tempered
his teaching with just enough humor to make his points interesting and easily remembered.

But Hutchins did not do so well on the school ground during recess periods. The older and bigger boys derided Bob's extreme height and slight weight.

They taunted Bob with remarks such as "shitepoke," "bean pole" and called him "too thin to make a shadow."

If Bob Hutchins had taken the liberty of bringing his six-shooter to school and had bounced a few tin cans around, or had shot the edges off a few shoe soles, as he was quite capable of doing, he could have been the cock of the walk, and the idol of many. But he was forced to achieve their respect the hard way.

He had never fought a fistfight before, but he learned to be quick and nimble. At first, he got his nose bloodied, his eye blacked and his face skinned, but he gave no quarter and refused to admit defeat. He learned that accuracy, skill and cleverness were as important to fistfighting as they were to gunfighting. He learned this fast, and applied it well enough to promote himself from the cellar of ridicule to the pinnacle of respect.

J. M. Carlyle was aware of what was going on, but he waited until Hutchins had established his right among the boys before he put a ban on fighting.

"Bob," he asked privately one day, "what do you want to be in this world?"

Unhesitatingly, Hutchins replied, "An officer of the law, sir."

Carlyle nodded sagely. "A likely profession for steady employment," he agreed, and added with a wry smile, "if a fellow can stay alive. Law and order are what this country needs until folks are settled and civilized. Then the laws will still need to be enforced. Where do you plan on working for the Law?"

"Indian Territory," Bob said. "That's going to be my home."

"It will be a fine state someday," Carlyle predicted. "I hope you live to see it. It's wild and woolly now though. Rougher than this part of Texas has ever been."

"I can make it," Bob told him. "The way I figure it, every man has a purpose in this world, and a certain time to die, anyway."

"How would you like to live in my house, young man?" Carlyle asked. "My wife is a very good cook, you know, and since you want to be useful in this world and a help to society, I can give your education special attention. And my wife is a pretty good schoolma'am, too!"

77

"I'll sure be much obliged, Mr. Carlyle," Bob said gratefully. "Why you're so generous to a thick-headed, clumsy cowpoke like me, I don't know. But I will be a thankful and willing student."

Bob Hutchins boarded with the Carlyles at Whitesboro and made the most of their kindness and attention. Mrs. Carlyle was a busy, buxom, energetic woman. She was a talented house-keeper and fine cook.

Bob Hutchins took Jackie Akers to a square dance in Whitesboro one night and met Belle Starr, who was pointed out to Bob as the outlaw woman from Indian Territory. She was not a beautiful woman, but Bob thought her rather attractive; with soft, dark eyes and long, jet-black hair.

He danced with her and found her fascinating. She was more than a score of years older than he, but somehow, as he danced and talked with her, she seemed gay and young. Her age meant very little. She said she was part Cherokee and Bob, himself, was part Chickasaw. She was able to speak the languages of both tribes, whereas Bob had by then learned only a fair working knowledge of Chickasaw.

They had much in common and talked about persons and places in the Territory known to both of them. When Belle learned that he planned to become a peace officer in the Territory, she accepted this information with interest.

"No doubt, you will be connected with Fort Smith court," she said. "You will be coming through Younger's Bend sometimes. Please come to see me."

"I sure will," Hutchins told her cordially, and to himself, promised to do so.

Later, Hutchins went to Fort Worth with Carlyle to see a rodeo during an officers' and stockmen's convention. While there, they saw Heck Thomas, the famous marshal of the Indian Territory, and Carlyle introduced the marshal and the future young peace officer.

Heck Thomas was a fearless man with sharp, grey eyes, great wit, and a fondness for laughter. He was closely built — narrow hips and broad shoulders — weighed about 175 pounds, was six feet tall and was ramrod straight in posture.

"Heck," Carlyle said, "this young maverick is going to school with me now. He has had pretty good experience for a young

78

fellow, got lots of brass and isn't a smart alec. He knows better than most youngsters what a six-shooter is for. He has his heart set on being an officer. Think you might help him?"

Heck Thomas sized Bob up seriously and shrewdly. Hutchins met his gaze with an eager, unwavering smile and proud poise.

"Young Hutchins," the marshal said frankly, "You're just a gawky boy now, but I reckon you'll pass. Come see me when the professor is through cramming your head full of arithmetic and common sense. I'll see Judge Parker about adding you to the force when you're old enough." He added, with a grin, "You got one advantage. You'll make a mighty narrow target."

These encouraging words to Bob, from a man like Heck Thomas, were quite satisfactory. "I'm much obliged, Mr. Thomas," he said quietly. "I'll be remembering what you said and reminding you about it one of these days."

Heck Thomas laughed. "Remember, too, young man, that you are asking for it. When the time comes, don't blame me if some of those Territory hoodlums shoot holes through your ears — or your guts!"

Hutchins grinned. He had been hardened to such talk from men who talked tougher than Thomas. He had even seen exactly the sort of thing he implied. "I don't scare easy, Mr. Thomas. I'll try to be around when the smoke clears away."

Bob Hutchins returned home a few months later with the blessings of J. M. Carlyle and Mrs. Carlyle, and a certificate that announced "that James Robert Hutchins has satisfactorily completed the prescribed course of education in the Normal School of Whitesboro, Texas, and has graduated." What pleased Bob most was that through special tutoring from Mr. and Mrs. Carlyle, he had accomplished it in half the expected time.

Proudly, Cassie Hutchins placed it inside a frame over a picture and hung it on the wall.

Within a few days, Bob grew restless. "I think I'll ride over to the courthouse in Paris," he told his mother. "Maybe I can find out where Heck Thomas is. He might have forgotten that he sort of promised me a job a year ago, but I haven't."

Cassie Hutchins knew the time he had spoken about when

79

he went off to school had now come. As he got out his bedroll and saddlebags, she asked, "Are you going away to stay?"

"I don't know how long I'll be gone," he said frankly. "I'll probably wind up for a while in the Chickasaw Nation with Uncle Bob and Aunt Sally."

She sighed. "Maybe we'll all be over there when your pa makes up his mind. Tell your Uncle Bob to write to him."

"Don't worry about me," he told her. "I'll write and let you know where I am and what I'm doing."

John A. laughed and predicted: "Your feet will quit itching some day, like mine did; and you, too, will settle down to a house full of kids."

All the children gathered around this big brother who was always coming and going and watched him prepare for the trip. Bob knew them all very well by now. There were seven of them in 1887: John, Andy, Sam, Dellah, Tom, Sallie Ethel, and Albert; the youngest, two years old.

Their eyes widened as their big brother strapped on his big six-shooter and thrust his rifle into the saddle scabbard. They were still yelling at him to come home again soon when he rode out of hearing.

The office deputy in the marshal's office in Paris didn't know much about Heck Thomas, so Bob Hutchins rode to his Uncle Bob Faulkner's place on Oil Creek in the Chickasaw Nation. He passed along greetings from his mother and father to Uncle Bob and Aunt Sally. Then he asked Bob Faulkner to write John A. and tell him the possibilities of this virgin country. "Tell him to get over here before the white settlers find some new way to cheat the Indians out of their birthrights."

He told Uncle Bob his plan to become a lawman.

"Why don't you ride into the new town of Ardmore and talk to Tom Coggins, chief detective for the Santa Fe. They have nearly finished the Santa Fe track from Purcell to Gainesville across the Chickasaw Nation. I plan to take Sally in to watch the first train come into Ardmore. Nearly everybody will be there. There will be federal officers there, too. You can bet on that. Tell Tom Coggins I said to help you. He knows me. He's a good man."

Elated by this news, Bob Hutchins rode into Ardmore and

80

hunted up Tom Coggins. He was pleased to see that Coggins was a friendly, kindly man. "Any nephew and namesake of my old friend, Bob Faulkner, is on the credit side of my ledger," Coggins declared. "Come with me, Kid. I want to introduce you to a real marshal, who's going to ride the first train from Gainesville into Ardmore with us. He's here on a circuit with some other deputy marshals."

They found Heck Thomas in Tom Nolan's refreshment place, and to Tom Coggins' surprise, Bob Hutchins said cheerfully, "Howdy, Marshal Thomas. Remember me?"

"I sure do, son! Did you get that gilt-edge education?"

"Got it signed and sealed, hanging on the wall at home."

"That's fine. What are your plans now?"

"That's what I brought this boy to see you about, Heck," Tom Coggins interrupted. "Where have you met him before?"

"At Fort Worth at the fat stock show and rodeo, about a year ago, wasn't it, Kid?"

"Yes, sir."

"This kid wants to be a lawman and he's just a button!" He turned to young Hutchins. "How old are you now, Kid?"

"I'll be sixteen years old this coming September eighth, sir."

Heck Thomas laughed at Coggins' amazement. "This kid has already done and seen more than lots of men in a whole lifetime. Old John Hall took him to the Spur Ranch in West Texas before he was really seven. He gave him a .41 calibre Colt to cut his teeth on. I tried to tell him what a risky, poor-paying job being a lawman is, but it didn't discourage him. He's not figuring on getting rich, and he's seen men gut-shot and gunned down before."

Hutchins had not told Heck Thomas this, but he knew that J. M. Carlyle must have.

"I'm going to let him ride the train with us from Gainesville day after tomorrow, even if I get bawled out from the main office. What are you going to do about making him a posseman, Heck?"

"I heard of a deputy sheriff down in Texas who was fifteen," Heck said, smiling. "You take him under your wing until he's sixteen, Tom. By that time I'll have my family moved to Whitebead Hill. I'll make him a posseman, if Judge Parker and Marshal Carroll will let me."

To Hutchins the conversation was almost like sitting in judgement, for his career was at stake. He thanked both these newly found friends fervently.

He was a proud young officer, by Tom Coggins' special appointment, as he rode the first Santa Fe passenger train from Gainesville, Texas, into Ardmore, Chickasaw Nation. There were a number of passengers from Texas and Indian Territory riding for the historical importance of the trip. With the bell ringing, smoke belching from the engine's stack and steam hissing from its pistons, the train came to a stop at the depot platform. It was twenty minutes after twelve noon, on June 28, 1887, when the shouting, happy passengers unloaded onto the platform and greeted friends in the crowd gathered to meet them. It was the largest crowd the new little town of Ardmore had ever seen.

Bob Hutchins rode the passenger trains; sometimes with, and sometimes for, Tom Coggins. When Heck Thomas came back through Ardmore again that fall, he joined him and his posse.

The "Hanging" Judge
and His Court

He rode with Heck Thomas and Colonel J. H. Mershon as posseman for the next two years. Deputy marshals were badly needed, but Hutchins was considered too young to take on the full responsibilities of a marshal and lead a posse on his own. Thomas and Mershon admired his courage and caution, though; and they knew that soon he could be trusted to lead a posse into the outlaw country or go alone. Heck Thomas introduced him to the judge and told about the youth's ambitions.

"You make good as *posse comitatus*, young man," Judge Parker assured him, "and you'll also make the grade as a deputy." His sincere voice was assuring to Bob. He sat in the courtroom during sessions of the court to get a first-hand knowledge of the workings of justice. He was awed at first by what seemed to be the cold, relentless intolerance the judge and jury seemed to show toward culprits. But he also learned that mercy was not as alien in Judge Parker's court as he had heard. It could be generously dispensed to deserving people.

The more Bob Hutchins came to know Judge Isaac Charles

Parker, the more he liked him. He was a Yankee ex-soldier, who carried himself with dignity and looked like a typical Southern colonel, with his white mustache and goatee and great grizzled shock of hair. Away from his bench, he could be jolly and jocular, and exceptionally interesting, somehow. Bob forgot the cold, accusing title of "Hanging Judge," which men had given him.

Judge Isaac Charles Parker was born in Belmont County, Ohio, in 1838. When he was twenty-one, he moved to St. Joseph, Missouri, and practiced law. In 1869, he was chosen city attorney and served in that capacity until he was elected prosecuting attorney of Buchanan County.

From the beginning in St. Joseph, Parker became active in politics. He was president of the Stephen A. Douglas Club in Missouri, but early in 1861, he supported the Republican Party and continued to do so until his death. In 1864, he was chosen presidential elector to cast Missouri's vote for Abraham Lincoln. He became judge of the Twelfth Judicial Circuit Court of Missouri in 1868, and two years later was elected to Congress from the Sixth Missouri District. In 1872, he was re-elected to Congress, and during this second term, he served on the Committee of Territories, of which James A. Garfield was chairman.

In 1875, Judge Isaac Charles Parker was appointed Chief Justice of Utah, but two weeks later, President U. S. Grant withdrew the appointment — at the request of Senators Dorsey and Clayton — in order to end the fierce Brooks-Baxter war that was making the Western District of Arkansas an unfit place to live. Parker was appointed judge of that district, thus establishing the unique precedent of appointing a judge from outside the state.

At the age of thirty-seven, Isaac Charles Parker became judge of the largest federal court in the nation. His stature of about six feet tall and 265 pounds weight impressed men with the idea that he was a battering ram of law and order on the border of the wild, savage Indian Territory.

During Judge Parker's almost quarter century tenure in Fort Smith, Arkansas, around 172 men were sentenced to hang, and 89 of these were actualy executed on the grim gallows in the prison yard. Some were killed trying to escape. The others were saved by appeals to the United States Supreme Court;

for Judge Parker was sometimes overruled. Many others were given life sentences or lesser terms.

Chief Justice Fuller, in Washington, at one time criticized Judge Parker's procedure, but Judge Parker flared right back with the reminder that he was on the ground and knew what he was doing. He went so far in his retort as to tell the Supreme Court to go to the devil and attend to its own business. He announced that it was his duty to rid a great, free land of outlaws and criminals. His court, he insisted, was making it possible for free-spirited pioneers to settle in this untracked region and fill a gap in westward expansion where life, liberty and the pursuit of happiness could be enjoyed in peace and good will.

Hutchins sat in the judge's court and saw him drop his head and weep after pronouncing the death sentence. But each time a man was convicted by the jury, Judge Parker carried out his duty.

Wherever Judge Parker went, his tall, broad figure, in his Prince Albert coat, was the symbol of authority to the law-abiding citizens. He was a flapping scarecrow of doom to the lawless. Court was held every day during the term, except Sundays and the holidays, for the flow of criminals from the marshals and their parties seemed endless.

The marshals and their deputies and possemen camped along the Arkansas River bottom, west of town. Boats ferried them and their prisoners over to the jail. By the time he was appointed deputy marshal, Bob Hutchins was familiar with every detail of life of a frontier federal officer.

Although there was almost always one or more parties of officers camped along the river, their forays into the Indian Territory generally lasted about ninety days. Marshals and acting marshals made regular quarter-annual reports to the "Chief" Marshal of the Court.

With bench warrants and firearms, these vigilantes went out like cowboys onto a range. They took along an extra grub wagon and a cook and camped at different locations for intervals of only a few days. The deputies and possemen rode out and searched the country, and rounded up criminals, sometimes for a radius of a hundred miles, chiefly looking for men on the warrants they carried with them.

85

They scouted relentlessly for killers, outlaws, whiskey runners and minor criminals. In the language of the day, the captured criminals were charged with everything from *crack-a-Lou* to *cold-blooded murder*. Many of them were arrested for distilling whiskey and selling and trading it to the Indians. Rape was a crime often committed and many times punished by hanging. Sixty-five officers were killed in the line of duty during Judge Parker's tenure; and many others wounded.

The prisoners of the deputy marshals were kept handcuffed and shackled in camp to the wagon wheels as they moved about on the circuit, or to convenient jack-oaks.

On Bob Hutchins' first trip with Heck Thomas, the marshal carried fifty-five bench warrants in his pockets. Most of the violators of the law were wanted "dead or alive." Besides Heck Thomas and Hutchins, there were Little Jim Wallace, Joe Cadel, Bub Trainor (a Cherokee Indian who was a deputy) and ten wagon guards. The trip took ninety-nine days, and they returned to Fort Smith with fifty-one prisoners. Three of the fifty-five criminals had been killed resisting arrest, and the worst one of the lot had eluded them. He was Jim Harbolt, known to the old-timers as a "bear-cat."

Occasionally on the trips, they arrested men for minor infractions and relied on them as *trusties* to help guard the hard-cased ones, and to do cooking and other chores. But it often happened that such trusted prisoners were rare; and on these circuits, they had to be very cautious.

During his twenty-one years' tenure as Judge for the United States Court of the Western District of Arkansas (which included both Oklahoma and Indian Territory for the first eight years), Judge Parker presided over the largest and toughest judicial district in the entire country. Judge Parker presided over the court for the first time on May 10, 1875, and continued in good health, hardly missing a day of court until early in July, 1896.

Then he inexplicably took sick and lingered in bed, racked with disease and pain, until he died on November 17, 1896. He had tried to carry on for the court and issue orders from his bed, but he grew too weak to do it. Cases piled up in the suspended court. Shorn of the twin territories to the west, the court diminished in grandeur and significance as the man who had so fearlessly administered it, diminished and passed away.

Judge Caldwell, of the Eighth Judicial District, had on August 24 appointed Honorable Oliver P. Shiras "in the place or in aid of Honorable Isaac Charles Parker, to preside over the Fort Smith court until December 1st, 1896."

Judge Shiras presided for two days — August 27 and 28. The grand jury reported on the first day and was discharged. Their bill of indictment consisted of 210 cases; 54 were dismissed after investigation, and the other 156 admitted as true. The next day, 33 of the prisoners indicted entered pleas of guilty; and 87 criminal cases were scheduled for trial a week later.

During Parker's term of court the first time, he soon found he could administer justice more efficiently and more economically than it had been done in the past. He reduced the annual cost of operating the court from $400,000 to $300,000.

In that first term, he tried eighteen murder cases, fifteen of which were convicted by the jury. On June 26, 1875, Judge Parker pronounced his first death sentences. Eight men were sentenced on that fateful day: Daniel Evans, James Moore, John Whittington, Edmund Campbell, Smoker Man-Killer, Samuel Fooy, Frank Butler and Oscar Snow. Judge Parker, in a measured, clear voice, pronounced the fatal words to Daniel Evans. Then, as he could hardly ever keep from doing afterward, he bowed his head and wept. Hutchins, in later years, witnessed this several times. The judge rapped with his gavel and he himself questioned the witness or defendant to bring out the truth. He seemed to always be able to know when a person on the stand was lying. Hutchins said: "If you were guilty, you had come to the wrong court for trial, but if you were innocent, you had come to the right court. Judge Parker would go as far to prove a defendant's innocence as he would to prove his guilt."

The records of Judge Parker's November term of court in 1875 show: criminal cases, 91, with 60 found guilty, 18 pleaded guilty; 61 sent to the penitentiary. Six were convicted of murder, while five were acquitted; four were sent to the old garrison jail. In all, the grand jury returned 150 indictments.

After the establishment of the United States Court of the Western District of Arkansas, including the twin territories, 13,490 cases were docketed before Judge Parker's court. Of these,

87

9,454 persons were either convicted by jury trials or pleaded guilty.

The official records for ten years — December 31, 1884 to December 31, 1894 — show the convicted criminal cases as 7,419; 305 for murder and manslaughter, 406 for assault with intent to kill, 1,910 for selling liquor to Indians, 2,860 for introducing liquor into the Indian Territory, 97 for illicit distilling, 124 for violating internal revenue laws, 65 for violating postal laws, 50 for counterfeiting, 24 for arson, 48 for perjury, 32 for bigamy, 27 for conspiracy to commit crime, 59 for stealing government timber, 24 for resisting arrest, 149 for unspecified crimes. What the other 1,179 were accused of and what became of their cases was not clarified.

During the next years, two thousand additional cases were placed on the docket. The federal arresting officers were kept busy, despite the hardships and risks involved, going out into a virtually untracked wilderness after unbelievably brutal criminals.

The court had final jurisdicton over all crimes committed in the Indian Territory and No Man's Land, except in those cases where the accused and accusers were Indians. The courts of the Indian nations at that time took care of their own people and maintained their own systems of law enforcement.

But the scope and power of the jurisdiction of this great court were hampered by acts of Congress.

The first act of Congress that reduced the jurisdiction of the court in the Indian Territory was approved January 6, 1883. It provided that: "*All that part of the Indian Territory lying north of the Canadian River and east of Texas and the one-hundredth meridian, not set aside and occupied by the Cherokee, Creek, Seminole Indian tribes,* be annexed to and form a part of the United States District Courts at Wichita and Fort Scott, Kansas. This gave these Kansas courts exclusive and original jurisdiction over all offenses committed within the limits of that territory. . . ."

These changes in Judge Parker's judicial area had no appreciable effect in lessening the work of his court. Though the federal officers had to police far less territory, they were able to do it more thoroughly, and the number of cases in Parker's court increased because of it.

But Congress was never satisfied with the *status quo* of the Fort Smith court. Other acts of Congress were passed until the final act sounded the death knell to the jurisdiction over the Indian Territory on September 1, 1896. So when the great court and the great judge expired in 1896, thousands of the twenty-five thousand people in Fort Smith assembled to mourn his death. People came from as far away as four hundred miles to pay their respects to the man whom they knew had made peace and progress of civilization possible. The largest cortege of mourners in the city's history attested their sorrow and their tributes to His Honor's death.

Bob Hutchins joined the enforcement officers of the Fort Smith court in 1887, about the time the new jail was built next to the courthouse. It had easy accommodations for 144 prisoners. On February 2, 1896, the records show there were 244 prisoners confined there. An unofficial rumor later claimed that there were 300 in number in the jail at the same time. But it does seem that the new jail could hold all the prisoners the industrious deputy marshals arrested.

The new jail was a considerable improvement in health and sanitation over the old garrison basement. It consisted of a large, three-story steel cage, with a run-around space seven feet wide between the cage and the walls of the building on two sides and the southwest end. The cells were five feet by eight feet in size and were fixed with iron doors, opening into a four-foot aisle, extending the entire length of both sides of the cage. On each floor, twenty-four cells, twelve on each side, were numbered alternately. There were seventy-two cells in all. The twenty-four cells on the first floor were called "Murderers' Row."

The second floor was used to confine men charged with robbery, burglary, larceny, assault, etc. The top floor held those charged with selling or introducing whiskey into the Indian Territory; for which severe punishment was meted to them.

Two years later, a new courthouse was built three blocks southeast of the old one. The old courthouse, or the first floor of the old military barracks, was devoted to jailers' quarters. The courtroom, itself, was converted into the jail kitchen; and the spectators' section was used to hold female prisoners, and was also used as a penitentiary for women sentenced by federal

89

courts in the Indian Territory to terms of imprisonment for twelve months or less.

On all three floors of the new jail, if there was a single prisoner remorseful about the death of "Hanging" Judge Isaac Charles Parker, he was silent; but even if he had screamed his grief, it would not have been heard above the whoops and the shouts and the laughter of those who rejoiced.

One Negro criminal put it very aptly for all of them when he laughed and shouted joyfully and declared, "The debil's sho' got de ole cuss dis time!"

This might have been the sentiment of the lawless, but the law-abiding citizens felt quite differently. The crowning irony of the court is the fact that Judge Isaac Charles Parker *was a jurist who was opposed to the death penalty.*

There is a story behind the coining of the term "bootlegger" which goes back to about the year 1888. The word was first used by Judge Parker in his court.

Bob Hutchins attended a square dance with his fiddle in the Spavinaw Hills of the Cherokee Nation. He noticed the boys and girls were getting pretty gay, and the attentions of the girls were mostly focused on a young man named Jack Spratt. Hutchins suspected him of selling whiskey.

Both Indians and whites knew it was a criminal offense to sell liquor to an Indian, and some of the people at the dance were Indians. Hutchins took Spratt outside and searched him, but found no whiskey. Hutchins danced a few sets, called a few sets and fiddled some. But all the time, he kept his eye on Jack Spratt. The girls kept paying attention to Spratt and growing happier all the time.

Then he heard it whispered around that "Jack Spratt was there with the goods, but the fiddlin' deputy marshal was not sharp enough to catch him."

The second time he took Spratt outside and made a thorough search but met with the same failure. Later, he saw a young Indian man sitting disconsolately in a corner by himself. Motioning for him to come over, Hutchins said, "Jack Spratt is selling whiskey here tonight." He gave the Indian a dollar. "Go buy yourself a bottle and have a drink. Maybe you will feel better."

After a while, the Indian came back by and thanked Hutchins. "You sure helped me out," he said.

"Where did Spratt get the whiskey he sold you?" Hutchins asked. The Indian didn't recognize Hutchins as an officer. "Out of his boot," he said. "It sure is good whiskey, too!"

Hutchins took Spratt outside again. "You'll wear my clothes out searchin' me," the first *bootlegger* complained.

"I think this will be the last search," Hutchins assured him, and raised a trouser leg above the boot top.

Out of the boot, he produced three pints of whiskey. Out of the other, he took two.

Hutchins took his prisoner to Fort Smith and placed him in jail. The next morning, he took the culprit before Judge Parker and stated the case.

The judge listened in silence.

"How about it, *Bootlegger* Jack?" Judge Parker asked.

"You've got me," Spratt said, grinning, "but I sure got by with it a long time!"

The Prince of Hangmen

It was late in 1887 when Bob Hutchins first met George Maledon, the hangman for doomed criminals sentenced by Judge Parker. Captain Heck Thomas introduced Bob to Maledon on his first trip to Fort Smith after he had become a posseman under Thomas.

"If you're set on being a lawman, Kid," Heck told him, "you might as well meet the Grim Reaper. You've met Marshal Carroll and Judge Parker, so you should meet with the man who opens the gates of hell. He's also called 'The Prince of Hangmen.' I got my belly full of hangin' right after I went to work for Marshal Carroll. I saw old Maledon hang 'em two at a time twice; but his record, I think, is six men twice through the gates of hell at once."

Bob Hutchins paused in his stride. "Now quit your bullragging me, Heck," he said peevishly. "You've tested me before, and you know by now I can take it."

"Just think," Thomas continued, chuckling, "old Maledon

earned thirty dollars both times. Five dollars a head for every neck broken. And he does a neat job, too!"

"You think I can't watch 'em swing? They all got it coming to 'em, haven't they?"

Heck Thomas grew solemn and serious now. "You won't like it none, Kid. I didn't. I'd much rather shoot 'em down when they are shootin' back at me."

Heck Thomas and Bob Hutchins found George Maledon puttering with his ropes and gadgets; oiling ropes and working coal-tar fluid into the best ropes that could be obtained from St. Louis, Missouri. After oiling them, he stretched them on the gallows gibbet by hanging two hundred pound bags of sand to them until the ropes reduced one-quarter inch in diameter to a good, strong one-inch "hanging rope."

Bob Hutchins was at first awed by Maledon's gaunt appearance. The skin was stretched tautly over his high cheek bones, leaving skeletonlike hollows beneath. His dark, graying and thinning hair and his graying beard, that swept downward around his mouth and under his chin, combined with his mustache in one hairy mass that nearly obscured the face beneath.

Maledon was a thin man, who looked tall because of his thinness, though he was only five feet, six inches in his high-topped boots. Hutchins judged him to weigh no more than 145 pounds. He had black button eyes that were alert and piercing. When he spoke, his voice rose gutterally from the cavernous depth of his chest and filtered through his beard.

He cordially shook hands with Bob, pleased and complimented that the young posseman would care enough about him to want to meet him. His tight features relaxed in a smile as he surveyed Thomas' protégé. "Why, you're just a button of a kid," he remarked. "You must be a nervy one at your age to want to track down bad men over in the Indian country. There's not much pay in it, even when you collect all your fees and mileage from Uncle Sam!"

Hutchins already knew this, but he was relying on the money he had saved to tide him through. He answered Maledon with a grin: "I reckon it takes more stomach and guts to do your job for five dollars a head. You don't expect to get rich, either. Do you, Mr. Maledon?"

A frown swept across his usually immobile face. Then he

93

laughed deeply. "No, Kid, I don't — salary and all," he confessed, "but somebody has got to introduce the wicked bastards to the devil!" He nodded at Thomas. "Men like Heck and you have got to bring 'em to me — through Judge Parker, of course!"

Then he summarily began to show Bob some of the tricks of his trade, all of which Heck Thomas had seen before. He showed Hutchins how he used different knots for men of various sizes and weights, and explained why. He skillfully tied the thirteen coiled knot which matched the thirteen steps to the gallows. "Now this," he said, tying a seaman's simple square knot, "is best suited for a man who is about one hundred twenty or thirty pounds. It breaks his neck easier." Then he showed Hutchins and Thomas a double clove hitch knot. "This one is my favorite," he said proudly. "It'll work for any of them. I learned these two seaman's knots from a customer of mine who used to be in the navy." He smiled and added, "He wasn't a very big man, and that reef knot worked just like he said it would."

Heck Thomas felt sorry for Maledon, because of his isolation. Everybody in Fort Smith shunned him, as if he carried bubonic plague. Hutchins, too, as he saw all this, felt pity for poor old, lonesome Maledon.

George Maledon came from Europe to Detroit, Michigan, when he was only a year old. He was born in Landau, Bavaria, on June 10, 1830. He was educated in both the German and English schools of Detroit. He had heard and read so much about the West that he set off to seek his fortune there, when he was twenty years old. Somehow, he wound up in the Choctaw Nation of the Indian Territory where, for years, he managed a sawmill.

The sawmill life proved to be too mild for him. He went to Fort Smith and hired out as a policeman in that turbulent town, called "The Swinging Doors of Hell." He mixed with the worst of criminals and bad men in that town and somehow managed to survive.

When the Civil War began, Maledon enlisted in the First Arkansas Federal Battery. He lived through the terrible conflict of many artillery duels.

Mustered out of military service at the end of the war in 1865, he was appointed deputy sheriff in Sebastian County, Arkansas, where he served under two successive sheriffs, Thomas F. Scott and John H. McClure.

When Fort Smith was established as the office of the judge of the Western District on May 2, 1871, Maledon accepted a commission as Deputy United States Marshal under Chief Marshal Logan S. Roots.

The marshal of the court of the Western District at the time Judge Isaac Charles Parker made his debut in May of 1871 was James F. Fagan. His successors, in order, were:

D. P. Upham, appointed July 10, 1876

Valentine Dell, appointed June 15, 1880

Thomas Boles, appointed February 20, 1882

John Carroll, appointed May 21, 1886

Jacob Yoes, appointed January 29, 1890

George J. Crump, appointed May 29, 1893

George Maledon worked under all eight of these court's marshals during his tenure of a little over twenty-three years. His job was not coveted nearly as much as that of United States Marshal.

He had become expert with shooting irons. He wore two large pistols in his coat belt, which he handled almost as dexterously as he later tied hanging knots. He was soon assigned the job of turnkey for the jail. A year later, because the other deputies refused the job, Maledon was appointed a special deputy, with salary and bonuses and put in charge of the execution of condemned prisoners.

He held this job four years before the arrival of Judge Parker. During his twenty-five years with the court, he had hanged over sixty men for their atrocious crimes. He killed three and wounded two men who tried to escape.

Frank Butler, a Negro, had been convicted of murder and his attorney had requested that Judge Parker hold a night session to sentence him. At that time, the old Fort Smith garrison basement jail was still in use. When the big, burly Butler stepped through the jail door, he suddenly threw back both his arms and knocked down the guards on both sides and sprang forward into the darkness.

Maledon quickly turned the key in the jail lock to prevent other prisoners from escaping. When he turned back to look for Butler, he skylighted him as he neared the east wall. He leveled his pistol, took a quick, unerring aim and fired. Butler fell dead on a spot that was later measured at seventy-five yards.

A horse thief, Frank Wilson, was a desperado who didn't even get to trial. When he was brought to the jail, he knocked the marshal down and ran. It was a dark and rainy night. Wilson zigzagged, thinking to dodge any gunfire, but Maledon's first shot brought him down with a bullet through the hip. Two days later, he died.

Three escapees were Ellis and Orpheus McGee — brothers — and John Werthington, who escaped by taking the stone mantle from the fireplace and using it for a battering ram on the outside door. They broke the fastenings. Maledon brought Ellis down with his righthand pistol. Jailer Charlie Burns now brought his gun into action, and they both shot down Orpheus. Then Maledon shot John Werthington down from the top of the gate with his lefthand pistol, in a single, fatal shot.

Ellis McGee, after being shot by Maledon, spent some time in the hospital and was sentenced to fifteen years in prison at Little Rock, Arkansas, where he again escaped. But he later met his death at the hands of George Hawkins in the northeast corner of the Choctaw Nation the Indians had named Skullyville, which means Moneytown; because that's where the United States Government paid them their annual annuities.

His brother, Orpheus McGee, tried, convicted and sentenced to hang, lived to be hanged by Maledon's favorite clove hitch knot. "Just to make sure," Maledon joked, "we didn't have to shoot him again."

The gallows stood in a corner of the prison yard; weathered, grim and unpainted, with a roof that sloped sharply back to the rock wall. The trap doors in the floor, directly under the condemned men's feet, opened in the middle and dropped the victims eight feet to break their necks on the "hanging knots" Maledon improvised. About thirty or forty minutes later, when it was certain that the last spark of life had left each victim, Maledon would have them taken down and laid in their coffins in their new suits, or death robes, furnished by the government.

Maledon always appeared on the scaffold neatly dressed in a black suit, white shirt and black necktie; his boots polished; and carrying his big pistols, strapped around his waist, over his coat for easy access. He had a peculiar mannerism of raising his beard to adjust the knot of his necktie at his own throat before he was satisfied with the black hood he had placed over the head and the hanging knot he usually placed behind the left ear. Then he sprang the trap doors that left his victims hanging between Heaven and Hell.

The crowds of thousands of people that gathered in the prison courtyard on "Hanging Days" to watch the gruesome spectacle, like spectators at a freak show, grew larger each year. This sadism drew so much criticism that in 1882, authorities in Washington, D.C., sent orders to Judge Parker to restrict the quota of witnesses to a reasonable number of officials. Six years later, Bob Hutchins saw his first hanging, when he was one of the forty selected to witness it.

The original beam of the gallows was used to hang eighty-two of the total of eighty-nine men hanged by the court. The last hanging on it took place April 30, 1896. Two brothers — George and John Pierce — and Webber Isaacs had murdered their boyhood playmate, William Vandever; but Maledon *did not* spring the trap. Prior to that, Crawford Golby — alias Cherokee Bill — had been hanged at 2:30 on the afternoon of March 17, 1896. The man who pulled the lever that sprang the trap on poor Bill was jail guard Eoff, whom Bill had tried to kill eight months earlier, at the time of changing guards for the night. He did kill another popular guard named Lawrence Keating, with a revolver that had been smuggled to him by Ben Howell, a trusty with the run of the prison yard. He was known over in the Indian Territory as a sort of straggler with the Dalton and Doolin gang, whom they used for petty errands, since he lacked the courage to join their raids. Cherokee Bill finally admitted Howell smuggled two pistols to him on June 27, 1895. They were put into his cell window from the outside on a pole. Bill hid one of them in a bucket, but it was found on July 10. The other, he concealed in a hole he had made in his cell wall by removing a brick.

Afterward the beam was replaced because it had grown weak from weather and strain.

Not long before he left Fort Smith, a little old lady visited the prison, and it was Maledon's duty to show her around. He took her out into the prison yard, showed her his ropes and

97

gadgets, explaining each patiently, and finally he showed her the gallows.

"Doesn't your conscience ever bother you about all the men you have hanged? Don't their spirits ever come back to haunt you?"

"Well, Madam," he drawled, "all the men I've hanged claimed they were innocent, but I've never hanged a man who has come back to have the job done again. The ghosts of men hanged here have never come back to hang around the old gibbet."

After Maledon retired in 1894, he went into the grocery business in Fort Smith, but he soon tired of the monotony and moved up near Fayetteville to take charge of an eighty-acre farm.

In the spring of 1897, Judge Parker's jurisdiction over the Indian Territory ceased; no more executions would be performed in the Western District of Arkansas, except where capital crime had been committed on a government reservation, or other government property.

When Congress ordered the removal of the old gallows, an enterprising territorial promotor got Maledon to sign a contract, gathered some of his ropes and gadgets he had used in his gruesome work and toured the territory with him. Maledon enjoyed it. For the first time in his life, people flocked around him and paid attention to him.

At last, Maledon had found popularity; sensational, of course, but he was now, at least in the eyes of the youth of that day, a hero.

When he talked to the kids, he tried to leave a moral lesson with them, but didn't preach any sermons. He did it in the casual way he had of talking to them. He showed them the ropes that had strung up twenty-seven men and eleven men and nine men, a small piece of the scaffold's main beam, and pictures of sixty men he had hanged. He lectured to young and old, for the admission of twenty-five cents. He loved to show them his favorite double clove hitch knot. "Just see how easy the knot slid on the neck," he would tell them.

Lucky was the youth who shook hands with the great hangman, or talked him out of a bit of fiber from one of the ropes. They could go away and say, "This is the hand that shook the hand that sprang the trap that sent sixty men to hell; and this is part of the rope that hanged twenty-seven men!"

He was often asked what reactions his victims had to his hanging them. He just smiled and replied, "None of them ever came back and complained to me about it," and this always drew a big laugh from his crowd.

A gentleman one day reminded him that the greatest executioner of all times was the Frenchman, Deibler, who decapitated 437 on the guillotine. Maledon retorted with one of his rare, tight-lipped smiles, "That may be true, but hanging them was so much cleaner, you know. I didn't mess around with my business at all."

Maledon's show became so successful that his manager decided to exhibit him in nationwide vaudeville. He tried to obtain from the city commission of Fort Smith the trap doors of the old gallows for the act. When he learned two museum promotors from Buffalo, New York, had made better offers than he had, he went to the newspaper editors and cleverly played on their civic pride and patriotism by telling them he was going to exhibit Maledon and the death trap and give Fort Smith a scandalous reputation as the "hanging" town. The newspapers stirred up such a frenzy of public opinion that the mayor indignantly ordered the trap doors burned. Even then, six-inch scraps of the burned trap doors were sold to souvenir hunters for ten cents each.

A few days later, Maledon died with his boots off, in bed.

Robin Hood of the
Boston Mountains

In 1889, some authority in the Department of Justice in Washington, D.C., decided Judge Parker's court was too slow in cleaning up the territories. He sent orders to Judge Parker and Chief Marshal John Carroll to appoint enough deputy marshals to make a clean sweep of all outlaws and other criminals.

Bob Hutchins was one of those mass appointees, even though he was still three years younger than legal qualifications, which is why the government records show his age as three years older than he actually was. He had proven to his associates that he would make a good lawman and had the ability to uphold the laws.

That same year several deputies died and several more were wounded. Hutchins was one of the casualties. From that time on, despite criticism from Washington, Judge Parker used his own judgment in upholding law and order.

The morning after the appointment, the judge sent for Bob. "Kid," he said, "I have a job for you. It will be your first test as a real deputy. I've sent for you because I think you can do it."

"I'll do my best, sir," Hutchins replied, restraining the eagerness that leaped up inside him. "What is the job, Judge?"

"Have you heard of the Boston Mountains and the activities of the moonshiners there?"

Hutchins nodded. "The source of a lot of firewater for the Indians, I'm told."

The judge regarded him carefully. "Are you game to go in there looking for someone?"

"Judge," Hutchins said recklessly, "I'll try anything once!"

"Yes, that's what I'm afraid of," Judge Parker rebuked him mildly. "But this is a job for brains, not daring. Horse sense will take you in and bring you out. Violence must be reserved for the last resort."

The expression on the judge's face changed to one of doubt. Hutchins felt the chance slipping away. He tried for a new angle. "Someone you want especially alive, Judge?"

"This man is good at heart. He's educated, and a man of good breeding and background. He's tired of lawlessness and wants to surrender to the law, stand trial in my court for all the charges against him. If he is cleared, he aims to try to live a respected life again."

"A friend of yours, Judge?" Hutchins asked softly.

"I barely know him, but I do believe he is honest and sincere."

"Then who is this gent?" Hutchins pursued.

"His name is Dunnegar. He's the king bee of the Boston Mountains."

Hutchins whistled through his long mustache. "How come he can't fork his horse and ride into Fort Smith and surrender to you?"

"Now you have put your finger on the trouble," Judge Parker declared. "His gang won't let him surrender. They have killed three revenue officers this past year, and they're afraid he will hang for it. He is charged in my court for murder, but he sent me word that he is not guilty and explained his predicament." The judge smiled. "Which goes to show certain friends are much easier acquired than they are to get loose from."

"Birds of a feather —" Hutchins broke off, smiling.

101

"You're a green officer yet, Kid," the judge stated flatly, "but that is the main reason I have selected you for this trip. Later on, enemies of society will spot you pretty quick as an officer. Your reputation will travel ahead of you wherever you go. But now it will be different. That's why I'm sending you into the Boston Mountains — alone!"

Hutchins caught the stress and meaning of the last word. The judge had paused and his eyes seemed to drive the word straight into him as he spoke it.

He waited patiently as Judge Parker studied his reaction to the assignment. "Yes — alone!" he repeated, shifting in his swivel chair. "Just a green kid on a tricky mission," he reflected. "You're sharp, Hutchins. I can't give you any advice, except to use your wits and bring this man in to see me."

"I'll do it, Judge, or you'll know the reason why," Hutchins promised.

"I'll have a racehorse saddled and waiting for you at sunup tomorrow," Judge Parker promised. "The rest is up to you, Kid. Good luck!"

The young deputy rode away from Fort Smith early next morning. The long-legged sorrel he rode was named Piebald, because of a big blazed spot on his forehead of that shape. All day long, Piebald kept up the same easy, tireless gait. He was much like Star Face in looks and traits, except that he was younger and had more endurance and speed.

During the long ride, Hutchins' ardor and enthusiasm had enough time to become tempered by thoughtful caution. He camped late that night in the mountains, and arose early the next morning with the sun. He cooked breakfast, washed in a nearby stream and broke camp when the sun was climbing over a hogback in the east. Down the trail a couple of miles, he met an old mountaineer in faded blue duck trousers, held up by one yellow yarn suspender.

"Good morning!" Hutchins greeted him cheerfully.

"Mawnin', stranger!" came the drawling response. The old codger looked him over curiously. "Where to?"

"Just looking around," Hutchins replied easily. "Know anything about minerals in these mountains?"

"The kind you're lookin' fer, I reckon."

102

"I'm interested in all kinds," Hutchins said glibly. "I'm making a geological survey for the government."

"Yeah, I know," the mountaineer replied with a shrewd grin. "The last three gents that came in here makin' a survey are planted over on that ridge yonder."

Hutchins felt a shock run through him, but he kept a straight face and stubbornly insisted, "You must be thinking about revenuers. I heard about that and I was warned I might be looked upon suspiciously. I don't care a hoot for stills. I'm a mineralogist, just out of college. I'm too young to be a lawman!"

The old mountaineer drew a long twist of homegrown tobacco from his pocket and offered it to Hutchins. The young deputy marshal took one whiff of the strong odor and declined with a grin. The old man chewed over Hutchins' last remark and looked at him with one eye squinted.

"You talk like a fust grade kid with yore line of bull, young feller," the old mountaineer declared bluntly. "What for does Jedge Parker wanta send a button like you into these hills? Did he run out of men?"

Hutchins felt a foolish grin steal over his face. He was flustered by the uncanny intuition of the old-timer. He decided to risk everything boldly. This old codger knew all about the moonshiners and he must also know the man he was looking for.

"Where can I find Dunnegar, the king bee of this gang of spirit makers?"

"What for do you wanta know?"

"I've got a letter of introduction to him from one of his old whiskey gang down in Texas," Hutchins lied.

He watched closely and saw the look of surprise in the mountaineer's eyes. Hutchins knew he had hit upon a lucky note.

"I ain't ever heard of your man," the old codger persisted, "but sit down and graze your hoss and wait here. If your man is in these hills, I'll find him." As he started off in a dog trot, he flung back over his shoulder, "I'm not promisin' that you won't regret it, young feller!"

After he had turned a bend in the trail, Hutchins boldly took pencil and paper, wrote a note to the king bee and signed

Judge Parker's name. Then he lay basking and napping in the warm autumn sun while his horse cropped the grass around him.

In about two hours, the yellow-suspendered man returned with a younger man, better dressed and neater in appearance. This man looked sharply at Hutchins and asked, "You got a note for me?"

"If your name is Dunnegar, I have," Hutchins retorted.

"That's my handle."

Hutchins watched Dunnegar read the note, and he noted the pleased expression that came over the man's face.

Turning to his friend, Dunnegar said, "Buck, you ride our bunch over to Blue Spring. We'll meet there and figure out what to do about this."

When Buck loped off, the boss of the Boston Mountains moonshiners turned to Hutchins with a grin. "Now, my young friend, you and I have got to do some smart figuring to work out a plan that won't get us both killed."

"I have a hunch," Hutchins told him, "and my luck always runs good on hunches."

"Spill it," Dunnegar said. "If it ain't the right card, we'll shuffle for a new draw!"

"Your friend, Buck, thinks I'm a revenue officer, and so will the rest of your gang. Let me just tell them the only authority I have in Arkansas is a permit from Judge Parker to arrest a fellow wanted in Texas for four murders. I'll say there's a reward of twenty-five hundred dollars offered. I'm just a Texas officer after the reward."

Dunnegar's face wrinkled in thought. "Might do," he agreed. "You got a quick mind and a glib tongue. Maybe we can both lie enough to back it up."

The moonshine gang was gathering at Blue Spring when Dunnegar and Hutchins arrived. Addressing them, Dunnegar introduced Bob as a young Texas officer, with an introduction from an old friend and a permit from Judge Parker to look for a man among them who was wanted in Texas for four cold-blooded murders.

Hutchins was impressed with the agility of Dunnegar's mind. He read off a great deal that wasn't in the letter and substituted another name for Judge Parker's. The way he

104

flourished the letter in their faces made Bob uneasy, until he realized not a man among them could read.

"Boys, this law button don't care a hoot about our business," Dunnegar assured them, "except he likes a little nip once in a while, himself. He promises to recommend our brand. There's a reward of twenty-five hundred dollars on the head of this killer he wants, and he said he'll split it with us. If there is a man in these mountains who has killed four men in cold blood, we don't want the snake hibernating among us! Do we?"

"No!" they thundered. Someone produced a jug and it was passed around. Soon they all relaxed. Rifles were confidently laid aside, and nervous fingers stopped drumming on the butts of six-shooters. Now they busied themselves stuffing pipes, rolling quirleys and lighting them.

Suddenly, Dunnegar turned to Hutchins with an inspiration. "I've been thinking," he said, "who this killer might be." He glanced over the faces around them. "He ain't none of this bunch. He ain't bothered us and we ain't bothered him all these months he's been in these mountains. Done nothing but hunt and tan hides. Seems to want to be alone all the time."

A few of the men approved Dunnegar's suspicions heartily.

"That sure takes a load off my mind to know this gent ain't no close friend of you boys," Hutchins declared with a broad smile. "Too many smoke-guns around here for me to buck. I'd rather drink your whiskey with you any old day!"

They all laughed and Hutchins decided he could get along with these men with no more trouble. Getting Dunnegar away from them was the only real problem now.

Dunnegar solved it easily. "Boys, hang around close. We may need you, if we run into trouble."

They rode off and Hutchins breathed easier.

"That's the fastest one I've put over in a long time," Dunnegar confessed with relief. "Now if I can be as lucky in that Fort Smith court —"

"We'll leave that to Judge Parker," Hutchins interrupted. "If you can convince him you didn't murder those revenue officers, you're as good as cleared now."

Riding down a canyon, they came to a big, flat rock. Here Dunnegar stopped, climbed down and drew a little cow horn from beneath the rock. Grinning up at Hutchins, he said: "I can give one loud toot on this horn and you would be shot out of your saddle before we get out of this canyon."

Hutchins didn't doubt it. He had already seen how the moonshiners gathered at his bidding and obeyed his orders.

The canyon led into a little flat, where there was a two-room log cabin just off the trail. By the trail stood a big oak.

"See that contraption hanging there in that tree?" Dunnegar asked.

Hutchins nodded, as he observed an old, rusty plow-sweep, suspended as a bell, with a rock hanging beside it for a clapper.

Dunnegar grinned again. "I can tug on that rope, ring that one time and you would be shot off your horse from that cabin. If the men are away, a woman would pull the trigger."

"I don't know why you're telling me all this," Hutchins said. "Let's get out of here."

"I'm telling you, my young friend," Dunnegar replied solemnly, "to help enlighten a bold, young officer." One eye closed slyly. "That letter you gave me ain't in Judge Parker's handwriting and it should have been written in ink. But I'm going with you, Kid, because I've got other ways of knowing the judge sent you."

Hutchins gulped back a gasp of surprise. He suddenly realized that it was impossible to be too cautious in dealing with desperate men.

As they spurred their horses, Dunnegar laughed. "I'm glad you get what I mean, Kid," he declared. "You're game and I like you."

Dunnegar got a thorough and careful hearing before Judge Parker in his private chamber. The questions which the judge put to this Robin Hood of the Boston Mountains were searching, for Judge Parker's main concern was to satisfy himself that Dunnegar was telling the truth about the revenue officers. Judge Parker became convinced that Dunnegar was guiltless of the murders.

If he knew exactly who committed the crimes, Dunnegar steadily avoided revealing their identity. He had not been present during the gunfight, and he assured the judge he could prove this by several witnesses. It appeared from the information he had gleaned from the mountaineers in general, however, that the revenue officers had acted rashly, and had simply invited their own deaths.

Finally, Judge Parker said, "Dunnegar, I'm going to stay this case for thirty days. You take the kid and go back to your mountains. Prepare your testimony, select your witnesses and hire a good lawyer. I predict you can beat the murder charges. In the meantime, I'll see what can be done to set aside the six moonshine cases against you."

So Hutchins and Dunnegar headed back for the Boston Mountains that evening. They arrived at Dunnegar's cabin in the middle of the next morning.

Their stay in the mountains lasted twenty-two days. During that time, young Bob Hutchins had the time of his life. The "hoe-down" square dances were the gayest and liveliest he ever attended. Bob was popular with men and women alike. As light as he was, the husky mountain girls could throw him over their shoulders and promenade home without missing a step.

Dunnegar returned with his witnesses, stood trial and walked out of court a free man. He returned to the mountains for his sweetheart, bid farewell to his illicit bootlegging comrades and settled down in Fort Smith to live a quiet life.

Belle Star—Friend
of Friend and Foe

Soon after his appointment as riding posseman for Marshal Heck Thomas, Bob Hutchins met Belle Star for the second time in his life.

Bell and her husband, Jim Starr, were in Fort Smith for one of their many cases in federal court. Belle was enjoying herself by shopping in town.

Bob was with Marshal Heck Thomas and Colonel J. H. Mershon when they met the Starrs on the street. When Thomas introduced his youthful posseman, Belle smiled and asked, "Aren't you the boy I met in Whitesboro more than a year ago? You were going to school there, and you played the fiddle for some of the dances."

Surprised that she remembered, Bob replied, "You've got me pegged right, Mrs. Starr. I told you then that I was going to be an officer. Marshal Thomas has taken the risk of starting me off as a posseman."

Belle Starr's alert and attractive eyes glanced at Heck

Thomas. "Mr. Thomas is a good officer. I hope you become as good as he is."

"Coming from you, Belle, that's quite a compliment," Heck Thomas said seriously.

"I mean it, Heck," Belle said. "Jim and I have never been mistreated by you."

"That's a fact," Jim Starr affirmed quickly, and added, "nor Colonel Mershon, either. You men and the kid will always be welcome at our humble home."

Bob realized that Belle's attractiveness was not so much caused by her good looks, but by her charm and the elegant way she dressed. She was wise enough to buy clothes that would accent her best points of attraction. Black and white were her favorite colors, and she wore them often. She rarely dressed in a man's clothes. Even at home, she wore feminine clothes, and rode a horse sidesaddle. She could ride this way better than most men could ride astride. Her favorite riding skirt was black.

Hutchins had never met Sam Starr, Belle's prior husband. He had been killed in a gunfight with a Cherokee Indian policeman named Frank West. Although the John West clan and the Tom Starr clan were cousins who owned adjoining land, there had been bad feelings between them for nearly three years. John West, Frank's father, had testified in Judge Parker's court against Belle and Sam, and had caused both of them to be sentenced to a year in the penitentiary at Detroit, Michigan, for stealing two horses. John West, a captain of the Cherokee Nation's Indian police, testified that the Starrs penned the two horses in his lot on April 20, 1882, and led them away. West had not known then to whom the horses belonged.

But even though this feud existed, the real crux of the trouble between Sam Starr and Frank West was the shooting of Sam Starr and the killing of Belle's horse when Sam had been arrested by Cherokee policemen a few months earlier. The two men had met at a dance at Aunt Lucy Sarratt's place a few miles from the Starr home, and had shot it out in true western fashion. Both men were dead in five minutes.

Marshal Heck Thomas dispatched Bob Hutchins and Bub Trainor with a warrant to pick up Jim July, whom Belle had married in a Cherokee tribal ceremony a few months later, even though she was fourteen years older than the handsome young Indian.

The young deputies found Belle Starr alone in her cabin in Younger's Bend. Bob Hutchins and Bub Trainor rode up the narrow trail to the cabin on a hill overlooking the South Canadian River.

Jim July Starr was not there. Belle had made him take the name of "Starr" as a part of their marriage agreement. The name "Starr" appealed to her much more than "Reed," the name of her first husband. Her daughter and oldest child, Pearl, was at Siloam Springs, Arkansas. Her son, Ed Reed, was also gone. They were "teen-aged" children then and they came and went as they pleased.

Bob and Bub still found the woman attractive, though not beautiful. She was very friendly and hospitable. She recognized both young men as officers as they approached her. To Bob she said pleasantly, "I knew that some day you would come to see me. Has that Hanging Judge got out another warrant for me?"

"He's left you out of it this time, Mrs. Starr," Bob replied as he looked steadily into her dark eyes. "The warrant we've got now is for Jim."

She didn't ask what Jim had done. Bob and Bub were sure that she already knew. She declared frankly, and without emotion, "I'll tell you the truth. I don't know where Jim is. You know, anyhow, I wouldn't tell you if I did."

"We don't expect you to, Belle," Bub Trainor said. "It's all in the day's work with us. If we don't find Jim July, some other officer will. We're riding circuit now, going south, and Marshal Heck Thomas is across the river with a pocket full of other warrants.

They smelled Belle's dinner cooking and it seemed enchantingly delicious to them. It was past high noon. Belle knew they were hungry and saddle-weary, so she graciously invited them to sit down and sample her cooking. Both men eagerly accepted her invitation.

Bob looked around the cabin and saw that it was nicely furnished. It was clean and tidy. According to Indian custom of the time, the walls were covered with cloth instead of wall-

110

paper. Muslin was commonly used, but Belle's walls were covered with white calico, decorated with sprigs of bright flowers.

She had a bookcase in one corner filled with books by authors such as Mark Twain, Nathaniel Hawthorne, James Fenimore Cooper, Edgar Allan Poe, Charles Dickens, Thomas Carlyle, Walter Scott, Robert Burns, Longfellow, Emerson and Tennyson.

During the meal, the two deputies plied Belle with earnest questions about outlaws believed to be in the vicinity of Younger's Bend, for whom Marshal Heck Thomas held bench warrants. Belle Starr was discreet about any information she gave the officers, but she ruthlessly hated those outlaws who had no honor or good principles at all. Two such men had been by her place very recently and had gone on south into the Choctaw Nation. Those two men were Bert Casey and Jim Harbolt, and as vicious as animals.

The two young officers thanked her for her hospitality, and respectfully took their leave, with cheerful invitation from her to come again whenever they came that way.

On a half dozen occasions, Bob Hutchins was a visitor at Belle Starr's cabin. One night he was caught out in a cold, hard rain and he spent the night with her and Jim July Starr. They kept him up most of that night, playing "hoe-down" and fiddle tunes.

There was one special favor Belle asked of him. She wanted him to help her plan the arrest and conviction of a man who had evaded the scales of justice too many times. The initials of this man were J. O.

J. O. was a big stockman who lived near Talequah, the capital of the Cherokee Nation. On one of his trips to Kansas City, he took with him an eighteen-year-old half-Cherokee girl, and "kept" her for about ten days. The girl confided her pregnancy to Belle Starr, and Belle rode to Boggy Depot, where she knew Bob Hutchins was stationed now, as a full-fledged deputy marshal.

They made plans to trap J. O. on one of his cattle-stealing forays. Belle got J. O. drunk in one of her tenement cabins, and Bob arrested him and took him to Fort Smith Federal Jail.

Belle appeared against him later as a witness, and J. O. was convicted and sent to the penitentiary.

The most vivid and most important recollection Hutchins had of Belle Starr was the night he fled from Bert Casey and three other outlaws who were trying to murder him. Hutchins had gotten separated from the circuit wagons and all the other deputies. He luckily managed to elude the outlaws by swimming his horse across the river while they took the road directly to the river crossing and tried to head him off. He approached Belle's cabin on foot.

Gun in hand, she let him in and they heard the outlaws' horses coming up the trail.

"Who are they, Bob?" she whispered.

"Bert Casey and some of his bunch. They skylighted me and shot a few times, and I shot back before I realized I was just leading them my way. I swam my horse across the river above the crossing and circled around through the woods. They don't know which way I went."

"I didn't hear your horse," Belle declared.

"I left old Star Face tied up out in the woods, so they'll think I just kept on going."

"Come with me," she said, led the way into the kitchen, lifted a rug and a trap door beneath the table. "Get down there in the cellar," she told him urgently. "They won't find you there!"

When they hailed the cabin, Belle took her time answering, as if just getting out of bed.

Hutchins could hear their voices faintly, but distinctly.

"Who is it?" Belle wanted to know.

Bert Casey answered. "It's Casey, Jim Harbolt and two friends."

"What do you want?"

"We're chasin' a lawman. Did you hear him go by?"

"I've been asleep," Belle told them.

There was a pause while the outlaws talked among themselves, then Bert Casey said, "We're hungry, Belle. Can you fix us some grub?"

112

"For the price," she replied indifferently. "I'm not in the habit of getting up in the middle of the night to cook handouts for tramps."

Bert Casey uttered an oath. "We'll pay," he said, and she opened the door to them. The four booted men clumped in, spurs jingling.

Bob saw a faint light through an overhead crack, as she lighted a lamp.

Soon he could smell side-meat, potatoes and eggs frying and bread baking; and he knew the outlaws left well fed, for Belle gave him some of the same supper an hour later.

She wouldn't accept pay from him, and when he tried to thank her and go on his way, she wouldn't hear of it.

She was alone again; Jim July Starr, Pearl and Ed were all away somewhere; but she insisted that he go to bed for a much-needed rest. Before he left the next morning, she fixed him a ham-and-eggs breakfast, with buttered hoecakes and hot coffee.

"I've got something I want you to taste before you go," she said enthusiastically as she set a dish of candy on the table before him. "This is some of my own concoction."

There were two kinds and Bob selected a piece of each. Belle watched him carefully as he sampled each piece.

"This is really good, Belle!" he exclaimed. "What are these?"

"Sugar and cream candy."

"With all the kids my mother has, she sure would be tickled to make candy like this!"

"I'll tell you the recipes, and you write them down for her," Belle said.

Bob took out his pencil and little note tab and wrote down the two recipes:

SUGAR CANDY

6 cups of sugar
1 cup of vinegar
1 cup of water
1 teaspoon of butter

Put in last with 1 teaspoon of soda, dissolved in water. Boil without stirring for one-half hour. Flavor to suit taste.

113

CREAM CANDY

4 cups of sugar
2 cups of water
3/4 cup of vinegar
1 cup of cream
Butter the size of an egg
2 teaspoons full of vanilla flavoring

Let boil till it crackles in water;
then work very white.

"I generally make up a big lot," Belle explained, "because candy is hard to come by here, and I never know how many will be around to eat it." She laughed.

"This will be just right for Mama," Bob assured her. "She always has a lot of kids around."

"Go get your horse and feed him," Belle told him, as he started to leave. "There's plenty of corn in the crib. Remember, young man, your horse is just about as important as you are. It takes a long time to get anywhere on foot these days."

Bob was not surprised at this admonition, for he knew Belle Starr was a zealous lover of horses. When he returned, riding Star Face, he found her at the stable feeding, currying and fondling her own black gelding. She had him do some tricks for Bob and rewarded him with a couple of pieces of candy. Then she gave Star Face a piece and patted his neck.

"You've got a racehorse here, Bob," she declared, noting his long barrel and long legs. "No wonder you managed to give Bert Casey and his pals the slip!"

"John Hall gave me this horse and saddle when I left the Spur in West Texas, about four years ago. Star Face is getting a little age on him now, but he's still fast and strong. I've taken good care of him."

"He's got the Steel Dust blood," she commented, eyeing him critically, "but how much Morgan is he?"

"Belle, you're a fine judge of horses to see that quarter strain of Morgan in him. Most people think he's all Steel Dust!"

"I like red horses," she said wistfully. "I had a fine little red mare named Venus, but the damned Cherokee policemen caught up with Sam as he was riding her through a cornfield. It wasn't enough for them to shoot Sam. They had to kill poor

114

little Venus! I've heard since then that it was Chief Bill Vann who did it, but Sam thought Frank West did it, and not long after that they killed each other over it. If I ever get Bill Vann in my sights, I — "

She broke off without ever completing the thought. "I ought to learn to keep my mouth shut!" she laughed. "You must think I'm as mean as every bad thing you've heard about me!"

"I judge people by the way they treat me," he told her. "I don't care what people say. You've been good to me, Belle — as good as my mother, and I'll never forget it."

As he rode away that morning, Bob Hutchins was thinking of all the warmth and charm he had found in Belle Starr. It was hard to believe the gossip and rumors about her. With him, she had always been gracious, generous and unselfish.

He didn't know then, when he rode away down the trail and across the river, that he was riding out of Belle Starr's life forever. That was the last time Bob Hutchins saw Belle Starr.

The Courtship

Bob Hutchins was making a circuit as a posseman with Heck Thomas when he met Louisa Ethel Price at a picnic at Lone Grove, in Pickens County of the Chickasaw Nation.

Ethel was attractive, though a shy young lady, and she thought Bob Hutchins was the handsomest man at the picnic. He was dressed in a neat, dark suit, string necktie, Stetson hat and high-topped, polished boots. He was lithe, quick and rather tall. Though he was young to be an officer, he was modest and discreet about it. He wore his badge and his gun concealed under his coat. If Ethel had not seen him with Heck Thomas, she would not have suspected that he was an officer at all.

They found each other enjoyable as they sipped lemonade together and watched the horse races, foot races, horseshoe pitching, wrestling, and other sports. In the evening, when the picnic broke up, Bob walked with Ethel to Sweet Price's wagon, where the family was preparing to go home. He asked her if he could call on her at home the next time he came back to Lone Grove, and she was openly happy about the idea.

Bob asked Sweet Price and Mrs. Price if he could come calling on their foster daughter, and they readily consented.

116

They did not see each other often, because Bob rarely got back to Lone Grove more than twice a year. They corresponded, for even the mail service then was much more frequent. In the meantime, Bob Hutchins tried every way he could to come to Pickens County often.

On one of his infrequent visits, he told Ethel he would be willing to bring a bench warrant to Pickens County to arrest the Devil — if he could see her before the showdown.

Only half-joking, she said, "How many lonely nights does a deputy marshal's wife spend; and how many of them are widows, with only their memories too soon in life? I cannot remember either my mother or my father, Bob, and I'd hate to become an orphaned wife."

Bob realized that she was thinking, as he was, about the unhappy prospects of being the wife of a Deputy United States Marshal. She knew he was definitely set on the law as his career.

Ethel broke the spell lightly: "Just get me a couple of six-shooters, Bob, and I'll be a Belle Starr on the side of the law and ride with you after the meanest ones!"

Belle Starr was alive then, and Hutchins had seen her a few weeks earlier. "I wish you could know her, Ethel," he told her gravely. "She is not all bad, and she has befriended me more than once." He told her about the night Belle Starr had put him down in her secret cellar and had saved his life.

"Bless her for that," Ethel said gratefully. "Tell her for me when you see her again I'm thankful."

"I don't know what else I would do, except be an officer," he mused. "Think how wild and brutal life would be without law and order. It's bad enough as it is. This country will always need men to enforce laws and keep the peace, I reckon. It's a great service for men like me, but men don't follow it just because of patriotism. There's sure not much money in it. I imagine it's the same with most of the other deputies as it is with me. It just gets into you. A bad man is the most challenging and dangerous animal to hunt. He is mean and clever and ornery and tricky; and he can fight back with the same weapons and the same tactics as the hunter and has a violent will to kill."

"Bob! You speak of them as wild animals!" she exclaimed with a gasp. "I know you are not heartless. If you were not kind and gentle, I wouldn't ever see you again."

117

"A criminal is different," he told her seriously. "Some of the real bad men in the Indian Territory are worse than animals. They are enemies of all decent-living people. When they live by violence, they have to die by violence. They won't trust anybody, and they can't be trusted. They fight to the death. They won't surrender."

Ethel saw in him now the very core of his dedicated spirit. His face was flushed with the passion of his convictions.

"I guess I would hunt them all down, one by one, until I got myself killed, if one of them attacked you the way that demon did who raped and brutally killed that little girl in the Cherokee Nation a few weeks ago!"

"Bob!"

"You ought to sit in Judge Parker's court and see some of the specimens that have caused him to be called the *Hanging Judge!*"

After that visit, Ethel Price knew that Bob's career was the most important part of him.

When Bob Hutchins became a Deputy United States Marshal, with more independence and direct responsibilities, he went to Oil Springs near Berwyn and lived for a while with his Uncle Bob and Aunt Sally Faulkner. His duties at the time were not pressing enough to keep him from calling on Ethel often.

Star Face was not too old yet, but Bob left him in the pasture during most of these trips, reserving him for official duty. He had another, younger horse, who was not yet completely saddle and bridle wise. He rode an Indian pestle-tailed pony from his Uncle Bob's ranch. His legs were so long they hung down ridiculously below the pony's belly. It gave him an Ichabod Crane appearance, and Ethel underwent much teasing about her long-legged cavalier.

The Prices were all fond of Louisa Ethel and were her only family. She had been born somewhere between Rocky Bluff and Wildcat Bluff, just across Red River, in Texas, on December 26, 1871. Her parents had both died of pneumonia when she was a baby. Some nearby relatives took her, but they showed little interest in her welfare.

News about the baby reached John Price at Lone Grove. He was her father's brother. He made the trip down across Red

River and brought six-month-old Louisa Ethel home with him. He found her half-starved and dirty, crawling around over a filthy floor. He and his family made certain Ethel would never want for essential things of life again.

When John Price died, Ethel was about ten years old, and she went to live with his son, Christopher Columbus Price, who was called "Sweet" by everyone.

Finally, after three years courting, Bob Hutchins drove to Lone Grove in a covered wagon to carry away his bride. They had planned an elopement, because neither of them wanted any fanfare about the event.

But at Sweet Price's gate, the young deputy marshal ran into unexpected trouble. Sweet and his wife had gone along with them approvingly during the courtship, but Louisa Ethel Price had been cherished by them as their daughter. Sweet bluntly informed Bob, "I'll be damned if you carry her away from here like a thief and a scoundrel."

Hutchins had met angry men before. "Ethel and I are going to get married, Sweet. No man can stand in our way and live," Bob told him truculently.

"Both of you have said too much already," Ethel interrupted hastily. "How foolish can men get?" She turned to her foster father, then asked, "Cousin Sweet, are you against this marriage? Is that it?"

"No, Ethel," he admitted candidly. "He's courted you like a gentleman, and I intend for him to marry you like one."

"It's as much my fault as it is Bob's. I should have told you."

Hutchins breathed a sigh of relief. "So you want to give the bride away, Sweet? Is it that important to you?"

"It is," Sweet grinned. "I raised her for you, didn't I? Let's make it something we can all look back upon with pride. How about a barbecue and shindig wedding? I've got just the steer I've been saving for it."

The day was set, and the banns were read. Although Bob had wanted to be married quietly, he found that he enjoyed immensely Sweet Price's well-laid plans and enthusiasm. No knight or lord of the middle ages, he thought, ever attached so much importance and good will to the "come one, come all" wedding, barbecue and dance he held for the happy union.

In 1890, Bob's parents at last moved to Oil Creek from

119

Texas. John Andrew had leased seven hundred acres of land from Tom Boyd, to farm and raise cattle and horses. Bob and Ethel established their first home near Oil Springs, too, in a small cabin, sixteen miles northeast of Ardmore. He still rode for both the Fort Smith and the Paris, Texas federal courts. On October 16, 1891, their first child was born, and they named the baby Viola Pearl. This was the first flesh-and-blood link to bind them just a little closer in their marriage vows.

The next year, they moved to Paris, Texas, where Hutchins took a business course, while still working for the federal court. A number of times, when his tenure of duty in a place seemed permanent enough to warrant, they moved to the new area. Ethel had expected this sort of life, and she now accepted it happily. When she could not be near him, she faithfully remained at home, prayed for him, and waited for his return. She worried about the gunshot wounds when he was unlucky in a shooting scrape, but she didn't nag him about his profession. If hot lead could not discourage him, she knew considered hot words could not.

Pearl was five years old when their second child was born at Nebo, Chickasaw Nation, on October 24, 1896. They called her Essa Edna.

The next year found them back in Paris, Texas, again for over a year, where their third child — Della Mae — was born and died in May, 1898. It marked the first sad and grievous misfortune in their happily wedded lives.

During the twenty years of their marriage, they lived in several places in the Chickasaw Nation and the other Indian nations. Bob held the position of "circulating deputy marshal" for a few years. He quit working out of Fort Smith and Paris courts, except for just rare occasions, after the federal courts were established in the Indian nations. Then most of the time, he worked out of the courts at Ada, Ardmore and Muskogee.

Viola Pearl was eleven and Essa Edna was exactly six years old when the last of their children was born at Mill Creek on Essa's birthday, October 24, 1902. It was another girl, and they named her Ruth Virginia.

About the time of Ruth's birth, Hutchins resigned from his job, because of a controversy with Marshal Ben Colbert about complaints by a preacher about the way he had handled the bootlegging situation at Mill Creek. He soon secured a commission as United States Constable for the Southern District. He kept right on working with the deputy marshals. Then he was soon again appointed Deputy United States Marshal.

Ethel Hutchins devoted her life to guiding her daughters. She taught them to be homemakers and sent them to school in Ardmore. Her health was failing her when her oldest daughter was old enough to marry, on June 23, 1910 to Will Eaves. She didn't complain, but bore her burden secretly. All three of the girls had been keeping house for her. She had taught them to cook and to sew and to keep house neatly.

Though Pearl and Will had moved to Newton, Kansas, she still had Essa and Ruth to keep her company when Bob was away.

Then after twenty years of intermittent, but still rewarding companionship, Louisa Ethel Price-Hutchins expired of tuberculosis on September 7, 1910.

Bob Hutchins saw his loyal, loving wife laid to rest in the Lone Grove cemetery, in the community where she had grown to womanhood. It was his thirty-ninth birthday, the saddest day of his entire life. The Prices and the Hutchinses were there, and other relatives. There, also, were many of his lifelong friends and men of the law; lawyers, judges, and officers with whom he had ridden some long and dangerous trails.

No one ever so close to Hutchins in that hour could even guess the stormy emotions within his breast. As much as he had been away from Ethel, Bob Hutchins had always expected her to be waiting when he returned. Now, even the trails seemed lonelier. His home was broken, because the firm and tender hands that held it together were now gone.

Part of the furniture was sold, the rest moved to Pearl's home in Newton, Kansas, where Essa Edna and Ruth Virginia had also gone. He visited his daughters there, but he was restless and lonely.

That was when he met Mrs. Helen Frances Wayland, who had also lost her first mate. Lou Bowers, a wicked, outlaw woman, enticed and deceived him, then shot him in the hip; and he was laid up in the Hardy Sanitarium in Ardmore for a while, where he met Mrs. Wayland, a nurse. In the very begin-

121

ning, he nicknamed her "Nellie," and called her that to his dying day.

"Nellie" Wayland was a professional nurse, and an able one, having graduated from Johns Hopkins University. She and Bob had much in common; many of the same desires and aversions, and both were lonely. They were married on May 16, 1911, and lived in Ardmore, where Essa and Ruth came to live with them.

Nellie took up with the girls right where their mother's influence ceased. She was a wonderful mother to them; and they learned to love her for her gracious and unselfish devotion.

"I don't believe I ever would have married Bob," she often said, "if it hadn't been for Essa and Ruth."

She, too, accepted Bob's career willingly. If the scrapes he had been in had not damaged him much, she could take care of him as well as any doctor.

But she teased him sometimes, and called him the outlaws' target. Or she would mimic some officer and say, "Now you meet him face to face and shoot it out with him, Bob, while I slip around and get him from behind!"

She outlived Bob Hutchins four years, made her home with Essa Edna Hutchins-Smith in Los Angeles the last years of her life. She died on August 8, 1955. Essa died on July 11, 1962. Both are buried in Rose Hills Cemetery at Los Angeles.

Belle Starr's Avenger

Belle Starr was dead — shot in the back with buckshot.

Edgar J. Watson was in the Fort Smith jail for killing her. He had been arrested at Belle's funeral by her husband, Jim July Starr, who was then a posseman under Colonel J. H. Mershon.

Bob Hutchins did not learn about Belle's death until he got back from a long circuit trip with a load of prisoners that were lodged in the federal jail. Remembering what a loyal friend to him she had been, he insisted on investigating the case himself.

The news shocked Hutchins at first. Then a slow, relentless anger grew in him against the man who had done the cowardly, cold-blooded killing. Ed Watson had been confined in one of the cells on Murderer's Row, and being superstitious, he was frightened. He was among men sentenced to hang, until his hearing.

"I didn't kill Belle Starr, Mr. Hutchins," Watson insisted, when the deputy marshal confronted him. "I've been framed by the very man who did."

Hutchins stared at him sternly. "Jim Starr?" he asked.

Watson nodded, and glanced furtively at the guard, who was

123

coming toward them along the runway. He lowered his voice. "Can you talk Chickasaw?"

"Yes," Hutchins said.

Watson switched to that language. "Mr. Hutchins, Belle was killed with my shotgun, but I swear before God — and I hope he strikes me dead right now if I'm lying — I did not murder Belle Starr! Jim July did!"

Hutchins thought about Belle Starr, lying in the mud in the road, where she had fallen from her horse after she had been ruthlessly gunned down. He listened coldly to Watson's words.

Looking at the man's haggard face and worried blue eyes, he decided Watson was not Belle's killer. Watson was about thirty-six years old, a man of medium height, fair complexion, with bristly, sunburnt whiskers and mustache. He was good-looking and seemed to be an honest man.

Hutchins often based his decisions on hunches, which were more or less inspirations and conclusions, from inborn thinking and emotions. He had one of these hunches now. "Watson," he said, "that's a pretty sensible statement; and a fool's oath, if it is not true. If you are telling me the straight facts, you'll never hang for the murder of Belle Starr." Hutchins looked him directly in the eyes, and his voice was icy as he added: "If you're guilty, you had better hang. If you're lying and they free you, when I find it out, I'll kill you if I have to track you clear to hell!"

Watson drew a long, deep breath and sighed with relief. He looked at the young deputy marshal as if he could not believe his ears. For the first time since he had been arrested, somebody was listening to him. He thanked Hutchins like a man who had found hope.

Now Hutchins took pencil and notebook from his pocket and said calmly, "As briefly as you can, give me all the details."

He jotted down the bare facts as Watson gave them to him.

Saturday morning, Ed Watson had been at the King Creek Store, swapping jokes and chatting with other men there. Saturday was the day people for miles around came to trade and buy; and Watson liked to meet people traveling through the country to Fort Smith and other places.

It was soon the noon hour when he rode home.

"Where have you been?" his wife, Mandy, asked. "Belle

Starr was here to talk to you. She ate dinner with me and the kids."

Belle owned the farm the Watsons were renting. With her Cherokee rights, as a member of the Cherokee tribe when she married Sam Starr by tribal ceremony, she owned much of Younger's Bend. She rented most of the land to white settlers, who cleared and cultivated it. When a family moved on, the farm and improvements reverted back to Belle for rental again. Ed Watson had been talking to her about a lease for more land to cultivate.

As Mandy was talking, Jim July Starr rode up and Watson went out to the gate to greet him.

"Wat," he said, "I want to borrow your shotgun. Wolves are catching my chickens. I want something so I can shoot them on the run."

Watson didn't like lending his shotgun, but he hated to refuse a neighbor. He brought out the double-barreled weapon and handed it to him.

"What's it loaded with?" Jim asked.

"Turkey-shot."

"Hell!" Jim Starr exclaimed. "I need buckshot. Do I have to go clear over to the store for shells?"

"I have some buckshot loads," Watson said, and went back into the house. He brought out five cartridges and gave them to Starr.

Jim Starr thanked him and his white teeth gleamed evenly in his handsome, bronzed face. "Now I'm going to kill me a bitch-wolf," he said with a laugh, and he rode off, with his long, black hair fluttering.

On Sunday afternoon, Ed Watson was visiting at the home of Jack Rowe, a neighbor, when Belle Starr stopped to talk to Mrs. Rowe. She said she and Jim had spent the night with Mrs. Richard Nail on San Bois Creek. That morning, Jim had gone on to Fort Smith, but Belle had decided to return home. She rode leisurely and stopped at the King Creek Store before going to Rowe's.

Belle did not speak to Watson and Rowe in the yard. She spent her time in the house with Mrs. Rowe and the children.

Belle had not been on very good terms with Watson for several days, but she was still friendly with Mandy and the children.

125

Soon after Belle Starr left, Mandy Watson came by from the store, and they both rode home together.

About an hour before sunset, Milo Hoyt rode up to Watson's gate with the news that Belle Starr was lying dead in the road.

Edgar Watson couldn't bring himself to believe it. But he went with him about a half mile and found Belle Starr lying with the right side of her face in the mud. Her left hand was flung outward, clenched. Her right hand still gripped the white bone handle of her Colt .45, which she had tried to use in her last convulsions.

The murderer had hidden in the brush behind a rail fence of the Hoyt farm, and had fired the buckshot into Belle's back as she passed. Then he climbed over the fence to fire a load of turkey-shot at her where she fell. This charge struck her in the left side of her face and in her left arm, while she was trying to draw her six-shooter. It was obvious that the first shot had not killed her outright. She had sat up, and had tried to fight back. She had died game.

Watson studied the tracks of the sharp-heeled boots and he knew they had been made by Jim Starr's boots. In the brush, he found more proof in the two empty shotgun shells when he recognized the peculiar nicks, more on the right side than center, in the percussion caps of both shells. He knew they had been fired from his own shotgun. He slipped them into his pocket and said nothing. He sent Milo Hoyt to Belle's cabin to bring back Pearl and Ed Reed.

A crowd was gathering when Milo "Frog" Hoyt returned with Pearl riding behind his saddle. Ed was not at home, nor was Jim Starr.

Pearl jumped to the ground and ran to her mother. She implored the men standing around to move her mother out of the mud. But the men insisted that the body should not be disturbed until an officer could check the situation.

The only two lawmen in Younger's Bend were Bob Stacy and Jim Starr; both possemen under Colonel J. H. Mershon, Deputy Marshal of Fort Smith Federal Court.

Both men were sent for, but Jim Starr could not be found, and someone said he was in Fort Smith. Bob Stacy came, looked the situation over, unbuckled Belle's six-shooter and had the body loaded into a wagon and taken home.

126

The *Fort Smith Elevator* published the following story the next day:

> Fort Smith, Arkansas. Feb. 4 (1889) — A telegram was received in this city today by James Starr, husband of the famous Belle Starr, announcing that she had been shot dead at Eufaula. No particulars were given and nothing to show who did the deed. . . .
> James Starr was in the city yesterday when the telegram announcing her death was received. He is a tall, well-formed Indian, with long hair falling around his shoulders. There was bad blood in his eye when he heard the news, and without delay he saddled his horse, provided himself with a quart of whiskey and struck out on a run for home, saying somebody was going to suffer.

Tuesday morning, Jim July Starr returned Edgar Watson's shotgun with no apparent signs of grief that Watson could see. He handed the gun down from his horse to Watson, along with three shells. "The gun's loaded," he explained. I shot twice at a wolf. She was too far away, but I burned her good, and she won't go after my chickens anymore."

"Too bad about Belle," Watson remarked. "When's the funeral?"

"Tomorrow at home. Belle's been high-handed for a couple of days now. She got mad at me the other day and threatened to shoot me. Guess she said the wrong thing to somebody else, too."

Abruptly, he rode off, but that night Edgar Watson, Jack Rowe, Hyram Barnes, Mr. Wallace and Milo Hoyt were discussing Belle's death at the King Creek Store, when Jim Starr rode up in a gay and drunken mood, and announced: "Well, boys, Belle's gone. We'll bury her tomorrow, and she won't cause anybody any more trouble. She won't be runnin' things in Younger's Bend now. You can all look to me, and I'll treat you all right. We won't have any trouble."

When he rode away, someone said, "Jim's trying to drown his troubles, but when he wakes up tomorrow morning and looks into that coffin, his troubles will still be with him."

Belle Starr's funeral was held three days after her death. Women of the neighborhood had washed the body, anointed

127

it with turpentine and oil of cinnamon, and dressed it in a fine, black, silk dress with a white, frilled collar and white waist.

A carpenter in Briartown built the pine coffin, which he dressed and finished with reverence and care. Belle was laid gently into it, clasping a six-shooter in her hands.

Some of Sam Starr's blood brothers dug the grave in the rocky clay soil in front of Belle's cabin. A large crowd gathered around to show their respects. Most of them were Belle's friends. Her two children, Ed and Pearl Reed, members of the Starr clan, white squatters, Cherokees, Chickasaws, Choctaws and Creeks were there. Indian police, deputy marshals and outlaws Belle had befriended and sheltered, mingled at Belle's graveside. The outlaws had dared to come there to pay their last tribute to the woman who had been a contact between them and the Law. Because of this, she had acquired the public name of the "bandit queen."

There were officers who had warrants in their pockets for the arrest of some of the outlaws who were also there, but today was a day of amnesty. Tomorrow would be time enough.

There were no religious services. No hymns were sung. No sermons preached, no tributes offered in eloquence. Although Belle was a member of the Cherokee tribe by marriage, the Indians did not chant and sang no dirges. Belle had wanted silence at her funeral. Heavily armed Indian pallbearers carried the coffin from the house to the graveside. There they removed the lid and stood aside for everyone to pass by and view the body for the last time. Symbolic of provision for the journey to the happy hunting ground, each Cherokee placed a small piece of cornbread in the coffin in keeping with their ancient tribal ritual. When everyone had filed by, the lid was quickly nailed on and the coffin lowered into the grave.

When the grave had been filled and the mound rounded and smoothed, the crowd was already breaking up and going each his respective way. As Ed Watson moved away with his wife and children, a cold voice commanded sternly, "Throw up your hands, Wat!"

Jim July Starr confronted him with a Winchester. Mandy Watson screamed, and the children began crying with fright.

128

Quietly, Watson raised his hands. "I'm unarmed, Jim," he said quickly. "What's the trouble?"

"I want you for murdering my wife!"

For a moment, Watson was stunned. Then he said, "I'm not guilty, Jim. Nobody knows that any better than you!"

Jim Starr jabbed the barrel of his rifle threateningly and viciously into Watson's stomach. The Indian posseman's eyes were bloodshot, and his voice thick from whiskey. He snarled, "You're lying! You murdered my wife and you're going to jail with me!"

"If you kill me, Jim, you know you'll be killing a man who has been your friend. You know who had my shotgun!"

"I'm taking you to Fort Smith Court Jail," Jim Starr repeated grimly. "I'm going to see you hang for Belle's murder!"

Watson called upon his friends in the crowd to go along to ward off foul play. He knew Jim would go even farther than framing him. He told his friends that Starr did not intend to take him to Fort Smith, and he would kill him, if he had a chance, and claim he had tried to escape. Several men agreed to go, including Ed Reed, and also his sister, Pearl.

Ed Watson had been in jail for about a month when Hutchins found him there. Hutchins took his notes to Judge Parker and read him what Watson had told him.

The judge leaned back in his high-backed, swivel chair and listened carefully. Occasionally, he ponderously nodded his massive head and tugged at his white goatee.

"Well, what's your opinion, Judge?" Hutchins asked, looking up from his notebook.

Judge Parker regarded him with a quizzical smile. "What do you think about all of it, Kid?" he countered.

"If Watson is telling the truth, Jim July Starr is a guilty man!" Hutchins declared with conviction. "And the man seemed to me to be so earnest, I believe him.'"

"Jim Starr was in town the day after Belle's murder, when the news of his wife's death reached here by telegram from Eufaula."

"He had plenty of time to get here," Hutchins pointed out. "It's only seventy-five miles to ride. The killing took place in the afternoon. The only thing that bothers me now is Jim's motive. Crazy or not, there's always a reason behind a murder like this."

"You know Jim has a case pending against him now for larceny, don't you?"

"No," Hutchins said. "Has he stolen another horse?"

"He has. He's under bond now. Been dismissed as a posseman, too."

Both the judge and Hutchins knew that Jim July Starr was quite capable of the crime.

"Judge," Hutchins said vigorously, "I want your permission to go to Younger's Bend and check into this case."

"Permission granted," the judge replied readily. "If it looks like a case, take your time, work it out. If it doesn't, come on back. Something else might turn up."

Hutchins rode up to Watson's house as Mandy and the children were sitting down to a scanty supper.

When he told them why he was there, Mandy Watson and her children greeted him happily. All they had to eat was cornbread and milk.

His horse corraled and fed, Hutchins sat down on the porch and rolled a cigarette. Soon Mrs. Watson joined him and he began asking about Belle Starr's murder.

She brought him the empty shells which Watson had found at the scene of Belle's murder. He saw the marks on the percussion caps where the plungers had driven in on the right side, just as Watson had described them.

The Watson family were wholesome and friendly and had good standing in the community, although they were very poor. Watson was badly needed at home to do the plowing and get ready for the spring planting.

Mrs. Watson told him her husband had tried to lease more land from Belle, but had failed. But there was no trouble between them, as Belle had often visited in the Watson home, and had been kind and neighborly.

From men in the community named Wallace and Rowe, Hutchins was told that Jim and Belle had been having domestic troubles. Jim had threatened divorce, and Belle was supposed to have told him, "When you file the divorce proceedings, I'll shoot you in the courthouse!"

Jim Starr had told them this when he was drunk. Scornfully,

he had referred to his wife as *Old Grandma Hag*. He never forgot that Belle Starr was much older than he was.

It was Milo Hoyt, nicknamed Frog, the community simpleton, who gave Hutchins the information about Jim Starr's *motive* for the murder.

"He met me in the road one morning," Hoyt said, "and offered me two hundred dollars to kill Belle."

"I don't want Belle dead," Hoyt had told him. "She's my friend."

"Was she your friend when she accused you of stealing her pig the other day?" Jim asked.

"She didn't accuse me of stealing her pig," Hoyt denied. "She asked me to help her find it, and we did."

"Hell!" Jim Starr grated angrily. "I'll kill her myself and spend the two hundred on whiskey!" Spurring his horse cruelly, he rode away.

"Why did Jim want to kill his own wife?" Hutchins asked.

"I reckon it was because she found out he was goin' with that good-lookin' Cherokee girl over near Briartown."

"Have you ever seen them together?"

"Sure! Lots of times, but I didn't let them see me! Jim Starr would have plugged me, I know! He's awful mean! 'Specially when he's drunk, and he sure drinks a lot!"

Three days of investigating around Younger's Bend gave Hutchins enough evidence to prove Ed Watson was innocent of Belle Starr's murder. He also had enough circumstantial evidence to convict Jim Starr.

Judge Parker examined the empty shotgun shells carefully. "If it wasn't so late in the day," he said, "we'd get into my buggy and drive out of town and shoot that shotgun a time or two."

"No need for that," Hutchins told him. "Just send for Watson's shotgun, and I'll prove it right here in your office."

The loaded shells Hutchins had brought back from Watson's home were exactly like the empty ones. Hutchins removed the wadding, shot and powder from one, slipped it into the right barrel and pulled the trigger. There was a small explosion, such as might be made by a cap pistol. When he and the judge examined the marking on the cap, they found it had been made by the same plunger that fired one of the shells which had killed

131

Belle Starr. They performed the experiment in the left barrel, and got the same result.

Judge Parker leaned back in his chair and quietly considered the information Hutchins had brought him. His white goatee rested on his chest, and he worked his fingers through his thick mop of white hair.

"It's *not positive proof* that Watson *didn't* murder Belle Starr, and *it's not definite proof* that Jim Starr *did*," he said, speaking with slow deliberation. "Jim Starr will deny he borrowed the shotgun and had it in his possession when Belle was killed. Watson and his family will naturally testify Jim *did* have the gun. But you've dug up enough evidence and enough witnesses to scare Jim Starr and to turn Watson loose. We'll call in your witnesses for a hearing."

The hearing was held before Commissioner Brizzolara in March, 1889. Belle had been killed nearly two months before, on February 3. The case against Ed Watson, nicknamed Warty, was too weak. Jim Starr was anxious to get an indictment of murder, but Watson's neighbors testified that he was a quiet, hard-working man, and had never been in trouble of any kind since he had lived among them. Even Ed Reed and Pearl would not testify against him.

Jim Starr had not expected this, for Hutchins' investigation had been quiet. Starr asked for more time to bring in more witnesses. Another hearing was set for an early day in April. By this time, Starr had skipped the country, because of his larceny case; and his bondsman was offering one hundred fifty dollars for his arrest and return to Fort Smith court for trial.

Commissioner Brizzolara released Ed Watson on the grounds that the evidence against him was insufficient.

But from that time on, Hutchins knew Jim July Starr would be gunning for him. Threats he made against Hutchins' life reached him from several sources.

The following year, Marshal Heck Thomas and his deputies and trusties were making a circuit through the Territory with their pockets full of bench warrants from Judge Parker.

Among the warrants was one for the arrest of Jim July Starr. Knowing about the threats that particular individual had made against Hutchins, Marshal Thomas gave him the warrant, saying, "I guess this will be a chore to your liking, Hutch.

We'll be going up into that neck of the woods this trip where he's rumored to be, and you might run across him."

On the night of January 21, 1890, they were camped at the brickyard at the north edge of Ardmore. Marshal Heck Thomas and two or three of the deputies were off scouting, and the camp was dark, except for a single lantern, swinging from a tree limb. The guards and their shackled prisoners were rolled in their heavy suggans to protect them from the brisk north wind.

Hutchins and one other man were the only ones awake. They had a roaring fire and hot coffee; and Hutchins was playing his fiddle when, around midnight, a small Indian boy rode up. Hutchins spoke to him in Chickasaw. "Hello, boy," he said. "What are you doing out on a cold night like this?"

"I'm looking for Mister Hutchins."

"I'm your man."

The boy handed him a folded piece of paper. "Ma told me to bring you this. You better read it, for you're about to be killed!"

Hutchins went over to the lantern, unfolded the paper and saw it was signed by the widow Lena Robinson, a Chickasaw Indian woman, who lived on Rock Creek, fifteen miles southwest of Ardmore.

> Bob, you and Bub look out! Jim Starr just left here. He rode for John Selsor's place a few minutes ago. He said him and John had been in Ardmore all day, watching for you to show up, so they could bump you off.
>
> He was drunk. Told me there would be two funerals tomorrow, and I would have some place to go, for he and John Selsor are going to fill you and Bub full of lead.
>
> — Lena Robinson

Hutchins knew Bub Trainor, his Indian friend, was included in the threat because they often rode together. Deputies usually went in pairs and, sometimes, in groups for their own protection; just as outlaws did.

He woke Bub Trainor and showed him the note. Trainor yawned and shivered in the cold. He read the note while

133

Hutchins held the lantern for him. Then he exclaimed, "What are we waiting for? Let's go accomodate the gents!"

Trainor drew on his boots and took a quart of whiskey from the confiscated stock in one of the wagons. They moved quietly to avoid disturbing the sleeping men, and left instructions for the guard to wake up his relief and turn in for the rest of the night.

Soon they had caught their horses, saddled them and were riding with the Indian boy for Rock Creek.

In the still hour before dawn, they came to Lena Robinson's cabin. She was awake, had a roaring fire in the fireplace and a fire in the cookstove.

While they sipped hot coffee, she told them how Jim Starr had pestered her and insisted that she drink with him, threatening to blow out her brains if she didn't.

He referred to his wife as *Old Grandma Hag* and drank a toast to her death.

"Jim, did you kill Belle?" Lena Robinson asked.

He leered at her mockingly. "What the hell's the difference?" he asked. *"Grandma Hag* is gone!"

Then he tried to make love to the widow and, when she resisted him, he cursed her, made his threats against Bob Hutchins and Bub Trainor and stalked out. When he had gone, the widow sent her son on a horse with the note.

As they rode toward John Selsor's place, Bub Trainor kept dropping behind, and Hutchins had to rein his horse down to a walk. Finally, he waited until Trainor came abreast of him.

"What are you lagging behind for, Bub?" he asked. "It will soon be broad daylight!"

"I'm looking at the tracks coming this way," Trainor replied thickly.

Hutchins looked at him closely and realized he was drunk. He checked the bottle in Trainor's overcoat pocket and found that it was nearly empty. Hutchins swore under his breath. They were riding for a showdown with Jim July Starr, and no telling how many more men, and his partner was drunk!

It was daylight when they reached old man Smith's corncrib near the road, within sight of John Selsor's house. There they took their stand and waited.

134

Trainor was just about unconscious. He drew the bottle from his pocket again, and Hutchins grabbed it.

"Just one more little drink, Hutch," he begged. "I'm about all in!"

Hutchins relented, but when Trainor tried to drain the bottle, he snatched it away and broke it over a fence post. Trainor dropped limply to the ground and began to snore.

Then the front door of Selsor's house opened. Jim July Starr came out and began saddling his horse. When he came riding down the road, Hutchins thought at first that Starr had seen him and was coming to shoot it out. He knew that Starr was game enough to try it.

Then Hutchins saw John Selsor come out and saddle his horse, too. When Selsor came jogging along behind Jim Starr, Hutchins shook Trainor roughly. "Stand up, Bub!" he urged. "Here comes the showdown!"

Trainor broke off snoring with a groan, and settled loosely back to sleep again.

Hutchins took off his gloves and stuffed them into his left overcoat pocket. Next he took his six-shooter from his holster under his coats and dropped it into his right overcoat pocket. Then he checked his Winchester.

He would give them a chance to yield to arrest, he decided grimly. If they went for their guns, he would shoot it out with them alone.

When Starr came abreast of him, Hutchins stepped out of the black-jacks with his rifle ready. "Hands up, Jim," he commanded, "or this will be the showdown!"

Jim Starr drew his six-shooter, at the same time digging spurs into his horse. He had ridden several yards past him when Hutchins aimed his rifle and squeezed the trigger. Starr straightened up and leaned over the neck of his horse like a jockey, and Hutchins thought he had missed. He fired a second shot, and the horse stopped dead in his tracks.

Hutchins walked closer, lowering his rifle and levering another shell into the chamber.

"Don't shoot me again, Hutchins," Starr pleaded. "I'm killed already!"

"Get off your horse," Hutchins ordered, and watched as he

135

climbed down. The horse fell with a grunt, and Starr stood wobbling on his feet.

Hutchins removed his belt and gun. "Sit down, Jim," he said.

From the corner of his eye, Hutchins had seen John Selsor whirl his horse around when the shooting started. Now he could see him back at home, unsaddling. Hutchins watched him go into the house. There would be no trouble with John Selsor today, he knew.

He walked over and woke Bub Trainor and told him what had happened. When he walked back to his prisoner, the horse was groaning pitifully.

"Take all the shells out of my six-shooter but one," Jim Starr pleaded, "and let me put my poor horse out of his misery."

Hutchins trained Starr's gun on the horse's head, but the trigger was rigid, and he looked at it closely. "The hammer is hung, Jim. You jerked it back too hard when you tried to shoot me. I'll take no more chances with you." He shot the groaning horse with his own gun.

He looked down at Jim's blood-soaked front coldly. "Your groaning is music to my ears," he told him grimly. "I'm going to get you into Ardmore where the doctors can patch you up. I want you to live so I can see you hanged for killing your own wife in cold blood. Belle was a good friend of mine. The best I had in Younger's Bend. This bone-handled Colt you were packing was *her* gun. I'm keeping it to remind me of her forever!"

Again, Hutchins went back to Bub Trainor and dragged him roughly to his feet.

"Bub!" Hutchins spoke sharply. "Go down to Selsor's and tell him to hitch up his hack and bring some blankets and help us get Jim to a doctor in Ardmore! He's pretty badly shot!"

Trainor staggered down the road to John Selsor's place, and the two men soon drove up in a hack.

Jim Starr groaned painfully as they lifted him into the hack on some blankets, and spread some more over him.

"Shoot me again, Bob," he pleaded, "and get me out of my misery, like you did my horse."

"You've been shot your last time, Jim. I want old Maledon to get you with a rope."

136

But when they reached Ardmore, Doctor W. T. Bogie and Doctor Booth examined Starr and found him to be in a very critical condition. The neck of his bladder had been shot away, and only an operation could possibly save him. They were not prepared to perform an operation as delicate as that in Ardmore.

Marshal Heck Thomas took Starr on the first train to Fort Smith. There in the prison hospital, the doctors said there was no chance for Starr to live. He sent for Pearl, and told her he had an important secret for Bob Hutchins, alone, to hear.

"If I can't tell it to him," he groaned, "I'll take it with me to my grave!"

A telegram was sent to Ardmore, but Hutchins was out of town running down another desperado. On January 26, 1890, while aboard a train to Fort Smith, Arkansas, Hutchins received word by telegram that Jim July Starr had died at 10:15 that morning.

Hutchins was there when he was buried in Potter's Field the next day. True to his word, Jim July Starr carried his secret with him to his grave.

But Bob Hutchins was convinced that he already knew the secret — that Jim had murdered Belle Starr.

Some people living today may have their doubts, because of controversial literature about it, but Hutchins was satisfied beyond a shadow of doubt that Jim July Starr murdered his own wife. There are points of quite definite information, which courts sometimes reject as evidence; but in their hearts, all good officers know that they are true.

The Dalton Boys
Come Calling

Bob Hutchins rode into old Boggy Depot to find that Heck Thomas and his deputies had gone on to Ardmore. There, he learned they were at Table Mountain, next at White Bead Hill, and finally caught up with them on a Sunday morning at Berwyn. He found Heck Thomas shaving, primping, fixing his hair and mustache, preparing to take a lady friend to church.

"Imagine a marshal attending church this day and time," Hutchins ragged his captain. "Why, the preacher and the congregation will kick the door down!"

All of the deputies were teasing Heck Thomas when Bob Dalton rode up with a hearty greeting.

"Looks as if my church-going is blowed up," Heck said. "Bob Dalton is here for dinner. He sent word a couple of days ago that he and his bunch were coming."

"Just detail me to take your lady friend to church, Captain," Hutchins suggested.

"Do I look that ignorant?" Heck retorted. "Risk you with my skirt!"

He nodded his head and walked out to meet Bob Dalton, as the other deputies rose up nonchalantly and sauntered out behind him.

Bob Dalton said, "Don't take any long chances, Cap'n. Wait until my crowd gets here for the handshaking." Then Emmett Dalton rode into the clearing. They both stepped down from their horses and, as they did, they slid their Winchesters from their saddle-holsters.

Pat and Morris O'Malley rode up next, and climbed down from their horses. Then came Grat Dalton and Kid Bannister, who dismounted with their guns.

There stood six outlaws, some of whom had once been deputy U.S. marshals, ready to fight or be friendly. Then Dick Powell and Tom Foster joined them, which made eight of them squared off against six United States deputy marshals. Dick Powell had been a Kansas sheriff, before he turned outlaw.

"Show your good feelin's now, Cap'n Heck, with a hearty handshake," Bob Dalton declared, extending his hand. Every man on both sides of the law knew that to start shooting now would be suicide.

So the two leaders shook hands. Heck Thomas called for four trusties to attend to the outlaws' horses. Then the fraternizing began.

The officers and the outlaws mixed and mingled, swapped news, told jokes, had a steak dinner and a grand time. Although the deputy marshals were carrying warrants in their pockets for most of them, they made no attempt to serve them; for this was a day of amnesty.

About three o'clock in the afternoon, Bob Dalton said, "Cap'n Heck, if you will have your trusties fetch our horses, we'll bid you gentlemen a friendly good-bye. You've been good sports, and we've had a good time. This may be for all time to come. We just wanted to let you know, Cap'n, that we bear you and your boys no grudges or bad will. We're going to Roff from here and stay all night with our old-time deputy marshal friend, Charley Roff. If you see any deputy marshals looking for us, just tell them where we will be tonight. From there, we're going north to Coffeyville, where we figure on explorin' a bank or two. If any of you boys have any funny notions you'd like to come along, remember that most of us are

139

a bunch of ex-officers ourselves, with good records while we rode for the law. We just elected to go the six-shooter route instead of dabblin' with petty larceny and crooked lawyers.

"We haven't built any churches to hide our lawlessness, but we have contributed to some and to some preachers, too."

He turned to Hutchins and said, "Hutch, I'll just forget how you outshot me one day — and how you can stick an M-T-Y shell in a tree, step off ten paces and the second shot drive it into the tree, or pick out a sapling and shoot first to the left, second to the right, and center the third shot to cut it down."

Hutchins laughed with him at his recollections. "You didn't do so bad, yourself, Bob," he said.

"Any of you fellows that want to come along on the square are welcome," he repeated, "but I'd hate to see any of you end up like old Ben Williams, who got the big idea to join us. We had Coffeyville in our sights, but Ben suggested Longview, Texas, first. He didn't show up at Longview, so we came on back to the Territory. It looked to me like a trap. I think old Ben is a double-crosser; but the rest of my bunch don't figure it that way. They think he's jam-up, and when we meet him again, he'll have a reason for not showing at Longview. But there's a bug under the chip somewhere."

Hutchins had liked Bob Dalton while he had been a deputy marshal. He had always been a friend to him, so he told him now, "Bob, you are the brains of your outfit. You're in the wrong business, but you've got Ben figured right. I worked under his brother, Marshal Sheb Williams, and he's a square-shooter, but Ben is a different stripe. I don't trust him, either."

True to their boast, the Dalton gang went to Coffeyville, Hutchins learned later, but their plans had changed. They re-shuffled their members, and they tried to rob two banks instead of one. Somewhere along the line, the O'Malley boys, Dick Powell and Tom Foster dropped out, or were finally rejected. The Dalton boys — Bob, Emmett and Grat — rendez-voused at a place called "Dalton Cave" twenty miles west of Tulsa, on October 2, 1892. With them were now Bill Powers, Bill Doolin and Dick Broadwell. Six riders left the cave early the next morning and rode twenty miles north toward Coffey-ville, where they camped in the hills on Hickory Creek, only twelve miles from their objective. On the night of October 4,

140

they moved on up to Onion Creek bottom, two or three miles from Coffeyville.

All six men were riding racehorses, and they were equipped with six-shooters, Winchester rifles and plenty of ammunition. But now there were only five of them, for Bill Doolin's horse had become lame. He left them to go back a few miles to steal a sorrel gelding they had seen in a pasture they had passed. He promised to follow them when he made the exchange of horses, which he did, but too late to take a hand in the robbery. The Dalton gang pushed on ahead about thirty minutes too soon. When at nine o'clock on that fateful morning of October 5, 1892, Bill Doolin had not returned, they went on into Coffeyville without him. The Dalton boys were known in Coffeyville, for they had lived several of their growing years near that town. So the three of them disguised themselves; Emmett and Grat with black, false beards, and Bob with a stage mustache and a goatee. Broadwell and Powers needed no disguise, since they were strangers to that town.

They had planned for Grat Dalton and Dick Broadwell and Bill Powers to take the Condon Bank, while Emmett and Bob went across the street on the east side to The First National Bank.

The alarm was given by Alex McKenna, who was standing in front of his dry goods store on a corner of the main street when the five men rode past. He grew suspicious when he saw the Dalton boys wearing false beards. He watched them split up and enter both banks, after they had ridden down the alley and tied their horses between Walnut — the main street — and Maple. He cautiously followed them, peered through the window of the Condon Bank, saw what was going on, then turned tail and ran up the street, shouting, "The Daltons are robbing the banks!" He really didn't know for certain at the moment that the bank robbers *were* the Dalton gang; but their reputation was prominent then, and he guessed correctly the robbers' identity.

A frontier town could arm itself in less time than it took to talk about it. Men came swarming out of their business places and homes like hornets, with six-shooters and rifles and shotguns; and, in a few moments, the Dalton gang knew "they had made a bull."

141

The account of the Coffeyville raid has been recorded numerous times in the last seventy years and published in newspapers, magazines, and books in various versions by men who tried to seek out the exact facts, which may never be completely known.

According to Bob Hutchins, who knew and associated with some of the eyewitnesses to the Coffeyville raid, a few points have been overlooked in the whole adventure.

The newspapers at that time recorded eight men killed on both sides and four wounded. The Dalton gang was wiped out, except for Emmett, who survived a bullet through one arm, another through his hips, and a dozen buckshot in his back. Hutchins talked with Emmett many times later, even visited him at his home in California.

Of the citizens in Coffeyville, those killed were Marshal Charles T. Connelly, Lucius M. Baldwin, George Cubine, and Charles Brown. Three others — Mat Reynolds, Thomas G. Ayers and Charles T. Gump — were wounded.

But there was another casualty that has not been mentioned in any account this biographer has read of the Coffeyville raid. He was Ben Williams, brother of United States Marshal for the Eastern District of Texas, avowed by Hutchins.

Ben Williams was a reward hunter. Since Coffeyville had known that the Daltons were planning a bank robbery there, Hutchins always believed, because of what Bob Dalton said at Berwyn, and what Emmett told him later, that Ben Williams was the one who warned them. In his own words in his memoirs, Hutchins wrote:

> Bob, Grat, Bill Powers and Dick Broadwell were snuffed out. Only Emmet survived, though shot from his horse while trying to rescue his brother, Bob, who was fatally wounded, but still alive. Bob's six-shooter was under his chest. Ben Williams appeared for the first time during the robbery. He came up to Bob Dalton, lying there on the ground, and rolled him over, face up. Bob, in his dying moments, fired a bullet into Ben Williams' heart, and both men were dead in twenty minutes.

The Chicken Peddler

The itinerant poultry peddler was a familiar figure and a good disguise for bootlegging, until too many chicken peddlers caught on and spoiled the setup.

Their method was to build a large-size chicken coop in their wagon bed, leaving enough room for pints of whiskey to lay flatwise beneath it. This space was filled with as many pints as possible. A trap door was made at the end of the wagon, and a stiff, chicken-catching wire was used to hook and pull the bottles out for sale.

Until the idea was spread around, a deputy marshal searching the wagon never discovered the false bottom under the chickens. His only chance was to catch the bootlegger in the act of making a sale. Then he would have only one pint for evidence, which wasn't much of a case.

Bob Hutchins arrested such a bootlegger near Ada who, with his wife and several children, was traveling around the nation, buying and selling and trading chickens. He even had an old milk cow tied to the endgate of his wagon, with a hound dog following. He was trying to rent land on which to make a crop, but he could not find a farm to suit him.

143

Hutchins crawled up close to his camp one night and hid in the bushes. In a short while, a customer appeared, a business man from Ada, and he bought a pint of whiskey. When the bootlegger went behind the wagon to "fish out" a pint, Hutchins came up and helped him unload the rest of it. In the whiskey trap of that particular wagon, Hutchins found nearly one hundred pints of Kentucky bourbon whiskey.

When he searched the old man, he found a card advertising a saloon in Violet Springs, Oklahoma Territory. Somehow this card was not produced as evidence in the case, or Judge J. T. Dickerson "would have thrown the law book at the culprit."

But being a tender-hearted man, "Judge Dickerson, after seeing the wife and group of half-naked kids, allowed him to plead guilty to possession of intoxicating liquors in Indian Territory. He fined him thirty days in jail and twenty-five dollars, which was about the least penalty possible.

Another experience Hutchins had with a similar bootlegger occured with a much-noted character named "Hookie" Miller. He derived his name from being trimmed by bullets *afterward* until he looked as if there wasn't a spot left on him that had not been punctured with lead. His real name was George Miller. Hutchins often laughed and said, "If he had all the lead that's been shot at him tied around his neck and was thrown into the Canadian River, he would have drowned as surely as Christ made little apples."

Hookie had only one finger left on his left hand, and he had a mechanical right arm and hand; but he could make a Winchester rifle talk. Miller always said, "Six-shooters are made to get a man killed by carryin' one around. If you really mean business, get a Winchester and get busy. Every time it barks, something jars loose."

Bob Hutchins and eight more deputies "shot it out" with Hookie Miller and the Bert Casey gang at Table Mountain, near Desperado Springs. He never weakened until he had nineteen holes shot through him. He lost his right arm, most of his left hand and pretty well "got bunged up in general." He spent nearly two years in the hospital before he got well.

Hutchins and the rest of the posse of deputies were hot on the trail of Bert Casey's gang when they ran up on them suddenly at the outlaws' favorite watering hole. They drove them

144

up Table Mountain with a hail of bullets, where a furious gun-battle took place. Hutchins never knew exactly how many were in the outlaw party, except there were as many as, or more than, there were officers. Bullets were crashing and ricochetting off rocks near him, and whining uncomfortably close to his head. He was pretty sure he knew most of the men in the gang: Jim Harbolt, Jim Hughes, Jim Moran, Jim Castleberry, Dad Bruner, Bert Casey, Hookie Miller, and a shady and illusive character named Simms.

There were serious casualties on both sides, and a few slight injuries, but Hookie Miller and Bob were the unlucky ones. The only one arrested was Hookie Miller. The rest got away. Bob had been dodging from rock to rock like every other man in the fight. It started so suddenly and ended so abruptly, it couldn't have been anything else but the wild melée of a fight. It was a case of "every fellow for himself, and the Devil take the hindmost!" Hutchins had just shot one man down when, to his left, he caught a movement out of the corner of his eye. He swung his Winchester around quickly, but a split second too late. Bert Casey had risen up with his rifle and fired from behind another boulder, and Bob caught the full impact of the bullet about three inches over his heart. He felt a stunning shock as it knocked him a few feet back down the slope, and when he was able to get back around to a crawling position, Bert Casey and his gang were "high-tailing it for points unknown."

They next had a "little first-aid society" and went back to the spring and got them all a cool drink of water, taking pains with Hookie Miller and Bob, after they had crudely bandaged his wound with his shirt tail. Then they took what was left of Hookie Miller on an improvised litter, made from two slender black-jack trees, and a blanket, to Dr. T. P. Howell at old Woodford. Bob Hutchins rode his own horse with his grit and strength.

Doctor Howell did all he could for both men. He cleansed and cauterized their wounds with medicines and equipment with which he had to work. Bob's wound was clean. The bullet had burned a hole clear through him. Doctor Howell bandaged him up well. "You'll be all right, if you will just take it easy," he advised.

"I guess we were tougher than boots in those days," Hutchins laughed and said, "To go the gait we went, we had to be!"

Doctor Howell told the deputy marshals confidentially, "You bucks didn't leave too much of Miller to keep alive! You fellows shot the devil out of him!"

Bob Hutchins afterward concluded that Doctor Howell was more correct than he knew. "Hookie Miller was a better man after that!"

When Doctor Howell had done all he could for Miller, he told the deputies, "You boys better get him to the sanitarium in Ardmore as quickly as you can, if you want him to live. He's lost a lot of blood from that shot-off arm!"

They borrowed a hack and rushed him to Ardmore to the hospital.

Hookie Miller had been a terror to deputy marshals for years; but this time, his career as an outlaw was ended for good.

When Miller was able to sit up in a wheelchair, he asked his nurse, Maud Murphy, to bring him a pencil and tie it to the stub of his right arm. Then he proceeded, with her help, to write Hutchins the following letter:

> Deputy U.S. Marshal Bob Hutchins
> Cob Town, Chickasaw Nation, I. T.
>
> Dear Hutch,
> You know the line-up, for you were there when it happened, with your Winchester smoking.
>
> Now please go to Desperado Springs, at the foot of Table Mountain, and make a strict search for my right arm. Get a large, flat solid gold ring off the third finger and save it for me. It was my mother's wedding ring and a treasured keepsake of mine. Do this, and I'll help you smoke out the rest of them tough shooting hombres.
>
> Your pal,
> HOOK

Bob Hutchins rode back to the battle scene and found the rotted, bony arm, with the solid gold ring on its finger. He

146

took the ring, cleaned it, buried the forepart of Miller's arm, and took the ring with him.

Hutchins enlisted help from other dignitaries of the court and marshal's office, and succeeded in getting Hookie Miller appointed a Deputy U.S. Marshal. Miller made an excellent officer.

"What he did to criminals from there on was misery every inch of the way, from start to finish," Hutchins declared proudly. "He was a lone wolf. He made all his raids alone, crippled as he was, but he always came to the aid of other officers when called upon."

The Negroes had a saying about Hookie Miller, U.S. Deputy Marshal, that Hutchins considered about as good a summary of the man's character and career as an officer as can be epitomized:

"Whar you thinks he is, he ain't; and whar you thinks he ain't, he is!"

He is Dead
Over There

Scar Faced Jim Watson was one of the most renowned whiskey peddlers of the Indian Territory. He was a man of good character and puritanical principles. He had unlimited courage, and he was as sympathetic in a way as a woman.

For ten years, Jim Watson peddled whiskey, while every deputy marshal held a warrant for his arrest, without being arrested. Jim was involved in many shooting scrapes with officers and outlaws. He went up against some men who were experts; men who could shoot a man with no more qualms than shooting a tree, and he was never touched by a single bullet.

Jim Watson attributed his luck to the fact that he sold the best of Kentucky bourbon whiskey at "living" prices, never robbed anybody or stole a horse or committed any deed that could be morally considered a crime. He did kill a few times in self-defense, but Jim didn't consider that a crime.

Another peculiarity about Jim Watson's bootlegging was the fact that he sold only one brand of whiskey, which was called John Hart, and he handled it only in pint bottles.

He landed at Sulphur Springs with a load of whiskey, and

two officers, named Buck Garrett and Bill McCarthy, decided to relieve him of it. Instead of confiscating Watson's whiskey, Buck received a couple of hot bullets through his coat, and Bill McCarthy had his hat shot off his head. Jim Watson shot his way to freedom, spurring his Steel Dust sorrel and laughing as he went.

From Sulphur Springs, he went to Ada, where he was met by Deputy Marshals Bob Nestor, Dick Couch, and posseman George England. England was shot, though he finally got well, and again Watson rode off laughing.

He had a wife, who helped him with his whiskey peddling by driving their wagon to the Corner Saloon and loading it full of John Hart pints of whiskey. Then she drove about the territory, camping at different places. All the time, Jim Watson rode horseback, with a pair of Methodist circle saddle riders, which he filled with whiskey, rather than Bibles for his customers.

His trading route reached from the Corner Saloon across the South Canadian River, the Indian Territory, Red River, and clear to Denison, Texas, where he could stock up for the return trip. He traveled this route each month, and sold only to regular customers. He would let his customers have an extra pint or two, and would even give a pint to the sick and the needy, but seldom trusted any kind of a risk.

"Whiskey," Jim Watson would say, "is darned good medicine when you are sick; but it's made to sell and not to drink, when I'm peddling it."

Another remark he often made was, "If any bootlegger drinks his whiskey, the penitentiary doors will open wide to welcome him sooner than later."

Bob Hutchins knew Jim Watson almost all his life. He was born at Sorghum Flats, and he began his career at what was then Hutchins' hometown of Dougherty.

The nights never got too dark, or the weather too severe, for Jim Watson to go to the rescue of his friends in sickness or in trouble of any sort.

From the revenue of his business, he cared for his aged mother and educated and supported two sisters. Bob Hutchins knew him so long and liked him so much, he never attempted to arrest him, except once; and he then thought it was Bert

Casey or Jim Harbolt. He and Deputy Marshal Henry Oats had received a tip that they could catch Bert Casey and Jim Harbolt in Cob Town, in the Chickasaw Nation. This settlement was on the trail for Long Riders, going from Doan's Store on the Chisholm Trail across Red River in Texas to Younger's Crossing on the South Canadian River, at Younger's Bend. But Bert Casey and Jim Harbolt were on their way to Nickel Hill, possibly to rob one of the big poker games constantly going on there. Also, there was a big gambling house at Cob Town that was tempting to outlaws.

When Hutchins and Oats reached Cob Town after dark, they learned of a big dance going on there. They also found out the two outlaws had been there all evening, and were said to still be at the dance. They heard some fellows laughing and talking about an incident that afternoon between Casey and a foot peddler. Bert Casey bought three pairs of socks from the man. When he picked them out, the peddler said, "That will be twenty-five cents." Bert Casey just laughed and stuck the socks into his pocket.

"Give me a quarter or give me back my socks, you god-damned son-of-a-bitch!" the peddler shouted, bristling.

Cold silence fell among the spectators, as they waited breathlessly for Casey's next move. But the outlaw just handed the peddler a quarter and laughed. Then everyone laughed. The peddler thought it was funny, too, until somebody told him who he had cursed.

Hutchins and Oats quietly scouted the dance, and as they went to the front door, they saw two people who went out the back door. They located their quarry in a clump of trees in the back yard. Several yards apart, they advanced in the moonlight. The deputy marshals knew they were taking a long chance. They were moving from tree to tree, but in the moonlit areas they were excellent targets, while their quarry were concealed in the shadows of the copse in hiding.

Directly, a voice came at Hutchins from behind a tree in the edge of the shadows: "Go back, Bob, I don't want to shoot you, but I won't let you take me. I won't go with you."

Hutchins kept silent and went on advancing. A six-shooter roared and he saw the flash of the gun and felt a shock in his leg almost at the same instant. He went down on one knee and

150

emptied his six-shooter into the clump of trees. Henry Oats did the same. Then Deputy Oats came running over to see how badly Hutchins was hurt, and their quarry escaped.

They learned later that they had "treed" Scar Faced Jim Watson and Lou Bowers, who had been selling whiskey at the dance. The dance had seemed too tame for Casey and Harbolt, who left earlier with some of the Long Riders for Younger's Bend, and had given up their project at Nickel Hill.

Bob Hutchins' wound was only superficial. He had a sore leg for a while, but nothing more.

Watson sent him a message:

> I'm sorry, Bob. You made me do it. I could have killed you, for you pressed your luck too hard. I don't like to be cornered. Don't ever try to walk me down like that again.

Later, Scar Faced Jim Watson made up for it by helping him. Hutchins was eternally grateful to Jim Watson for a service the bootlegger rendered to him when he needed it.

Morris Sass had twenty-one head of cattle stolen from him near Dougherty. Sass followed the rustlers to Roff, where he met Deputy Marshal Hutchins and told him about the theft. Together, they followed the trail to Ada and learned they were about three hours behind them, and the cattle were tired.

The thought of being only three hours behind dangerous cattle thieves made Sass deathly sick. He was unable to go on, despite urgent need to retrieve his cattle.

Hutchins had earned a reputation for never turning back when after a thief or an outlaw, and he did not intend to do so now. He tried to get help from a deputy marshal in Ada, but both officers stationed there were in court at Stonewall that day. Hutchins stubbornly rode north, by himself.

Near Allen Blackburn's gin at the outskirts of Ada, he encountered Scar Faced Jim Watson. Warily they rode to meet each other. Jim was smiling, but kept his right hand resting lightly on the handle of his six-shooter.

"Howdy, Hutch!" he greeted, and when Bob replied in the same friendly way, they shook hands — lefthanded.

"Jim, I'm certainly proud to meet you," Hutchins said

151

earnestly. "I don't know any fellow in this wide world I'd rather meet up with right now."

Watson grinned, "That so?" he asked. "You gettin' short of shootin' scrapes? How many warrants are you carryin' in your pockets for me, Hutch?"

"Ten," Hutchins said, without batting an eye. "All for selling whiskey, but let's can the skeleton-digging and get down to business, Jim. I'm on the trail of a bunch of cow thieves that stole all the cattle a poor nester had, and while we're saddle-sitting here right now, they're headed for the Seminole Nation. Let's forget I have any warrants to arrest you, Jim. Just take those old saddle riders stuffed with John Hart whiskey and hide them some place where they'll be safe until we get back." Hutchins grinned now. "All but one pint to use if one of us gets shot. I'm appointing you a full-fledged deputy marshal to help me catch some cow thieves."

Jim Watson's eyes opened wide. "What the hell do you mean, Hutch? Have you gone nuts?"

"I mean just what I said. We're losing time. It's only twelve miles to the Canadian River and the Seminole line, where my jurisdiction ends. We've always been friends, and I know how much you hate cow thieves."

"Let's go then," he yelled, wheeling his horse around. Off they went in a long lope.

As they rode, Watson said, "I've never let a friend down yet, and I'm damned sure you mean what you say. Your cow thieves are lettin' them cattle graze over by Oakman, and they are asleep now. I passed them a little over an hour ago. I know one of them, who's ridin' a big dun horse. He tried to kill me at Atoka about a year and a half ago. There are at least three of them, all together."

Hutchins laughed. "Well, three or six makes no difference. The odds ought to be about even. We'll surprise them."

"I want one thing, Hutch, before we get there. It's why I decided to side you."

"What's that?"

"Let me take the feller with the yaller horse, and we'll both do our best with the rest."

"All right, you go after him while I cover the others."

They spurred their horses to a faster gait.

152

As they dropped down into a wooded draw, they proceeded cautiously. When they topped the next hill and looked down into a grassy hollow, they saw the cattle grazing contentedly, and three men.

Two of them were lying on the south side of the cattle. The man with the dun-yellow horse was about three hundred yards to the north.

"Go get your yellow-horse man, Jim," Hutchins said in a low voice. "I'll get the other two before you get back."

The two that Hutchins stalked were sound asleep. When they awoke from his prodding, they were looking into the smoke-end of his Winchester.

"Unbuckle and drop your six-guns, gents," he ordered firmly, "and don't make any wrong moves."

When they had obeyed, he threw them a pair of handcuffs and told them to put them on themselves.

Several shots rang out beyond the herd, and they did as he asked, hurriedly.

Jim Watson rode back with a determined grin and reported, "He's dead over there!"

"Just like that!" Hutchins retorted accusingly.

"Hell, Hutch, the son-of-a-bitch tried to kill me again! When I told him to stick up his hands, he decided to shoot it out. He got the first shot, but he couldn't shoot straight enough!"

"I'm glad you explained it, Jim," Hutchins replied dryly. "I didn't really think you would use your authority to end a grudge."

Hutchins left Watson with the two live cow thieves to guard, and he rode to the Oakman post office and found a farmer and hired him and his wagon and team to haul the dead man to Ada.

Jim Watson identified the corpse as John Flowers, nicknamed "Short Arm John" by the officers. "Short Arm John" Flowers was known to be one of the hardest men in the entire Chickasaw Nation. He had been involved in several shooting scrapes with deputy marshals, and had always been lucky, except for one time when he was captured and did time in a penitentiary for stealing cattle — and this time, when he ran up against Jim Watson.

Bob Hutchins contacted Morris Sass at Ada, who was fully

recovered from his illness, and sent him and the farmer back to gather up the cattle. They had stampeded and scattered when the shooting took place.

For five days, Scar Faced Jim Watson was posseman and guard for Deputy Marshal Bob Hutchins. A preliminary trial was held in Ada; and Hutchins, responsible for his posseman's actions, was exonerated for the killing of John Flowers while resisting arrest, and Jim Watson was the star witness.

A number of deputy marshals came around and talked to Jim. They joked with him about themselves being bad shots, and having nightmares about bad men. All of them carried warrants for Watson's arrest as Hutchins did; but no officer would butt into the business of another. If a novice ever undertook to do so, the shooting started; and the novice usually got the blame and the most bullets.

The two rustlers were taken before United States Commissioner B. F. Talbott. Hutchins signed an affidavit that John Flowers was shot and killed while resisting arrest. He paid Jim Watson the two dollars per day the federal government allowed for guards, and had him sign receipts for it. Then he escorted Watson to the spot near Blackburn's gin where he had met him, paid him a dollar for a pint of John Hart and told him good-bye.

"Jim, come to my home any time, and don't worry about ever being arrested by me, no matter what the charges are."

"You are a good scout, Bob," Jim replied. "I'll never forget this, and I'll help you again any time you need me."

Bob Hutchins always thought of Scar Faced Jim Watson as a man who hated a thief worse than the devil hates holy water. Jim did not believe there was any harm done in selling whiskey. He insisted it was a legitimate business and an accommodation, For some strange reason, he would never sell whiskey to a man when he knew the man's wife objected. He also would sell no whiskey to a man whom he thought could not afford it.

About three years later, a notorious outlaw woman — Lou Bowers — found out how John Flowers was killed. John Flowers had been her common law husband for several years. She "framed" Jim Watson by telling him that Zack Runnels, her Choctaw Indian husband, was trying to steal her life's savings and little farm in the Kiamichi Mountains of the Choctaw Nation. He

154

wanted to put her out, so she would be homeless in her old days.

"Jim, I want you to go with me," she pleaded. "You've got plenty of brass, and I need your help."

Being a chivalrous type, Jim Watson agreed, not suspecting treachery from this woman.

They were riding along peacefully when Watson was ambushed and shot from her wagon seat.

Hutchins was sure that his old friend had been double-crossed and murdered in cold blood. He knew Lou Bowers would do anything for vengeance.

As he was known occasionally to remark, and as he told this biographer: "Lou Bowers was so cold-blooded, hard-boiled and bull-headed, she had to kick the bucket and go to her eternal reward to get warm!"

The Big Fight

The most prominent national sport before Oklahoma became a state was boxing. Football, basketball, tennis, hockey, even wrestling and baseball had not begun to equal boxing's popularity in the Oklahoma and Indian territories. More important than all of these sports was horse racing; and Indian ball, which had been originated by North American Indians, possibly even before Columbus. It was called *baggataway* by the French-Canadians. They named the game after the cupped end of the catching and throwing stick *la crosse,* because it looks like a bishop's cross. It was a beloved sport of all the Five Civilized Tribes, and was interesting to the white people, because the game usually ended in a free-for-all fight, with participants beating each other with their cupped sticks until the side that got the worst of it retreated on foot, on horses, or in their horse-drawn vehicles to a distance of one mile from the playing field.

Bob Hutchins attended these games and sometimes had to arrest white men who intruded into the sport, unless they were on one of the teams.

He kept up with boxing from occasional copies of the *Police*

Gazette and local newspapers, most of which were published weekly.

There was much talk in the barber shops and gaming parlors and at crossroads stores about the impending fight between Peter (Dutch) Maher and Robert (Bob) Fitzsimmons.

In November, 1894, Fitzsimmons, fighting his way to become the world's heavyweight challenger, killed Con Rierdon in a bout. It had such an effect on Fitzsimmons that he publicly announced he was going to quit the ring.

Peter Maher fought Steve O'Donnell on February 11, 1895. "Gentleman Jim" Corbett, the heavyweight champion, became so enthused at Dutch Maher's defeat of O'Donnell that he jumped into the ring, congratulated Maher, resigned his championship and gave it to Maher. However, Corbett was officially still the world's heavyweight champion.

In 1896, therefore, when Bob Fitzsimmons decided to return to the ring, sports writers of the metropolitan newspapers conceived and pressed for a battle between Fitzsimmons and Dutch Maher.

The fight was scheduled to be held somewhere in Texas. The promotor was Dan Stuart, a reporter for the *Police Gazette*. Bob Fitzsimmons and Dutch Maher were both signed for a ten thousand dollar purse.

Bob Hutchins was on duty at Ardmore, Chickasaw Nation, when he decided to take a vacation in Dallas to see his first prizefight. He had seen many fistfights and rough-and-tumble fights. He had even participated in some of these, but they were different. A prizefight of worldwide interest was to be held in Texas, and the contenders were two of the best prizefighters that lived. He decided it would be good for him to get away from his job for a few days.

In Dallas, he learned to his dismay that Governor Charles A. Culberson had called a special session of the state legislature and had passed a law forbidding such fights in Texas. A number of big church people had created a furor that prompted the legislature to do this.

Hutchins heard that plans to stage the fight in Old Mexico were brewing in El Paso. A couple of days later, he walked into Al Howard's Coney Island Saloon in El Paso.

"What'll you have, stranger?" asked the bartender. Hutchins' hand moved to his hatband and brought away the trainfare tag at which the bartender was staring.

Crumpling it and tossing it aside, he looked again at the bartender who was still patiently waiting his order.

"Whiskey straight," said Hutchins.

He casually glanced at the men bellied up to the bar beside him.

He grinned as he recognized the lineup. Thugs on one end. Bankers and merchants on the other. Cowpokes in the middle, where he, himself, stood.

The bartender sized him up and shoved out the bottle with good whiskey in it. Hutchins knew he was being given special attention. It wasn't only because of the six-shooter and big belt around his waist and his big hat and boots. He was aware he had been judged to be some other character than a cowboy.

He knew how to carry a gun and use it. He was six feet tall and didn't look ridiculous in a big hat. His boots didn't pinch his feet any more than they did any cayuse-riding cowpoke.

During another lull, the bartender returned his attention to Hutchins, intent on being friendly. "Have a drink on the house," he invited.

"Thanks."

Carefully, the bartender wiped the bar in front of him. "Here for the big fight?"

"I was till I heard Texas had called off prizefights. I'm hanging around a little longer to see what happens. I've come a long way to see this fight."

"I'm Al Howard," said the bartender frankly, extending a hand. "I own this place." He grinned easily as they shook hands. "I'm putting my bankroll on Bob Fitzsimmons against that flat-footed Dutchman, Peter Maher!"

"Is that how it's going to be?" asked Hutchins.

"That's how my money talks, if the bout comes off."

"Well, my name is Hutchins. Just to get your sights straight, I *am* an officer all right, but not a Ranger. I'm a United States Deputy Marshal from Ardmore, in the Indian Territory."

"Make yourself at home, Hutchins," said Al Howard. "Take a drink any time you want it. Keep your money in your pocket. It's no good here, unless some ornery cuss yells 'hooray for

Maher!' Then out with your money and cover him. He's a sucker for a hook!''

Hutchins was now at home in many different ways. A giant of a man moved up to the bar beside him. Glasses and bottles rattled and the bar shook as he banged on it with his huge fist.

He let out a cowboy yell. "Belly up, boys, and tell your troubles!"

"Hutchins," said Al Howard, "this is John L. Sullivan."

Hutchins was too surprised at first to notice the crushing grip on his hand from Sullivan's big paw. He should have known who this huge man was. He had seen many pictures of him. But he had been expecting to see Fitzsimmons and Maher here in El Paso.

"Glad to know you!" he managed to say.

"Sure thing!" boomed Sullivan. "The pleasure is all mine."

Al set out a half-gallon bottle of private stock. "Nothing but whiskey here!" he announced to the house. "No beer or mixed drinks. You can get that across the street. And water, too! That's for washing your feet in. It'll rust your guts if you drink it!"

After the third drink, Sullivan said, "Kid, I like your grey eyes and your mug. They're clear and frank. I like 'em that way!"

Hutchins could think of nothing to say.

"Yes, sir!" declared Sullivan, swigging down another shot. "You are a kid from the forks of the creek. I don't fall for britches, except for use. Come on, Kid! I'll show you my skirt."

He bolted from the saloon, with Hutchins trailing him. He banged on the door of Room 28 in the Paso del Norte Hotel with his big fist.

Who's there?" asked a feminine voice inside.

"Who — hell!" Sullivan exploded. "Open this door before I kick it in!"

The door swung open and there stood a ravishing brunette in her negligee. She was one of the loveliest women Hutchins had ever seen.

"Kid, this is Trixie!" boomed Sullivan. "Trix, meet my pal, Kid Hutchins!"

"Hello, Kid!" Her voice was soft and rich.

Hutchins stared in dumb wonder.

"Bury your modesty and shake hands, Kid!" Sullivan urged.

"Then I'll take her across my knee and spank her bottom for not being dressed."

Hutchins shook hands with her, and then looked on in stunned silence, while the spanking was being administered.

"Now jump into your duds and get ready for dinner," the world's ex-heavyweight champion said when he released her. "I told you what you'd get, if you weren't ready when I got back!"

She retreated into her bedroom, rubbing the spot that had been spanked.

The dinner Sullivan ordered for them would have been enough for a threshing crew. Hutchins never saw a man eat like John L. Sullivan. Back at Al Howard's Coney Island afterward, in a private room, Al bewailed the fact that the governor of Texas had outlawed prizefighting. Dan Stuart had become disillusioned by this and had made a deal with John L. Sullivan to find a way to promote the fight.

"You haven't heard from Mexico, have you, John L.?" Al Howard asked anxiously.

"Not yet. I'm still waiting."

"Mr. Howard, I'd like a little syrup and lemon in my drink," Trixie said sweetly.

Sullivan eyed her sternly. "Cut out the funny talk and swig it down, Trixie. Don't you know where you are?"

"That's all right, John L." Howard assured him hastily. "With her, it's different. I can break rules for her. I'll send out and get — "

"No you don't!" Sullivan stopped him emphatically. "If she can't drink it, she can leave it alone!"

Just then, a Western Union boy came in with a telegram.

"Are you John L. Sullivan?"

"That's me."

"Gosh! Glad to meet yuh, Mister Sullivan! Sign here."

Sullivan took the telegram and gave him a silver dollar.

"Gosh, thanks!"

They watched Sullivan's face grow long and sober as he read. Silently, he laid the message on the table for all to read:

160

"SPECIAL LEGISLATURE CALLED. NO FIGHT IN MEXICO."

GÓMEZ, PRESIDENTE

"That's that!" Sullivan announced. The news left him limp. "My time and money gone to hell!" he moaned.

"Keep a stiff upper lip," said Trixie. "We set out to promote this Fitzsimmons-Maher fight for Dan, and we're still going to do it!"

"How?" Sullivan's voice was weak and defeated.

"We'll die hard or not at all," Trixie declared, feeling her drinks. "The Kid and me will pull this deal, or break both trace chains trying!"

Sullivan snapped erect. Hutchins squirmed under his wild stare.

"Now listen, John L.! "I only met your girl today. You introduced me yourself! I — "

"Kid!" Sullivan's voice was like a shot. "You're grabbing the first train for Phoenix. You're a United States Deputy Marshal. You know something about dealing with hard-hearted men. If you fail in Phoenix, head for Santa Fe. By Jeshosephate, this fight is going to be held!"

"Wait a minute. You got me wrong. I ain't — "

"Spare no money! Pull the deal, Kid. Don't overlook a single bet!"

In vain, Hutchins protested. "Listen, John L., I'm a peace officer, not a fight promoter."

"For me, Kid. Do it for me," he begged. "I've got to promote this fight for Stuart. I've got all my money tied up in this deal. It means a lot to you, too, Kid, or you wouldn't come this far to see it."

Sullivan and Trixie were staring at him like hypnotists trying to control his mind.

"All right, John L.," he yielded, "I'll do it for you. As you said, I don't like to miss what I've come so far to see."

Trixie hugged him with fervor, and Sullivan's big ham of a hand slapped him on the back with painful enthusiasm.

"Sullivan, you're a tricky old bull!" Hutchins grinned as the big fighter stuffed a fat roll of greenbacks that would choke

161

a calf in his pocket. "I sure didn't know I would have to promote this fight in order to see it, but here's to it!"

They all drained their glasses. Howard handed Hutchins a grip containing four quarts of Kentucky's finest bourbon. Forty-five minutes later, he was aboard train, headed for Phoenix, Arizona, while three hopeful people waved good-bye and good luck to him.

In answer to his knock, the governor, himself, opened his office door.

"Hello, Kid!" He called the cards on the spot: "If the prize-fight is all you have on the brain, you can move on. You can't pull bare-fisted manslaughter in the glorious Territory of Arizona."

Hutchins realized the governor was shrewd. He had thrown a bombshell at him before he got his feet planted firmly in his office. Remembering John L. Sullivan's stricken face when he had read the Mexican president's telegram, he stubbornly persisted.

"Your talk and money won't get you anywhere with me, son," the governor warned. "Neither will your whiskey. Just move on!"

"Now wait a minute, Governor! Let me talk. This is no rot-gut. It is the very best bourbon Kentucky ever made. It's been selected special for you. Let's talk this fight over."

"The whole thing has already been threshed out right here in this room till I'm batty. No fight — no bets! The good Christian people of Arizona Territory won't permit it. It's too brutal and too primitive. Good day!"

The door bumped Hutchins' heels as it closed firmly behind him.

His four quarts of bourbon untouched and his bankroll hardly peeled yet, he took another train for Santa Fe.

The governor of New Mexico received him with open surprise and amusement.

"I've been expecting you, *hombre joven,* but you're certainly not the person I expected."

"I don't know just what you had in mind, Governor," said Hutchins, "but I'm here to fit the frame. How about a good swig of bourbon before we get down to business?"

Laughingly, the governor said, "Here I was thinking you

would be a big, two hundred pounder, nearly seven feet tall, with diamonds all over you and a banker's recommendation a yard long. In walks a *muchacho,* with a big six-shooter buckled on him!"

The governor laughed uproariously. When he stopped laughing, he started joking: "Have they got any *hombres* left where you come from, *Muchacho?*"

Hutchins took all this badgering good naturedly. This was, after all, the Governor of New Mexico Territory talking, and he had important business to do with him after he had finished laughing and joking. The fight had to be staged. John L. Sullivan had his heart gambled — his life's savings — on that fight.

Then the governor remembered the dignity of his office and suddenly became polite.

"*Perdoneme Usted, amigo!*" he apologized, then switched back to English. "What's on your mind, Kid?"

"The Fitzsimmons-Dutch Maher fight," Hutchins declared stolidly. He came straight to the point, but was careful not to say anything that might start the governor laughing again.

"What about the fight?" The governor's eyes probed him sharply.

"Dan Stuart of the *Police Gazette* and John L. Sullivan want to hold it here in Santa Fe." Glowingly, he described the prosperity the fight would bring to the territory. "I'm here now to plank down a sizeable guarantee on the barrelhead, Governor!" Hutchins said.

"Why pick on New Mexico?" asked the governor. "It seems to me I heard that fight was going to be fought in Texas."

Hutchins swallowed hard. Now was the time for confidential and earnest pleading of the case. "Texas turned them down flat, Governor. Arizona, too. John L. Sullivan needs your help. He is on the spot, and committed to promote this fight. *You* are his best and last prayer. Why, even Gómez over in Mexico has turned him down!"

That last remark was Hutchins' fatal mistake. The governor had been interested, leaning his way. Now he jerked erect.

"I'm Old Mexico born and bred, amigo!" he exclaimed. "That is my real home, even if I am the high, exalted governor of this fine territory soon to become the state of New Mexico. If my forefathers said 'No!' then my answer is the same!"

163

"Listen, Governor, don't be sentimental. Think of the red-blooded men who will enjoy a good prizefight."

"I am thinking of them — and the other people who won't. No, Señor! No dice!"

Hutchins knew his decision was final. Bang! went the last chance. Reluctantly, he wired Sullivan:

> BLOWED UP SUCKERS ARIZONA AND NEW MEXI-CO. TAKING FIRST TRAIN FOR EL PASO. SORRY!
>
> — HUTCH

When he reached the Coney Island Bar, Al Howard told him he would find John L. and Trixie in the dark cell. Howard shook his head sadly. "He's gettin' drunker than a boiled owl! He was a great fighter, Kid. This is trail's end for him. The way they've messed him up and wallowed him on promotin' this fight is a dirty shame!"

John L. and Trixie were fixing to swig another drink as Bob Hutchins joined them. He remembered then he hadn't had a drink himself in a couple of days. He still had the four quarts in his grip.

"Not good enough for governors, huh!" exclaimed Sullivan. "Well, it's good enough for you and little Trixie and me!"

Sullivan was in a bitter mood.

"I'm sorry, John L. I did my best!" Hutchins apologized, as he pitched Sullivan's roll of greenbacks onto the table. "I guess I make a better deputy marshal than a promoter."

" 'Sall right, Kid!" Sullivan smiled feebly. "I love you just as much just the same!"

"I guess I'll trot along back home," said Hutchins.

"Must you?" Trixie asked. "Stay on, Bob," she coaxed. "Something will turn up. It's got to!"

"You don't really have to go, Hutch, old kid," Sullivan said. "Stay on. I still have enough money left for a few more days of good times."

"Thanks, John L.," Hutchins said, "but I'll mosey along back to the Indian Territory and report to headquarters. My vacation will soon be over, and they haven't heard from me

164

since I left. If you and Trixie ever come through that territory, stop off to visit me."

Sullivan sat in moody silence. Trixie smiled a reluctant farewell. "Thank you, Hutch. Maybe some day we will."

Hutchins stopped at the bar to have a last drink and say good-bye to Al Howard.

Somebody prodded him in the side and an old, familiar voice said, "Hutch, old kid, how yuh doing?"

Turning, Hutchins saw The Law West of the Pecos.

"Judge Roy Bean, as I live and breathe!" he cried.

"Tell Al your troubles, Kid. I'm not sittin' court today!"

"I'm at your service, Judge. Any arresting you need done around here? Tell it to Hutch!"

"I've never been short on peace officers in my life!" Judge Bean grinned. "I got enough help around here now tuh handle the whole kit and caboodle in this joint!"

"I've got them spotted, too," declared Hutchins. "Want me to point them out to you?"

"Not now." Judge Bean laughed. "Heard yuh had quit workin' for Uncle Sam and had gone tuh promotin' prizefights. When did yuh get back?"

"Today." Hutchins' grin was sheepish. "I sure didn't impress those governors, Judge. I just now checked in to John L. and resigned. I'm on my way back to Indian Territory. I came this far to see a fight, but it's all off. I have had some fun, though," he admitted.

"I met Sullivan for the first time while he was reading your telegram," said Judge Roy Bean. "Hutchins, yuh couldn't have addled him any more, if you had hit him over the head with your six-shooter!"

"I knew it when I sent the telegram," Hutchins said, "but he had to know. I could telegraph it easier than I could face him and tell him. What we need around here, Judge, is some of your kind of law and justice about things. Two men standing up in the middle of a ring, beating each other, ain't any worse than a bunch like this, standing here burning their stomachs out with rot-gut."

Judge Roy Bean studied his glass in deep thought. "You know, Hutch," he said deliberately, "I've got a hunch me and

165

my six-shooter bunch can pull that fight off — if we wuz properly seed to!"

His words brought Hutchins to intense attention. *Why hadn't he thought of Judge Roy Bean before?*

"Ante, Judge, and sit in for the game," he invited. "Don't pass the buck, like three governors and a *presidente* have done!"

"I have some unfinished business with a lady friend," said the judge, looking at his watch. "See me in Langtry on Friday."

"Do your best!" Hutchins urged enthusiastically. "We'll see you Friday and pull the deal."

Back in the dark cell, he told John L. Sullivan and Trixie. She seized him fiercely, put her soft, warm arms around his neck and kissed him long and tenderly.

"I told you Hutch and me would come through. Just like two little old maverick branders!" she explained, twitching Sullivan's mustache. "Come alive, John! Yippee-ti-yee! Hoof along, little dogies! Hoof along!"

John L. Sullivan grew bright and cheerful again.

"Watch our smoke," said Trixie. "Get me a pearl-handled forty-five and belt like Hutch's, and one hundred rounds of ammunition. We're off to the shindig!"

She hugged and kissed them both again and said, "Whiskey straight, please! Booted and spurred, we're headin' for the world's famous roundup on our little old cayuses!"

Judge Roy Bean first set up his saloon and Justice of Peace court in a tent at a railroad camp called Vinegarroon, located near the juncture of the Rio Grande and the Pecos rivers. During the early years after 1890, the Gulf, Houston and San Antonio Railroad was being extended beyond San Antonio westward to meet the fast approaching Southern Pacific Railroad.

The point selected in West Texas for two railroads to meet was known as Langtry, just a few miles from Vinegarroon. Roy Bean moved to Langtry, where he established his bailiwick, which consisted of a combination saloon and a J. P. court. It was roughly built, with a log front and box-board, weather stripped sides and back, with plain planks running up and down. A covered porch ran all the way across the front, and the roof was shingled.

Inside was a long room, with the Jersey Lily Saloon on the

166

right. There were plain, but sturdy, tables and chairs in the place. The saloon, itself, was built of plain lumber. In the back, a ladder ran up to a sleeping loft in the attic. Outside, at the top of the porch, were the celebrated signs: "Judge Roy Bean" and in letters a little larger beneath: "Justice of The Peace, Law West of The Pecos."

Judge Roy Bean liked to brag that the railroad tycoon, Jay Gould, and the famous English actress, Lily Langtry, were his intimate friends. He claimed to have named Langtry after the actress, which was how the mistaken origin of the little town's name came to be known. But, according to files of the Southern Pacific Railroad, Langtry was named after a railroad contractor for the El Paso division.

That Friday, the meeting was held in Judge Roy Bean's famous court and Jersey Lily Saloon. The judge sat in court, surrounded by his gunmen. Among them were Smokey John, Kiowa Jones, Bart Goble, Two-Guns John, Hell Roaring Taylor, and some of lesser renown.

The judge cleared his throat and thereby signified that the court was in session. Then he announced the deal:

"For four carloads of Lemps beer set off on a convenient siding in Langtry, the fight goes on. Does the court hear an acceptance to the offer?"

"It's a deal!" cried Trixie, jumping up happily.

"Then I hereby do declare the big sandbar in the middle of the Rio Grande near here to be No Man's Land. The fight shall be fought there under the protection of this court. My men will assist in making the preparations for the big fight. Court dismissed!"

Trixie rushed upon the judge and gave him a hug and kiss on the cheek.

"We won't call that contempt of court, young lady," he told her, with a hearty laugh. "There will be no fine nor punishment!"

"We'll just keep our little project secret among ourselves," the judge cautioned, "and go about our preparations quietly. No noise and no fanfare. We have to put this deal over without any trouble with Rangers or the Mexican soldiers."

The ring was set up on the designated sandbar island. Many Mexican laborers were hired for one American dollar each

167

day. Two-Guns John arranged for boats to take the spectators to the arena-island; but they used them to lay down a pontoon walkway bridge, which would be the easiest way to control traffic.

The judge's four carloads of beer arrived on time, and were immediately taken to the Jersey Lily Bar. Barrels and cases were stacked all over the place, ready to sell to the workers.

Sullivan was in El Paso looking after other affairs, and Trixie managed things in Langtry. She played both ends toward the middle, relying on Hutchins and the judge to back her every move. With a bank account and a check book, she got things done. Finally, she wired John L. Sullivan:

> COCKED AND PRIMED. CHARTER TRANSPORTA-
> TION. ARRANGEMENTS ALL MADE. STAGE SET
> FOR BIG EVENT. RING FINE SHAPE. LOVE.
>
> — TRIXIE

People asking where the fight was to be held were told not to worry. Just hang around, wet their whistles. They would be informed in due time. Ringside seats could be had for reasonable rates on the island.

Smilingly, as she paid the expenses, Trixie told Hutchins, "I don't mind. I've got some more in the bank. Pulling this fight will put John and me on easy street the rest of our lives."

The day of the big fight, February 21, 1896, Langtry had the biggest crowd in history. Sullivan chartered two trains from El Paso, and one from San Antonio.

Beer and red-eye flowed freely at the Jersey Lily. Judge Bean's bar had not done as much business in a total of many months. In honor of the event, special prices prevailed. Beer was sold at the bar for one dollar per quart; red-eye, fifty cents a shot. For spectators' convenience, beer sold at the ringside for one dollar a bottle, and red-eye for the same price per shot.

The fight had been so secretly arranged that only two Texas Rangers made it to Langtry that day. They barely caught the special train from San Antonio.

The Rangers accosted Judge Roy Bean, dressed in his Sunday best, as he and Trixie were about to lead the parade to

168

No Man's Land. Bob Hutchins and the judge's gunmen stood by, ready for trouble.

"Yuh cain't stage that fight here in Langtry!" one of the Rangers told him.

Judge Bean fixed them with a judicial stare. "Gentlemen, who told yuh we're stagin' a fight here in Langtry? This is an international situation — it has been decided by this court — which you boys don't understand. You'd best stick to catchin' outlaws and hoss thieves!" Then he smiled broadly as he added, "By gobs, if yuh like a good fight, follow me!"

The Rangers, bewildered and undecided, watched for an hour as people crowded to the river and paid a dollar each to cross the toll bridge to the dry sandbar.

Hutchins collected silver dollars and greenbacks at the landing until his coat pockets sagged with the weight and threatened to rip off before he could transfer it to money bags. Others collected the admission fees at different ringside sections of seats.

Dutch Maher had trained at Las Cruces, New Mexico, and Bob Fitzsimmons had trained at Juárez, on the Mexican side of the river from El Paso.

Fitzsimmons had boasted there would be only two blows struck in the prizefight. He would hit Maher and the Dutchman would hit the floor.

The Rangers stood among outlaws and horse thieves on the Texas shore and watched the event. Mexican authorities stood on a bluff on the Mexican shore. Judge Roy Bean and his henchmen were in command of that previously insignificant little island for the day.

Some spectators went away rich. Some went away penniless. Some didn't even remember just when they did go away! But Sullivan, Trixie and Hutchins went away with two bags of silver and currency that required two burros to carry. But Sullivan and Dan Stuart made their big money above expenses on bets.

The prizefight was far from equal to the elaborate plans. It lasted almost exactly as long as Fitzsimmons boasted — one minute and thirty-five seconds, giving Fitzsimmons unofficially the crown; which he would have to win again the following year from James C. Corbett, to make it official.

The two fighters tore into each other in grand style. Maher caught Fitzsimmons on the mouth and drew first blood. From then on, the fight was the British Australian's. In one of Maher's fierce drives, Fitzsimmons caught the Dutchman squarely on the chin; and Maher stretched out on the canvas. He came up finally to one knee, but thinking better of it, lay back down for the count.

Some said Maher took a look at all the six-shooters and rifles around him and just wilted.

Anyhow, it left Sullivan, Trixie and Hutchins very happy, even with some twenty-five hundred dollars paid out for expenses, in addition to the ten thousand dollar purse.

No spot on the Rio Grande ever rang with more yelps and loud cries, even in battle, than that little island, neglected before and forgotten since.

Bob Hutchins left Judge Roy Bean, Sullivan and Trixie in fine spirits, with their praises and thanks ringing in his ears, and Trixie's last lingering kiss on his lips.

Handcuffs and Code of Honor

Bob Hutchins got word at Ada that Jack McDonald was coming home. Jack had been on the dodge about three years. He had a wife and five children, the youngest of which was about two and one-half years old, and Jack had not yet seen it.

His family had lived "from hand to mouth" for the past two years. His wife had worked hard and she had done the best she could to feed and care for her children.

Jack had been charged, with others, by the United States government for the burning alive of three Seminole Indians who had raped a white woman. The rest of the men involved had managed to squirm out of it by improvising evidence which shifted the entire blame onto Jack McDonald, after he had been persuaded to run away. Jack, an innocent, ignorant farmer, had been given money and guaranteed that his wife and children would be provided for, if he would leave the country until the affair died down.

On the night of his return, Bob Hutchins, Bob Nestor and Dick Couch went out to watch the trails into Jack's home.

171

Hutchins was on the extreme east end of the house, Nestor on the west, and Couch on the south. The South Canadian River was on the north side. All of them were stationed about 250 yards from the house.

About midnight, they heard a voice singing a hymn clearly and cheerfully: "I am coming home to die no more." The voice rang up and down the river, as if in a cathedral. Jack McDonald had a splendid voice. In the quiet of the river bottom, it was full and strong and melodious. He knew Jack was signaling his wife he was coming home.

There were at least ten pairs of ears listening as Jack's wife and five children and the three deputy marshals waited anxiously for Jack to appear.

The officers knew, also, this man they were waiting for would shoot at the slightest provocation.

As Jack came forward, Hutchins moved near to the cabin in order to directly intercept him. When he was twenty feet away, Hutchins rose up with his Winchester ready and said loudly, "Put up your hands, Jack!"

"All right," he said, and dropped his own rifle to the ground. Hutchins quickly stepped forward and handcuffed him. By this time, Bob Nestor and Dick Couch, and Jack's wife and children, who had waited faithfully three long years, had gathered around them.

Jack raised his handcuffed hands above his wife's head and dropped his arms around her neck. The eagerness with which his wife and children embraced him was pathetic. Hutchins looked at them a few moments and heard their sobs and said, "Jack, a man whose family is this much devoted to him after being gone three years must be pretty good. I'm going to release you. I'll take those handcuffs off and leave you on your honor and your promise that you won't run away again. I'll place you in the custody of your faithful wife and children and let you stay here tonight with them. Will you meet me in Ada at noon tomorrow?"

Jack let out a long sigh of relief. "If I live," he promised, "I will be there."

The three deputy marshals walked back to their hack and returned to Ada without their prisoner.

"Suppose he does not come?" Couch asked. "Hutch, you

can be sent to the penitentiary, yourself, for arresting and releasing a wanted man without proper authority."

"Nobody knows that better than I do. I'll take the blame, if he fails me."

But Hutchins had been right. True to his word, Jack McDonald was on time the next day. Hutchins brought him before Commissioner U. G. Winn, and he was committed to jail without bail. In due time, he was tried and sent to the penitentiary for five years.

Hutchins hired John Crawford, a lawyer, to take the case. A petition was circulated and signed by a number of people who knew about the case, including the jury and other officials of the court who convicted him. John Crawford was sent to Washington, D.C. to state the facts to President Theodore Roosevelt, who pardoned Jack McDonald after he had served a year and one-half of his sentence.

Al Jennings—
the Outlaw Imitator

Deputy Marshal Bob Hutchins went to Courtney Flats on Mud Creek, which was a community in the rich Red River bottomland in the Chickasaw Nation. Hutchins was after a much wanted criminal, but he failed to find him. The trip took him three days, with a buggy and team, and he got caught in a hard rain. He finally went home to Ardmore, feeling completely exhausted. He unhitched and unharnessed the team, fed them, and had just gone inside the house and had sat down on the side of the bed to take off his boots, when Ethel came in and told him that Al Jennings, the outlaw, was at the gate.

Hutchins had known Al Jennings many years, long before he had decided to outdo the Jameses, the Youngers, the Daltons, Bill Doolin and Bert Casey, and become the legendary badman of them all.

Hutchins went to the front porch. "Hello, Hutch!" Al greeted him. "Come out, I've got a word for you. It's important."

"You come on in, Al," Hutchins invited. "I just got back off a long, wet trip, and I'm just about sick."

"No, I'm too well known here to tarry long, Hutch," Al insisted. "It won't take me but a minute to tell you."

Hutchins went out to see what Jennings had on his mind. He knew it must be important for him to ride right up to his front gate in broad daylight.

"I've come to talk to you, Hutch, because of our many years of friendship. I want you to be out of town next Wednesday at eleven o'clock in the morning. Me and my bunch are going to hold up the First National Bank, and I've got a bunch of hard shooters. I don't want you to get hurt."

Hutchins looked him squarely in the eyes as he sat with one leg hooked around his saddle horn. "Al," he warned, "with all due respect for our friendship, I say *no* to you. This is one deal you will not pull. That bank has stayed with me through thick and thin. You and your bunch try to rob that bank, and I'll pull the trigger to stop you."

Al wasn't ruffled. He smiled. "Well," he said, "if that is the lineup, she's off, and I'm still your friend." As abruptly as he had come, he rode away.

But the more Hutchins thought about it, the more he decided that Al's gang might have another notion. They might decide Al Jennings just had cold feet and try to pull the hold-up on their own. They had no qualms about any friendship with Deputy Marshal Bob Hutchins. They knew Al's word was his honor, despite his reputation.

Hutchins went to the bank the next morning and told Charley Anderson, the vice president, about Al Jennings' visit and what the situation might be.

"You know where we stand and what to do, Hutchins. What do you suggest?"

"Charley, knowing the worldly greed of such men, I think we had better go over and see Steve Douglas about a gadget he can make for us."

Hutchins told the village blacksmith what he had in mind. After listening to the details, he told Hutchins, "Draw it on paper. I'll close the shop and begin work on it at once. Come back tomorrow night and it'll be ready."

What Steve Douglas built was a breastwork, or shield, six feet square, out of two-ply, cross grained hardwood lumber, containing four well-spaced portholes, large enough to accommodate four gun barrels, and two peep-holes about the size of dollars. To camouflage it, Douglas had covered it over neatly with cardboard.

He had the contraption placed in a strategic but inconspicuous place in the bank; and for eight days, he sat behind his death deflector, with his bone-handled .45 *Belle Starr* six-shooter and his Winchester rifle.

But Al Jennings' gang had gone off to rob a Rock Island train on October 1, 1897. This, too, was done in broad daylight; and it wrote finis to the brief career of the Jennings gang.

Wells Fargo had posted two thousand dollars reward for the capture of Al Jennings. Many federal officers up north were looking for him and his gang, which included Little Dick West, the brothers — Pat and Morris O'Malley — and Al's brother, Frank. Among the officers hot after them were William D. Fossett, Bill Tilghman, Bud Ledbetter and Heck Thomas.

But the gang eluded them for awhile, and Al Jennings came south alone and contacted Bob Hutchins, whom he seemed to trust. He was willing to make a deal to surrender, plead guilty and take possibly a five year sentence and bring an end to his brief, unsuccessful outlaw career. Hutchins agreed to use his influence to get two other cases against Jennings dropped, or pigeonholed, to let the statute of limitations run its limit. Al Jennings and his brother, Frank, had been aspiring lawyers before their innate feelings for showmanship caused them to find expression as outlaws. Their father, J. D. F. Jennings, was a lawyer and their brother, John, was legally inclined. Their father became Probate Judge of Pottawatomie County at Shawnee in 1899, and John became Clerk of the County Court.

Hutchins talked the matter over with United States Commissioner Arthur Walcott, who agreed to help in the case, if he could be sure that Al Jennings was sincere.

Then Hutchins sent a telegram to the Wells Fargo Express Company that he had a deal on with Al Jennings to surrender to him, if the company would agree to pay the reward and not prosecute to the fullest extent of the law.

The company had two cases against Al Jennings. One was a cinch for conviction, but the other involved too much uncertain evidence.

Instead of replying to Bob Hutchins' telegram, Mr. Wells of

the Express Company appeared in person at the United States Marshal's office to talk the subject over.

Mr. Wells began by saying, "Mr. Hutchins, I have investigated you and I have determined that you are both honest and brave in the execution of your duties. In the First National Bank here in Ardmore. I will deposit *not* two thousand dollars, but *three thousand* dollars for Al Jennings —" He paused a moment, then said, "Feet foremost! Otherwise, the reward of two thousand dollars will be withdrawn. What is your answer?"

The first thing Hutchins could see in the proposition was that he was deliberately being bribed to betray a friend and commit cold-blooded murder.

"My answer is *you can go to hell,* Mr. Wells," Hutchins replied grimly, looking him straight in the eyes. "You are talking to the wrong man. Your money, prestige and political pull cannot induce me to kill a friend in cold blood."

He picked up his hat and walked out of the marshal's office and went outside where he could get a breath of clean, fresh air, leaving Mr. Wells staring after him.

Hutchins learned afterward that Wells told Marshal Hammer, "You have one deputy that is ten times meaner than any man he ever arrested, Al Jennings included." But Captain Hammer merely laughed the matter off later with Hutchins.

When Hutchins went home, he found Al Jennings down on the floor, playing with Pearl and Essa, his daughters. He and Al had never withheld any information from each other and, naturally, he told Jennings the whole story. Then he realized it might have been a mistake. He had to restrain Al Jennings from going downtown to see how many holes he could shoot in Mr. Wells before he fell.

When Jennings finally calmed down, he admitted that such a rash act would land him in the penitentiary for life, and ruin his chances to put his outlaw career behind him.

Hutchins promised him that he and Judge Walcott would keep working on the case, and he cautioned him to go carefully when he rode north again, for he was a marked man.

Up north again, Al Jennings contacted his brother, Frank, and the rest of the gang. The pursuit grew warmer as the various groups of officers closed in on him. Deputy Marshal Bud Ledbetter and his posse finally cornered them between the Arkansas River and Snake Creek, on the old Spike S Ranch, on November 29, 1897. The two factions fought it out bitterly, and Al Jennings and his entire gang escaped, except for Morris O'Malley, who was captured.

But Bud Ledbetter and his posse were more relentless than the outlaws were resourceful, and they finally captured them at a Rock Creek crossing, one week later.

They were disappointed that their dragnet did not include Little Dick West. He was the real outlaw of the whole Jennings gang — the only one, as far as the officers were concerned, that made the gang a potential threat to public welfare and safety. They considered him to be the actual brains of the gang, and Al Jennings the figurehead.

Dick West drifted into the Cottonwood Creek country and, using an alias, he hired out as a farm hand to Ed Fitzgerald. When work was slack on the Fitzgerald farm, he found odd jobs on the adjoining farm with Harmon Arnett. All seemed to be going well for him, but he didn't reckon with the resourcefulness of the veteran officers who had tracked down worse and more clever outlaws than he.

In the early morning of April 7, 1898, marshals Bill Tilghman, Heck Thomas, William Fossett, and Sheriff Frank Rhinehart surrounded West in the Fitzgerald barn. He gave battle, and in the crossfire that followed, the last of the Doolin and Jennings gangs was killed.

The rest of the Jennings gang finally came to trial. Al Jennings received a life term sentence. The others received a term of five years each. Because of the influence and efforts of many respected citizens in high positions, President William McKinley was induced to commute Al's sentence to five years — the same sentence as the others had received.

Deputy Marshal Bud Ledbetter and his posse had fought the outlaws so hard at the Spike S Ranch when they captured Morris O'Malley — and later the trouble they had running down the rest of the gang at Rock Creek on December 6, 1897, except West — they felt the President was wrong in commuting the sentence; but President McKinley no doubt considered five years sufficient for stealing two gallons of whiskey and a bunch of bananas, which was reported to be all that was actually taken from the express car of the Rock Island train robbery.

President Theodore Roosevelt, in 1902, seemed to feel more strongly about the melodramatic career of an actor and imitator, whose wild adventures lasted only four months. He issued Al and Frank Jennings citizenship pardons, which Al used to his advantage in public appearances in the movie theaters to publicize a story he had drummed up in Hollywood from his book, *Beating Back*. Al Jennings had at last found a safer and more lucrative medium for showmanship.

The high points in Al Jennings' career and exploits can best be completed by citing here a speech he made, which was reported by a news reporter when he came to Del Rio, Texas, to visit his old friend, Bob Hutchins.

VAL VERDE COUNTY HERALD
Friday, December 3, 1937

AL JENNINGS, EX-BANDIT AND FORMER CANDIDATE FOR GOVERNOR OF OKLAHOMA, TELLS OF ROBBING TRAIN AND INTERESTING POLITICAL ACTIVITIES

By Ima Jo Fleetwood

The sight of a former United States Marshal greeting a former train robber with every sign of affection on the part of each was witnessed by a number of Del Rioans Wednesday, when J. R. Hutchins, now caretaker at the Pecos High Bridge, greeted Al Jennings, now of Hollywood, California.

Jennings, who was notorious early in the century as a train robber and leader of the Jennings gang, was en route to Mexico, looking for a location for a motion picture. He was accompanied by A. M. Baker of Hollywood, and left Del Rio early Thursday morning for Laredo, where he will cross into Mexico.

Hutchins was in Del Rio on one of his two monthly visits from the Pecos High Bridge. Jennings had written he would visit with him, but had been unable to locate him on the Pecos.

"I could have found him if I had been on a horse,"

179

Jennings stated, "but you can't find anything much in an automobile, especially down a canyon."

Admires Roosevelt

Jennings, who is 74 and who has been "honest for 34 years and awfully lonesome," spoke freely concerning government conditions and practices, but is an ardent admirer of President Franklin Delano Roosevelt.

"He is one of the few honest politicians I have ever known or heard tell of," he stated. "Those around him might be dishonest, but I believe he is a square shooter. At times I have thought, when I heard of some appointment he had made, 'How can he be honest and put *him* in?' But still, I think he's honest, all right."

Jennings ran for the office of Governor of Oklahoma *(against Robert L. Williams, who afterward became United States District Judge of Southern Oklahoma, in which capacity he remained for many years of his career)* in 1914; and Jennings' friends, including Hutchins, stoutly maintain he was duly elected, but that he was *counted out.*

"I saw some of the ballots they burned, myself," Hutchins declared Wednesday. "They hadn't been counted, and Al was just done out of the Governorship of Oklahoma."

For the past twenty years, Jennings has made his home in Hollywood, going there shortly after his race for Governor of Oklahoma ended unsuccessfully for him.

As interesting as his political ventures might be, however, the most interesting part of the man's career, as he related it Wednesday, was when he was a bandit.

Striking Personality

Standing about five-feet-two in tall-heeled cowboy boots and ten gallon hat, Jennings is a striking personality and a commanding speaker. Educated to be a lawyer, he served as county attorney before his foray into lawlessness.

With breath-taking frankness, Jennings related one of his train robberies.

"There were five of us," he told listeners with a grin and a twinkle of his bright blue eyes that still maintain an amazing vitality. "I knew everybody in that country very well and for that reason, I wore a mask. I didn't usually do that, but I did on this occasion, not because I

180

was *afraid,* but because I was *ashamed* of holding up my friends.

"We surrounded the station house and called to the station agent. When he didn't come out, I let go a blast with my Winchester, shooting the top off the door about six inches above his head. I could have hit *him* just as easily, so he decided to come out.

"He came out babbling so fast and so crazy you couldn't understand him, and he was shaking all over. 'What are you so excited about?' I asked him.

"Then I told him I wanted the key to the switch. 'What for?' he asked, and I told him it was none of his business. He told me it was in the right pocket of his pants, but he was shaking so bad he couldn't get it. And I had to perform the distasteful task of putting my hand in another man's pocket!"

Blew Up Car

"When the train had been stopped and we made all the crew get off, I nearly gave myself away, because I knew them all so well I almost spoke to them. Then we blew up the baggage car, but we did such a good job of blowing it up, we din't find anything to amount to much.

"So we just did like they do in church: we lined the passengers up against a barbed wire fence and took up collection. We never took watches or jewelry; the only thing we had any use for was money. There was a lawyer I knew in the bunch, and he kept fingering an old yellow diamond stickpin in his tie. I knew it wasn't worth anything, even though it was about three carats, and after watching him trying to hide it for some time, I said, 'Lawyer, let that paper weight alone. We don't want it.'

"One of the passengers was a Catholic priest, and the poor man had only 50 cents with him, I couldn't take that, so I gave him a $5 gold piece and returned his half dollar.

"After awhile, I heard some one walking and it was just who I thought it was, that station agent. He looked so pitiful and so scared, I gave him a $5 gold piece and told him to forget all about it."

Cleaned Smart Guy

"Later, we cleaned out a smart guy who had been talk-

181

ing about us. He had a little store, and we took everything he had; hams, flour and everything else, and loaded them in the wagon. We rode our horses and after awhile stopped at a farm. I got down and was picking up peaches off the ground. All at once, I heard somebody say, 'Don't take those, they ain't no good. I'll get you some good ones.' I wheeled around and there stood a woman with sore eyes. We were so grateful we gave her enough hams and flour and other things we had stolen to last her all winter.

"When I was on trial, they called up the Catholic priest and put him on the stand. He made a lot of nice remarks about me, saying he had known me when I was county attorney. But he didn't identify me. They put the station agent on the stand, and he failed to identify me, not because of the $5 I had given him, but because I hadn't killed him, I guess.

"While I was in jail, it was awfully cold. One morning early, the jailor told me to come out and warm myself at a fire. I knew he wanted someone to see me, but I came out and there stood the woman with the sore eyes. Her husband was with her, and I felt pretty bad. After awhile though, she said, 'Paw this ain't the man that stopped at our farm.' Was that a relief!"

Plays With Baby

"Those people all stood by me. But a funny thing happened. While we were waiting at the station house for the train before we robbed it, the agent's baby was playing around and I picked it up. The mask scared it, so I pulled it down and began *booing* at the baby. Pretty soon it was playing with me and when I'd put my mask back over my face, it would poke its fingers in the eye holes. Directly, the baby's mother came in and she nearly had a fit: her baby playing with a train robber!"

At one time, Jennings recounted, the gang decided to rob a bank. "I was going to get the plan of the bank by asking for a $25 loan," he explained, "but when the cashier, who knew me well, actually loaned me $25, I gave up. Any man who would lend me $25, knowing me, was all right, so we didn't rob the bank, but robbed a train instead."

Jennings laughed frequently as he related his story, but became serious as he said: "Penitentiaries accomplish no good at all. I know. The public is one of the reasons why criminals persist in their meanness. Once a man has been imprisoned, he is shunned and can not find work. By this attitude, the public becomes the greatest reason for the high percentage of criminals in this country today. The laws make no difference. You should publish all the laws needed for the well-being of a country in a small book. It isn't the law, it's the enforcement of it. And you can't get it fully enforced, because the higher officials in politics want a cut."

From time to time, Jennings turned to Hutchins for verification of the story he told concerning the train robbery and his subsequent trial. At last, Hutchins exclaimed, "Of course I know it . . . I have the records out at the Pecos, if you want to see them!"

Testifies At Hearing

Jennings was called to testify at the Teapot Dome hearings and made use of his law training there. His testimony had involved the late President Warren G. Harding, whom he described Wednesday as a "good fellow." Senator Walsh, in conducting the prosecution, inferred that Jennings was testifying against a dead man, unable to answer allegations.

" 'You know Harding is dead, don't you?' " Jennings said Walsh asked.

" 'I don't know anything of the kind,' I told him. Everyone in the room gasped. 'Do you mean to tell me that at the time you gave your testimony, you did not know the President of the United States was dead?' Walsh demanded. 'I didn't know it,' I answered. 'I read about it in the paper, but to my certain knowledge, I didn't know he was dead: I didn't see him dead and I didn't see him buried, so I didn't actually know he was dead: I just heard about it.'

" 'Oh, so you're a lawyer as well as a train robber,' Walsh sneered. 'Yes, but I never conducted a congressional investigation,' I told him." Jennings laughed.

Jennings, after being imprisoned in Leavenworth penitentiary, was granted a full and free pardon by Theodore Roosevelt, President of the United States at the time.

"I went to Washington to see the President about my pardon," Jennings stated, "and after appearing before a cabinet meeting, I went into Roosevelt's office with him.

183

'You have excellent recommendations from the governor of your state,' he told me, 'and I am inclined to pardon you. You were not even at the scene of the robbery, were you?' — 'Yes,' I said. 'I was there and held up the train.' — 'Then what in the world did you come up here for after a pardon?' Roosevelt demanded.

" 'Because,' I told him, 'I was convicted of holding up the United States mail and taking a box containing $10,000. I didn't hold up the mail. I held up the passengers. I didn't get the $10,000, because I didn't know it was supposed to be on the train. If I had known it, I would have taken it: I just didn't know it was there.'

" 'Well,' Roosevelt told me, 'you are truthful. What is your brother's name?' — I told him 'Frank Jennings.' — 'All right, I grant you both a full and free pardon. And you have given me your word you will be honest from now on.' I told him my word was my bond, and I have been honest now for 34 years. But I've been lonesome!" he concluded with a grin.

Al Jennings failed to mention in his speech that in 1915, he had been robbed, himself. *The Weekly Ardmoreite* published a little article that was picked up by the Associated Press under the date, Wednesday, July 14, 1915, as follows:

AL JENNINGS HELD UP IN LOS ANGELES

Former Oklahoma outlaw was among passengers on Interurban Car held up by two masked men last night. Los Angeles, Calif., July 12, 1915.

Al Jennings, former Oklahoma bandit, was among the passengers held up and robbed last night on an interurban electric car by two masked men.

The robbers collected a total of two hundred dollars.

An Ivory-Handled Mountain Belle

"Trusting a deceitful woman is like going into hell," Hutchins remarked more than once with bitterness. "Easy to slide into, but hell to get out!"

When he made this remark, he had in mind an outlaw woman, who was about as important in his career as Belle Starr had once been.

Hutchins knew both of them well enough to evaluate and give this candid opinion of the contrast: "Belle Starr had a warm heart. Lou Bowers was mean as the devil. Belle couldn't even have held her a light to go by, if they had been together!"

The exact words of Lou Bowers when she surrendered to Deputy Marshal Hutchins for the first time were: "You are the only scoundrel in which I have enough confidence in five years to hand this old tried, trusted and true ivory-handled six-shooter. Take good care of it, for I shall call for it when I come again upon the green. Only by your insistent request, while looking into the smoke-end of your forty-five, am I induced to

185

take this step. I can assure you it is not through any courtesy to you, you low-down son-of-a-bitch of a scoundrel!"

Hutchins said nothing. He knew she would rave enough without his saying anything to agitate her more.

"Anybody can buy brains, but it takes more than money to buy guts. Who sent you after me?"

This was in Kansas City, Missouri, in an apartment house, which Lou Bowers owned. Hutchins knew she had bought the real estate with tainted, bloody, double-cross money.

Within five minutes after her surrender, Henry Starr, who afterward became notorious as an outlaw, came in. Then, he was only a young boy. This boy got his early training from Lou Bowers. He made no effort to interfere, but listened silently to their conversation.

When Lou seemed to have run down a bit, Hutchins talked.

"Lou, I've got you now. What did you do with that loot that was taken from the passengers of that Rock Island train near Chickasha?"

"Why, the nerve! What are you belching up?"

"Al Jennings is now in the pen. Frank Jennings, Pat O'-Malley and Morris O'Malley are in jail in Chickasha, waiting trial. Come out of the paw-paw bush, Lou, and tell me what you did with the money from that train. During that robbery, you held the horses and took charge of the drag."

"This conversation doesn't interest me in the least."

"Well, I will tell you a funny story that might interest you. Only last week, while I was acting as circulating deputy of the Southern District of Indian Territory, I, with some other deputies, had been detailed at Paris, Texas, to take custody, there and at Ardmore, of Morris, Pat, Frank and twenty-six other hombres charged with the category of crime. We took them all to Chickasha, where they are now in jail."

Hutchins held her attention and the immobile interest of the Indian boy, Henry Starr, as well.

"At Gainesville, Texas, I had previously jumped off the train, hurried to the H and R Saloon near the depot and returned with a quart of whiskey. I knew those boys had been in the Ardmore jail about five months without a drop. On the train when we left Ardmore, I went into the men's room, poured out a tin cup full and handed it to those boys on the sly. Naturally, it tasted good to them, and it also loosened their tongues."

Now Hutchins' voice became accusing. "Lou, you know very well the part you played and how you double-crossed those poor boys. My business with you is to see that they get justice, and that you do, too. When we get back to Indian Territory, tell the truth, or else you will suffer more than some of the rest of them. You framed the game. You double-crossed the whole bunch. You are the girl who posed as the section foreman's wife. You cooked the biscuits in the section house just before the train robbery. Does that strike you as funny, or don't you like to hear the cold facts?"

Under later grilling by W. B. Johnson and R. A. Howard, Lou Bowers broke down and confessed. The consequence was a compromise, which resulted in a full pardon being granted to Al Jennings by President Roosevelt. To make this possible, Frank, Pat and Morris pleaded guilty to a crime they did not commit and were sentenced to five years in the penitentiary.

Some time after that, Deputy Bob Hutchins had another encounter with Lou Bowers in Mill Creek, Chickasaw Nation. She rode up to him on the street, wearing a man's clothing, riding *his* horse, with two six-shooters buckled at her waist.

"These are Bert Casey's clothes, his guns and his horse. He's at my house now drunk and in bed. Let's go get him, Hutch, and collect the reward!"

Her hair was honey color, sparkling like gold in the sunlight, and her eyes were dark blue. In her Amazonian way, she was a very attractive woman. He looked into her lying blue eyes now and said, "Not today, Lou. I don't feel lucky."

Her eyes blazed and her curved red lips twisted. "You're just a damned coward! Your wife has more guts than you. I just came from your house. Ethel didn't like it because I called you what you are — a scoundrel — and I asked her where you were. She reached back inside the door and brought out a Winchester and told me to get. Why don't you take her with you, Hutch, when you go after the bad ones?"

When he checked up on his hunch about Lou Bowers' proposition, he discovered that Bert Casey was at her house all right, but Lou also had three men waiting in ambush between Mill Creek and Bert Casey. Her scheme was to have Hutchins

187

carried to her house, kill Bert Casey and claim the two men had killed each other. Then she intended to claim the reward. It was just as easy for her to double-cross two men as it was to double-cross only one.

The first time Hutchins met Lou Bowers was at a camp meeting, just before he started riding posseman under Marshal Heck Thomas. Then he had later seen her at other meetings. She was likely to get sentimental and give the preacher all the money she had taken from some man. Hutchins knew she would betray a man any time for money or for liquor.

His next encounter with Lou Bowers was between Monroe, Indian Territory, and Hartford, Arkansas. He was after W. P. (Sandy) Martin, who was wanted for several crimes in the Indian Territory. Sandy Martin could preach a sermon, play stud poker, shoot craps, seven-up, or handle a six-shooter. He could rope a stray yearling, pick a brand; but he could not even read the alphabet.

"Lou, where is Sandy Martin?" he asked.

"I'm through talking and double-crossing. You learned me my lesson in Chickasha," she said angrily.

"Do you know Gene Moss?"

"Why do you ask?"

"Curiosity. He runs a saloon in Hartford."

"Yes," she admitted. "I know him."

"Let's go down there and talk this over. It's only about seven miles' ride."

"All right," she agreed.

In Hartford, she asked, "What do we do tonight? Do we go back home or stay in Hartford?"

"We stay in Hartford."

She looked at him with a curious smile and said nothing.

With a bold hand, Hutchins wrote "J. R. Hutchins and Wife" in the Campbell Hotel register in Hartford, Arkansas. This was the only plan he had worked out so far to guard her until he had gotten from her some more information. He would just sit up all night in a secluded hotel room, while she slept. He knew better than to be off his guard one moment, or to go home with her that night.

They had been to the saloon to have a few drinks together. Hutchins said, "Lou, there is no difference between the man

188

who will assassinate your character and the man who will shoot you in the back. If there is any place in hell that is a little worse than the rest, it ought to be reserved for the former ones. You know Sandy Martin. You know his game, and you know where he is, and I want him."

But Lou still held her tongue and insisted she did not know where Martin was.

The next morning, he took her back to the saloon. In the wine room, they had another heart to heart talk, and Lou finally broke over and told Hutchins everything he wanted to know.

Hutchins thought he was through with Lou Bowers. Several years had passed and Hutchins was on duty in Ardmore, when she appeared suddenly in front of him.

She offered him her hand, smiling and glad to see him, as if she bore him no grudge. Then she told him what she wanted.

"I need twenty-five dollars, Hutch."

"I'm no first national bank, and I have neither money nor time to donate to your cause, Lou."

"I need the money, Hutch," she pleaded earnestly. "I will give it back in six hours. I'll pay you back double."

Hutchins was curious about her anxiety. "Lou," he asked sternly, "what is your game?"

"Nothing, except I'm broke and I need a stake bad. I know you're not stuck on me, but you're the nearest to a friend I have in this town. I'll pay you back and get out of town."

"You'll sell no whiskey in this town," Hutchins told her, on a hunch. "If you do, I'll put you in jail."

"Come on, Hutch, be a sport. I'll show you I am right. Others will be none the wiser, and I'll do you a turn that will do you good."

"No dice, Lou!"

"All right," she surrendered. "I'll leave town."

Hutchins fell for her game. They went to the bank together, where he cashed a check and publicly handed her twenty-five dollars.

"Where will I see you about six o'clock tonight?" she asked sweetly.

"I generally go home about that time, but I thought you are leaving town."

"I will come to your house with the money."

189

Hutchins instantly remembered the run-in Ethel and Lou had that day in Mill Creek.

"Never mind," he said harshly. "I'll be on the street." Then he walked away and left her.

About thirty minutes after that, he was walking down main street when he saw a very prominent businessman and Lou Bowers talking in a stairway entrance. Hutchins had business up the stairs just in time to see Lou raise her dress and pull a pint of whiskey out of a false skirt to hand to her customer. Lou was back in business. Hutchins pretended not to notice the transaction as he walked to the top of the stairs. When the businessman left, he nodded for her to come up to him. When she reached the top landing, she gave him an innocent look with her baby-blue eyes and asked, "What's the trouble?"

"Lou, you have tricked me into staking you to sell whiskey in my own jurisdiction."

"I certainly have," she taunted, "and I'm getting the dough. Don't worry about me, I will be gone before tomorrow. You'll never see me again. Just give a good old sport one more chance."

Hutchins left her without another word at the top of the stairs, walked down to the street front and walked away.

Not but about a half hour later, he walked into the Blue Front Store and noticed three little street urchins sitting on the counter, getting fitted for new shoes. He walked across to the west side of the store and observed the situation. He saw Lou Bowers buying three pairs of shoes for three little street ruffians who needed them. She was paying for them out of the money for which she had sold whiskey on the streets of Ardmore.

Later, on a Sunday night, she sent a message for Hutchins to come to see her, for a wanted man was there. A reward was being offered for his return to Arkansas. The name of the fugitive was Oscar Coulter. He did not know, when he responded to her summons, who she really wanted him to arrest, but he did know Lou was always ready to betray anyone for part of the reward money.

When he arrived at her house, the front door was securely fastened. It was built of cross sections of tough cottonwood lumber. He couldn't afford to raise a disturbance. He needed to talk to Lou Bowers. He knew she usually slept in the south bedroom.

190

He went to a south window, raised it easily, and started to climb into the room to talk the situation over with Lou as to where to locate Coulter.

A .45 calibre six-shooter shattered the night's silence, and the slug tore into his hip and embedded in the bone. This proved to be the worst wound he received in his entire fifty years of public and private service. Even for years before he had to yield to its crippling insistence and go to bed permanently, he walked with a noticeable limp.

Oscar Coulter was not even there. Lou Bowers had set him up for revenge over the Rock Island train robbery arrest and other accounts.

When Hutchins was finally able to travel, he and Marshal Heck Thomas, with the aid of a Cherokee woman, managed to capture Oscar Coulter. They laid a trap one night and Oscar Coulter rode into it, not suspecting treachery from the Cherokee woman. Heck Thomas and Bob Hutchins were waiting for him, sixty yards apart, and they had him covered both ways. They took his six-shooter off of him and his rifle from his saddle scabbard, then took him to their camp near Boggy Depot.

Coulter told them the killings had been forced upon him by the Arkansas sheriff and deputy sheriff, his victims. He declared he was not afraid to face charges. He didn't want to go back to Arkansas without his guns to protect him. He had run away to go back when he could get a fair trial.

Before they moved camp and went on their circuit, Heck Thomas asked Hutchins in all confidence, "Hutch, what do you think about Oscar Coulter?"

"Captain," Hutchins replied, "he's the hardest man we have in camp."

"Yes, I realize that," Thomas agreed, "but he is dead game. When you look at those steel-grey eyes, that straight Indian stature, and watch his movements, there is a man who will never give you the worst of it. Kid, we're going to take those handcuffs off of Coulter, give him back his guns, make him a trusty, and take him to Fort Smith as a gentleman."

They did, and he was helpful to them as a trusty.

Oscar Coulter stood trial for the alleged crimes and came clear. For the rest of his life, as long as Hutchins had news of him, he lived in Fort Smith, Arkansas, a respected citizen.

191

Among the better recollections which Bob Hutchins had of Lou Bowers were these:

She could ride anything on earth with hair on it. She could shoot rings around a tree in a gallop. She could rope a yearling, take her little circle and maverick-brand it without any trouble at all. She could rope anything. She had no trouble in forefooting a horse, transferring the saddle and riding it off while the horse was in the air.

She had blue eyes and a convincing way of talking that would persuade a man against his own will. She had two brothers who were horse rustlers in the early days in Fannin County, Texas. The name Carpenter in those days was familiar to many old-timers of Bonham.

When Lou Bowers was just a teen-aged girl, horse rustlers had their meeting places, and she was a good courier rider for them. She rode the circuit and carried the news, far and near.

Once when she was in jail, she said to Hutchins: "It's a helluva pity to waste a moonlight night like this in jail. I could fork a horse and ride seventy-five miles from now until daylight. Instead of doing that, I lie here and wait for the gong to go off in the morning, and get up and get my coffee and 'dobe and fat meat."

The last account of Lou Bowers and her activities in Carter County, after statehood, was reported by Cecil Crosby:

"While I was serving as a deputy sheriff in 1927, I had an occasion to arrest Lou Bowers and a shell-shocked war veteran, whose name was Norton. Lou was old and gray-headed then, but she had a very modern .45 automatic. They were asleep in a car two miles east of the Fair Ground. She was mugged and fingerprinted by T. E. Carson.

Triangle Trap at Hell Hole

Around the year 1893, Bob Hutchins moved with his wife, Ethel, and his daughter, Pearl, back to Oil Creek and was again connected with the Fort Smith Federal Court. He had been assigned to keep law and order in that district. He received his insructions and warrants from the U.S. Marshal by mail; or courier, if urgent.

Near where he had moved, there was a famous hangout for badmen, known as Hell Hole. About the year 1884, an old settler named Queen came to Hell Hole, built a good cedar house, lived there about a year and then mysteriously disappeared. Nobody knew or cared where he went, for he and his family were not neighborly with anyone, which didn't make them too popular in the Indian Territory.

People only noticed that the house was vacant and a big padlock was on the front door. Five or six months later, they casually noticed that someone would move in, stay a few months, and leave as suddenly as he came.

Hutchins received word that traffic in stolen horses was

being carried on between horse thieves in West Texas and Arkansas, and that the swapping was taking place somewhere in the Chickasaw Nation. They were meeting in the Arbuckles to exchange horses, so they would have strange horses to sell in their own neighborhoods.

Hutchins decided the first thing to do was to check his own neighborhood. He knew all the *nesters* for miles around. He began trying to recall what settlers had been visited by occasional strangers.

When this came to nothing, he tried to think of people who had lived around that part of the mountains and had moved. The area was only good for range country. Farming in the folds of those rugged hills was impossible, except for garden patches. But in the foothills and along the bottomlands of the creeks and rivers, farmers prospered. Virgin soil was never richer anywhere than in the Washita River Valley.

Cattle were about all that could provide a living in the Arbuckles where the grass was good. Although white gold was known to be in the veins of the mountains, prospecting had failed. Hunting and trapping were good; but not lucrative, because of local prices offered for the pelts.

Hutchins' first day of prowling around netted him nothing. The sun was slanting far down its western steep when he rested for the night in his little log cabin. After feeding his horse, he turned him loose to graze. He never had trouble catching him when he wanted him. A whistle would always bring him loping. Next, he brought up a fresh bucket of water from the spring, while Ethel prepared supper.

After making an inventory of every cabin, occupied or empty, he could remember for miles around, he went to sleep with a tired mind. Queen's cabin was now not in the running. He could only think of two likely ones as possible rendezvous places. One of these belonged to an old Chickasaw Indian, called "Hermit George," who lived alone with his two dogs, a hound and a greyhound. Hutchins dismissed the likelihood of Hermit George, but decided to keep an eye on Queen's cabin for sudden visitors. On his scouting tour the next day, he dropped in at old Shane's, farther down Oil Creek. Shane was sitting against the side of his cabin, with a plug of tobacco in one hand and a jug of corn liquor in the other.

194

Shane wiped his tobacco-stained beard with the back of one hand and set the jug down with the other. His grey eyes squinted up at the deputy marshal, as he bit off a chew and thrust the plug into his Levi's.

Slowly, he tongued the chew into one cheek and drawled, "Howdy, Hutchin! Who's missin'?"

"Just looking around," Hutchins answered tersely. He eased a leg across the pommel of his saddle. At that moment, Shane's nosiness and curious habits were on his mind. Hutchins had just remembered that if anyone came into the neighborhood in the past three days, Shane would know it. The old fellow always had plenty of time on his hands and went nosing about a lot on his Indian pony. He was generally unwelcome, because he was too curious. Some people considered what their names were before they came into the Indian Territory was nobody's business.

"Have a drink?" The deputy marshal smiled and shook his head.

The little man stirred uneasily. "Yuh ain't got me under suspicion, I hope!" he blurted.

Hutchins dragged his thoughts back to the little nester and smiled again. "Nope!" he assured him. He had been staring at Shane without realizing it.

"Shane," he said bluntly, "you seen any strangers around here right lately?"

"Nary a one," Shane declared.

"How about Hermit George? He at home?"

Shane snorted. "Jest him and his two old hounds. Was by there yestiddy. Got three grunts outa him!"

Hutchins grinned. He knew just how much that kind of reticence infuriated Shane.

"How about the Queen cabin? Still padlocked?"

"Tighter than a jug when I rode by," Shane said.

Hutchins sighed.

"Who you lookin' fer, Marshal? Maybe I'll know 'em when I see 'em."

Hutchins laughed. "I haven't seen them myself yet, Shane. I just got orders to look out for some bad customers."

"Bank robbers?" Shane's imagination had gone to work.

"Might be, and other crimes," Hutchins told him vaguely.

"If you see any suspicious-looking strangers, Shane, come and tell me at once." Hutchins rode away and left the little old curious-minded man in a quandary of speculations.

Hutchins spent the rest of the afternoon at his customary lookout on a vantage point on the highest peak. He had a bird's eye view of the beaten trails winding through the narrow valleys. He could see his cattle grazing down in a draw in back of his own cabin. Star Face and a young horse he was breaking to ride were with them. He saw Ethel come to the back door to look after Pearl, who was sitting on the porch.

It was a quiet, hazy day, with just enough chill in the air for him to wear his overcoat. The air was quite brisk at his lookout. Nothing seemed to be stirring down there below. The sun was dipping behind the rim when he gave up and rode homeward.

He was neither restless nor disappointed. He was doing his routine duty and patrol. As he rode home, he concluded that he would have to look farther west through the Arbuckles for his quarry.

But action came sooner the next day than he had expected. From his lookout, Hutchins saw a large group of riders. He watched them turn off toward his own cabin. He forked old Pal and rode down the opposite side from his lookout. Then he scouted around cautiously and came up to his cabin from the rear. It wasn't likely that owlhoots trying to hide would come riding boldly right up to anyone's door, but he had seen many foolish deeds. He decided he would continue being cautious.

Although he rode carefully, he rode swiftly, for Ethel and Pearl might be in danger. He was at home when they drew up to his front door. Old Shane was leading them. Hutchins recognized most of his neighbors.

"Light and jingle your spurs, men," he greeted them warmly, as he stood in the doorway. "What's going on? A shindig?"

"Shindig your foot!" Shane sputtered. "Them damned tough hombres air roostin' in Queen's cabin this minute. Musta come in there right after I passed yestiddy. Or last night!"

"Are you sure?" Hutchins asked. "Not new settlers?"

196

A lanky fellow named Smith laughed raucously. "Is he shore? Tell 'im, Shane! Tell 'im!"

Hutchins looked at the old-timer again.

Shane spat indignantly. "Rode over that way early this mawnin'," he explained. "Saw smoke comin' outa the chimney, so I thought new neighbors had come amongst us. I rode down tuh give 'em a glad hand of welcome — "

Lanky Smith interrupted with another loud guffaw. "Right friendly folks! Waren't they, Shane? Tell 'im, Shane! Tell 'im!"

"Wal," Shane blurted out, "a hard-faced feller showed me the front end of a smoke-wagon!"

Hutchins looked over the group of armed men and stared hard at Shane. "So you told everybody in the neighborhood before you told me," he said accusingly.

"Jest savin' yuh some time and trouble, Hutch," he whined. "Them are bound tuh be the outlaws you're after." Then he bristled. "Besides, that hard-faced owlhoot made me plumb mad!"

"How many?" Hutchins asked crisply.

"Doggoned if I know," Shane exploded. "All I saw was the mug behind that smoke-gun! But the corral is full of horses!"

Hutchins couldn't repress a smile. "You'd make a fine lawman," he said mockingly. "But maybe that six-shooter looked so big, you couldn't see behind it!"

The posse laughed and Shane looked at the deputy marshal with pleading eyes.

"All right," Hutchins said in a forgiving tone. "But it would be better to know how many are in that cabin, even if we do have a sizeable posse."

There were twenty of them. It was the most oddly armed group of men Hutchins had ever seen. Those nesters had every kind of shooting weapon since the invention of the old flintlock. He identified the ragmouth shotgun, the .44 and the .45 calibre Colts, the squirrel rifle, Sharps rifle, the Iver Johnson, Smith and Wesson, bulldog and pepperbox seven-shooter revolvers, three or four Winchester models, and God only knows what other makes.

Hutchins grinned. "Got plenty of ammunition for those antiques?"

Some patted their belts and pockets. Others pulled out fists full of cartridges.

"Good enough!" Turning to Ethel, he remarked, "I don't know whether to feel like Washington or Napoleon!"

"You'd better be as careful of them as the outlaws," she warned.

It was about four o'clock that afternoon when Hutchins halted his posse on a scrub-cedar mountain west of Queen's cabin. There they could get the only cautious view of the cabin down there in Hell Hole, before coming right up on it.

The cabin was in a flat and was completely surrounded by draws and mountains. Nothing was stirring down there. Back of the cabin in the corral was a herd of twenty-four horses. Hutchins checked the rail fence for saddles, but it was clean. The saddles, blankets and bridles were evidently in the cabin. He eyed the big oak tree in the yard, some distance from the house, and was satisfied with the layout.

"It's not likely," Hutchins told his men, "but I sure do hope there's not a rider for every horse." He paused and looked into their faces. "If there is, men, we're in for a hot time!"

No man backed down, nor looked uneasy, and he admired their grit. The thing that worried him most was their eagerness for a fight. He led them to the off side of the ridge, where they ground-hitched their horses, and sat down to plan.

Hutchins decided to form them into two groups of five and one of ten. He sent the first group around a slope of the ridge east of the house. The second group was told to halt halfway around on the north side. The largest group of ten, under old Shane, was to remain right where they were.

His plan was to go down on foot, keeping in line with the great oak, and order the horse thieves to surrender. If they refused, he would have his men placed for attack in a **v**, or triangle formation.

Experience had taught him that inexperienced men such as these often got excited under fire. He had taken the precaution to safeguard their shooting each other in a cross fire.

"Now don't shoot unless I start it," he warned, and the two small bodies of men set off to take their positions. Hutchins gave them plenty of time.

Armed with his two Colts, he set off down the hill at the

right time toward the cedar cabin in Hell Hole Flat. Within seventy steps of the tree, one of the outlaws in the cabin spotted him and opened fire with a rifle. He sprinted for shelter, spurs jingling. No sooner had he reached the big oak when Shane and his men came over the hill in a wild cavalry charge, yelling and shooting wildly each time their horses' hoofs hit the ground.

"The damned fools!" Hutchins muttered, and rooted his nose into the ground as their bullets began cutting the bark just over his head. Other firing burst from the cabin, but Hutchins was safe from the men cornered inside.

Just then, the other two sections of his posse brought their assorted weapons into the fight, and the deputy marshal was caught in his own triangular trap.

The man who dashed out of the cabin, shooting rashly, fell before the fusillade and was killed outright. Hutchins lay there in the tightest spot of his life and cursed that posse of nesters every time he was hit by their crazy shooting. Fortunately, most of the bullets that struck him were buckshot from those ragmouth shotguns; and they were shooting from two hundred yards. His heavy overcoat provided enough protection, but it was cut to ribbons.

They shot all the bark off the tree just above the ground and part of the lower leaves. They mowed the grass around him for a space of two or three feet. He didn't breathe easily until their ammunition ran out. He rose up in tatters, dripping blood, and roundly cursed his posse as they closed in to inspect the kill.

There had been only three horse thieves; far too few for that furious onslaught. One was killed. Another — Hutchins couldn't even imagine how — got away in the mix-up. The other was severely wounded, but he lived to serve ten years in the penitentiary at Leavenworth, Kansas.

Hutchins lived, too, after the doctor had picked twenty-five buckshot out of him and gouged out one large calibre rifle bullet. Fortunately, the buckshot were spent by the distance, and warded off by his heavy overcoat. They had lodged just under the skin.

The owners of seventeen of the stolen horses were found. Nobody ever claimed six of them. The twenty-fourth was a dun

Hutchins picked out and rode for two years. He was one of the best horses he ever rode. One day in Fort Smith, Arkansas, he found the owner and reluctantly gave the man his horse.

He never saw a man more pleased to get a horse back. It was a well-trained horse, with plenty of stamina and endurance. Generously, the man insisted that Hutchins take fifty dollars reward, even after he had ridden the stolen horse for two years.

Stand Off at Buckhorn

Months of watching, waiting and expecting had sharpened the eyes of Hell Roaring Jones and kept his mind hair-trigger alert. As he chopped the breakfast wood on a cool, autumn morning, he spotted the buggy down the road, just before it burst through the clump of jack-oaks where the road made a bend around the creek at Buckhorn Crossing.

Hell Roaring stood tensely with his axe poised in mid-air. Then he swung it down hard into the chop log. He whistled a low warning at the open cabin door. The door slammed shut. Two of his sons darted across the road and the yard from the corral and disappeared inside through the back door of the kitchen. The other one hurried up from the spring with a bucket of water.

Hell Roaring Jones took no chances on visitors who came to Buckhorn. These men might be from Texas. If they were . . .

He set his jaws hard and tight. He could see the men now close enough to recognize them. Three.

The big man in the middle was Lee Stewart, United States Constable, who worked out of Ardmore. The driver was Lon Bigman, the general store merchant from Davis. The third man was Hugh Ledbetter, the young lawyer who had arranged the buying contract for his deal with Bigman in the spring.

Frowning, Jones remembered that he had received a notice of foreclosure on his note with Lon Bigman a few days ago. Because of his wife's illness, he had failed to get into town to see about it.

The buggy was coming up. "Hello, gents!" he greeted them politely. "Git out! I'm cuttin' a little wood for the little woman. You men are out early this mawnin'. Had breakfast?"

"Before daylight, Jones, thanks," Constable Stewart said cheerfully. The three of them climbed down from the buggy and stretched their legs.

Abruptly, Lee Stewart announced the purpose of their visit. "Understand, Jones, I'm acting under orders," he said apologetically. He cleared his throat and waited.

Hell Roaring Jones looked at Lon Bigman's sullen face. The merchant regarded him grudgingly, accusingly.

"My wife has been purty puny," Jones explained. "I couldn't git into town to renew my note, Mister Bigman."

"Renew it!" Lon Bigman echoed indignantly. "What makes you think I'll renew it?"

"Well —" Jones paused. Why did he? He could read nothing in Bigman's eyes now but hard and relentless speculation. "The drouth got my money crops — cotton and corn," he said lamely. "I ain't got no other means of raisin' the money right now. I just paid off my wife's doctor bills. Sort of figured they come first. Expected to pay you fifty dollars and let you know about me and my boys' plans to pay the rest of the five hundred I owe you."

Bigman's face was scornful now, his voice harsh and skeptical. "You got stock here to sell and pay off all the debt right now," he declared scoffingly.

"Ain't got none to spare," Jones shot back. He was feeling grim, stubborn opposition now. "We only been here on Buckhorn a year. Sell our work stock and saddle horses? What could me and my boys do without them?"

"Look here!" Hugh Ledbetter spoke up, producing the contract. "You've listed a dozen head of stock to guarantee your note with Mr. Bigman."

"I have?" Hell Roaring leaned over and looked at the list.

202

"They don't all b'long to me, if I did. Three of them saddle horses b'long to my boys. You cain't expect us to sell our horses and be left afoot! We're dependin' on them yearlin's and hogs for winter meat and to sell and buy other provisions."

"But you've got them all listed here in this chattel mortgage for security," Hugh Ledbetter argued patiently. "Mrs. Jones signed the note and mortgage with you. That means Mr. Bigman can confiscate all your stock and hold public sale to collect on the note."

"Now wait a minute!" Hell Roaring warned angrily. "Them animals are worth lots more than the stuff I bought from Lon Bigman last spring. Hang it all, men! I cain't afford to sell 'em!"

Looking straight at Bigman, he added, "What sort of new trickery is this thing you call a chattel mortgage?" He turned back to the lawyer with a roar. "Cain't a man in this territory be trusted anymore?"

The young lawyer had cleverly introduced the chattel mortgage into the Indian Territory. Until this time, businessmen had traded with the farmers and cattlemen with simple, signed bills of goods, itemized purchases on the backs of notes, or just oral agreements. Jones knew this deal was an ironclad, legal transaction, but he hadn't realized what he had put up for security.

Hugh Ledbetter was talking, " — won't take all your stock to pay off the note and costs, but they will have to be sold at public auction, unless Lon —"

"Like hell they will!" Hell Roaring spat sharply and took a solid stand. "I've always paid my debts," he said proudly. "My credit was good where I come from. Without a chattel mortgage!"

"What other way do you expect to pay me then?" Bigman asked testily.

"Two of my boys have jobs with Bill Washington for winter range. They'll hold down a line-shack for his Cross O L in the Arbuckles. The other one and me aim to run traplines on Buckhorn and over on the Washita. Trappin' will be right good this winter on both streams."

Constable Lee Stewart nodded approval. "Well, Bigman?" he asked. "Looks like you will get your money all right. Willing to grant Jones an extension?"

203

Bigman's eyes blazed rashly. "Hell, no!" he thundered. "Best thing for Jones to do is settle this debt right now. He can buy more stock later!" He sneered, and added, "When he gets rich trapping!"

His tone was ruthless and final. A shock of helplessness ran through Hell Roaring Jones. He shifted his gaze to the disapproving look stamped plainly on Constable Lee Stewart's face.

"I'll have to ask you to help me round up your stock, Jones," Stewart said softly.

"It ain't right, Stewart!" Jones grated between clenched teeth. "Me and my boys cain't do our jobs if yuh put us afoot. My wife, she's just up from a sick spell! In case of more sickness, how can we fetch a doctor, or help in a hurry without a horse?"

Jones watched Constable Lee Stewart's eyes clash with Bigman's for a moment. They sharpened to a severe, critical scowl. Bigman turned away.

Stewart said firmly, "It's the gosh-danged law! You mortgaged the stock, Jones. Now you've got to pay!"

Resolutely, he made for the corral gate. "Come on, Jones!"

Hell Roaring felt his world crashing down around him. He'd fight for his stake in this wild, new country, and for his right to hold now and pay later.

"Wait, Stewart!" he cried sharply. The constable stopped abruptly and turned on his heels.

"Leave them horses alone, Stewart!" Jones ordered grimly. "You git these men back in that buggy and git out of here!"

"You're resisting an officer, Jones!" Stewart reminded tensely.

"I know what I'm doin'," Jones retorted. "I'll pay the debt just like I said. Them horses, and what else me and the boys have, stay right here on Buckhorn!"

Jones was unarmed, but he didn't waver when Stewart's hand fell firmly on the butt of his six-shooter. "I don't want any trouble," Stewart warned. "I've got a duty to perform!"

"Meriah!" Hell Roaring roared at the closed cabin door. "Trot out them ragmouths!"

Promptly, the door opened. Meriah Jones appeared on the porch. She was lean, pale and anxious, but she grimly trained her shotgun on Constable Lee Stewart's breast. Flanking her appeared three stalwart sons — grim, alert and silent — all similarly armed.

Constable Lee Stewart was no coward, but he was also no fool. The officer and his companions climbed quickly back into the buggy and beat a dusty, hasty retreat back to Davis. Constable Stewart wrote a long letter about what had happened to Captain John S. Hammer, U.S. Marshal at Ardmore. Stewart urged him to send help at once.

When Marshal Hammer finished reading the letter, he laid it on his desk with a grin.

"That's the case," he declared, "and that's where it hangs right now. Hutch, I'm sending you and Buck to help Lee Stewart arrest Hell Roaring Jones!"

The captain shifted and his chair squeaked sharply. "Arrest the whole Jones family if you have to!" he ordered. He picked up another letter and added, "This letter from Texas, according to all description and details, indicates that Jones is an alias, wanted over there in Young County for the murder of three officers." He handed the grim letter to the two deputies to read.

Looking up from the letter, they found Marshal Hammer grinning ruefully. "You two locoed, headstrong trouble-hunters might find your match in Hell Roaring Jones and his boys. I'm sending you because my other deputies are highly prized. I can't afford to risk getting them bumped off."

Bob Hutchins tugged at his long, black mustache and winked at Buck Garrett. Buck shrugged and made a wry face at the marshal.

"You won't get rid of us that easy," Buck challenged. "You know how bad pennies always turn up."

Captain Hammer's firm handshake belied his teasing. They knew he was counting on them to bring Hell Roaring Jones back a prisoner.

The two deputies found Lee Stewart and Hugh Ledbetter in Davis just about dark. Despite their long ride on horses through the Arbuckles, Constable Stewart insisted they should all swoop down on the Jones cabin that same night, to make a surprise arrest.

Soon the three officers and the young lawyer were rolling toward Buckhorn Crossing in a double-seated rig. As they approached their destination, smoke from the rock chimney of the Jones cabin drifted lazily toward a bright moon.

The front door was open and a flickering shaft of light reached out to them from a briskly burning fire in the big fireplace. As the rig rolled to a halt, the door went shut, blotting out the cheerful red glow. Even the moon seemed to grow chill with the abrupt, unfriendly welcome. A cloud slid over it like a grey veil.

Horses snorted nervously in the corral. The four men sat staring at the dark, foreboding cabin now.

"Hello!" Bob Hutchins' deep, loud and cheerful voice rang out. "Anybody home?"

Somebody stirred inside. A narrow shaft of light shot out at them from a small porthole to the right of the door. "What do you want?" a woman's voice asked.

"We want to talk to Mr. Jones," Hutchins replied.

"He ain't home!"

A horse in the corral neighed softly and the mares hitched to the rig answered him. The cloud slid off the moon. Hutchins checked the corral in a sweeping glance and saw four horses distinctly.

"We'll talk to one of the boys, Mrs. Jones. Send out the oldest!"

"There ain't no menfolks here tonight," she insisted. "They've gone fur hunting. I'm all alone, and I ain't lettin' no strangers into my house. You go 'way!"

The small shaft of light winked out.

Buck Garrett stepped from the rig and stretched his big, lanky frame. "She's lying!" he snapped impatiently. He strode deliberately to the two-ply raw cottonwood door and banged on it with his big fist.

"Open this door in the name of the Law!" Buck roared. "We know you're in there, Jones. Come on out peaceable and give yourself up.

"You git away from that door and be quick about it!" the woman shouted angrily. "I'll fill your hide full of buckshot!"

This time, a porthole opened to the left and right of the door, and two ragmouth muzzles shoved through.

Buck Garrett went back to the rig in long, quick strides. "Well," he defended himself gruffly, "she's a woman!"

The other men laughed. Hutchins said, "She surely is mighty long-armed and spraddle-legged to man both them holes at the same time!"

They drove down into a thicket on the creek, unhitched the horses, built a fire and waited for daybreak. At sunup, Hutchins was sitting on the rail fence of the hog pen, the only guard on duty, while the others slept. His morning meditations were interrupted suddenly by the woman's voice. "What are you doing out there?"

"Thinking to buy this nice bunch of hogs," he answered.

"Well, they're not for sale, and if you feel lucky, fall off that pen, or I will gut-shoot you off!"

Hutchins fell off, without debating or waiting for a second invitation. He went down to the thicket to wake up his companions. All of them were hungry and chilled by the frosty morning air. Constable Stewart went over to the rig and brought back a quart of Kentucky Colonel.

Three or four swigs of whiskey warmed them up a bit. They felt inspired to call upon the Jones family in force and demand immediate surrender.

Buck Garrett agreed to do the talking again. He held the bottle up and squinted through it at the rising sun, just above its almost depleted contents. "Hutch here has conscientious scruples," he declared, grinning at Bob.

Three of them waited cautiously in the yard as Buck Garrett leisurely strode up to the cabin. He produced a sack of Bull Durham and papers and proceeded to roll a quirley.

"Mr. Jones," he called, pausing on the doorstep, "come out and bring me a match."

A porthole opened immediately and a half dozen matches fell at Buck's feet. He bent his tall frame and carefully picked them up. Then he very gravely lit his cigarette and deliberately sat down on the step to smoke.

"Now, Mr. Jones," he declared, puffing calmly, "we don't want to hurt anybody, but if you don't come out with your hands up, I'll kick your door in. When the smoke clears away, we'll have some Jones funerals."

Five gun-muzzles appeared instantly from many slits in the log wall. "You young fool!" came Hell Roaring Jones' guttural, thunderous roar. "Git off my porch and hit for the tall timber. Bluffs don't go here!"

The four men lost no time in getting back down under the hill to their camp on Buckhorn.

Filled with anger and chagrin, Buck said, "Hutch, you take the rig and go to Dougherty. Bring back five gallons of coal oil and two dozen sticks of dynamite. We'll make Hell Roaring come out of that cabin or blow the whole damned family to Kingdom Come."

Dougherty was a small settlement on the new Santa Fe railroad, close to Buckhorn. Hutchins was just about to drive out of town when the idea struck him to wire Captain Hammer about the events at Buckhorn.

At the Santa Fe depot, he handed the telegraph operator the following message:

JOHN S. HAMMER, U.S. MARSHAL
ARDMORE, I. T.

    WHOLE GOVERNMENT STOOD OFF BY JONES FAMILY AT BUCKHORN. WIRE INSTRUCTIONS.

                    HUTCHINS, DEPUTY
                    DOUGHERTY, I. T.

In just about thirty minutes, he received this answer:

J. R. HUTCHINS, DEPUTY U.S. MARSHAL
DOUGHERTY, I. T.

    BRING JONES FAMILY TO ME OR STAY AT BUCK-HORN REST OF YOUR LIVES. WILL WORRY ALONG WITHOUT YOU.

                    CAPT. HAMMER
                    U.S. MARSHAL

As he was ready to leave town, Hutchins spotted a bootlegger for whom he had a warrant. He pulled the warrant out of his pocket and showed it to him. "Listen," he said, "I haven't got time to arrest you now. I've got something more important to do. You go get me a quart of good whiskey, and I'll let you go another thirty days." The bootlegger took less than ten minutes to come back with the order. Hutchins had sampled it a couple of times and was halfway back to Buckhorn when he remembered that he had failed to get fuses for the dynamite.

When he reached camp, he was surprised to find Meriah Jones handcuffed to a tree. Buck Garrett had granted her permission to come to the spring for a bucket of water. Then he had captured her. By doing so, he had hoped to force the Jones men to surrender, but they were still holed up in the cabin.

Hutchins suggested that Buck free Mrs. Jones, show her the coal oil and dynamite, then explain what they were going to do, if she didn't go to the cabin and talk her husband and sons into surrendering.

With a grin, Garrett tossed the key to Hutchins. "You've had so much good luck with that woman," he declared with sarcasm, "you do it."

Hutchins smiled as he approached her. "I'm sorry, Ma'am! You and your sons have aided your husband's resistance. You have all made it unpleasant for us and more dangerous for you."

He unlocked the handcuffs and stepped back, smiling again to make her feel at ease.

Meriah Jones, however, was staring in open surprise at the keystone dangling from his watch chain. She gave him the Eastern Star sign, and Hutchins responded to it.

"Is your husband one of us, Mrs. Jones?" he asked hopefully.

"Yes," she replied, "and all the boys."

"Will you go back to the cabin and tell your husband and sons that I will personally see that all of you are treated justly, if he and the boys will give themselves up?"

She hesitated. Hutchins said gently, "I know your husband is bound to have heard of me. I am an active Royal Arch Mason. My name is Bob Hutchins."

Anxiously, she said, "I believe you, Mr. Hutchins, but my husband — . This here can be settled easy, but he got into a scrape in Texas over politics, and — "

"I know," Hutchins interrupted softly. "He's wanted for murder in Young County. We have the information straight

209

from the Texas Rangers. Go tell your husband and boys that I'm coming to talk to them, as a brother Mason — unarmed."

There was a glow of gratitude on her face as she took her bucket of springwater and returned to the cabin. Hutchins walked over to his companons at the fire.

Unbuckling his gun belt, he handed his belt and six-shooters over to Buck Garrett. "Hold these, Buck," he said briefly. "I'll be back directly with our prisoners."

Buck Garrett looked at him in blank amazement. None of the men had heard his conversation with Meriah Jones.

"What do you aim to do, Hutch?" Buck demanded suspiciously.

"I've made arrangements to talk to Jones and his boys."

"You crazy fool! Have you lost your mind?" Buck snapped, scathingly. "Old Hell Roaring, himself, will gut-shoot you and throw you out to die like a dog!"

"I'll take my chance," Hutchins replied, enjoying the secret solution he had figured for the stand-off.

But, as he neared the cabin, his heart skipped a beat with the sudden realization that he could be walking into a death trap. It was too late to turn back. The cabin door flew open, and Hutchins halted stiffly. Hell Roaring Jones faced him with his shotgun cradled in his left arm. Hutchins' empty hands raked skyward. "I'm unarmed, Jones!" he cried hoarsely.

Hell Roaring's searching eyes swept beyond him and then rested on the keystone fob, swinging from his heavy gold watch chain across his vest. Jones bearded face wrinkled in a wide grin. His deep voice roared approvingly. "I see you've been east, Brother Hutchins! Draw down yore hands and come in. Yuh're welcome!"

Hutchins shuddered with relief, acknowledged the signal Jones gave him, stepped forward and clasped the nester's calloused hand in a Masonic grip.

But Hutchins' feelings were nothing compared to the flabbergasted look on Buck Garrett's face when the whole Jones family marched out, and he learned how Hutchins had arranged for their surrender.

"Talk about brotherly understanding!" Buck Garrett smiled ruefully. "I'm going to throw my six-shooter away and join the

Masons, if they'll have me. A lodge like that beats a six-shooter more than hell!"

Commissioner S. B. Bradford was a Mason and Marshal Hammer was a Knights Templar; and the Jones family had no trouble in settling the local case. Hell Roaring Jones went back, of his own free will, to Young County, Texas, stood trial and was cleared of the charges against him there. A free man again, he returned to Indian Territory, where he became a prominent citizen in the Chickasaw Nation, and later Oklahoma. He became an active member in the Masonic Lodge at Dougherty. He assumed his right name, which Hutchins did not reveal; but the nickname, Hell Roaring, stuck with him the rest of his life.

The Checker Checked

An unwritten rule among U.S. deputy marshals of the Indian Territory was: "Love thy fellow officer as thyself." But this rule did not apply to the United States inspectors from Washington, D.C., drawing handsome salaries and all expenses paid to check on some poor, underpaid U.S. Deputy Marshal who might have chalked up a questionable quarter now and then, when he turned in his expense and mileage accounts.

Occasionally, Hutchins came in contact with some of those inspectors, who were so supercilious and disdainful he considered them less than human.

In one instance, a U.S. Inspector named Ocean Rider landed in Ardmore, registered at one of the best hotels in town, and set to work with an unlimited authority and expense basis in order to "give the deputy marshals in Ardmore and the Chickasaw Nation in general a bad time."

He came abruptly into the marshal's office one morning, singled out Hutchins and told him he wanted a thorough and complete explanation of his expense accounts.

"In what particular?" drawled Hutchins, unabashed and unperturbed.

"You will know more about it when I get through with you," Inspector Rider countered belligerently. Inwardly, Hutchins was boiling mad, but didn't show it.

"I'm here on the ground first," Hutchins declared truculently. "I take the risks, sweat the dangers and bleed the blood behind my accounts, and I can explain anything you want to know."

Ocean Rider opened his briefcase and brought out a small bundle of receipts, held them in his hands tightly and asked, "Are these bona fide?"

"Are they signed?" Hutchins asked firmly.

Questions and answers flew back and forth in red-white argument, as Inspector Rider took up first one receipt and then another for expenses Hutchins had paid.

Finally, Rider challenged: "Mr. Hutchins, we will hire a buggy and team and make the rounds to talk to some of the people who signed these receipts; and while I'm at it, I will check up on the other twenty-six deputies in this Southern Indian Territory District."

"Just how much are you allowed to pay for a buggy and team each day?" Hutchins asked.

"Five dollars and expenses."

"That's pretty good," Hutchins stated flatly. "If you see fit to employ my services while crooks and criminals are running free, I'm just the man to go with you."

They left Ardmore about two o'clock in the afternoon, and the first place to which Hutchins took him was the ranch of Uncle Pink Collins, who lived fourteen or fifteen miles west of Ardmore on the Walnut Creek Bayou. Uncle Pink Collins was an intermarried citizen of the Chickasaw Nation, and it was known all over the nation that he never charged a deputy marshal a cent for staying all night, eating supper, breakfast, and feeding his horse. Invariably, he signed each receipt, though, and would say, "I'll collect it some time when I come to your office in Ardmore."

Deep down in his heart, the old settler knew that all the deputies were underpaid and that their expense accounts were too often cut short. He considered his accommodations as a contribution to law and order by helping to keep bodies and souls of officers together. And there were a number of other

213

settlers and nesters who did the same thing with the same logic.

Inspector Rider presented Uncle Pink with four receipts. "Did you sign these receipts?"

Uncle Pink looked them over carefully, handed them back to him and said dryly, "I did."

"Did the deputy marshals pay you money for their board and keep?"

"Now I'd be a damned fool to sign anything without getting value received, wouldn't I?" Uncle Pink retorted indignantly. "For your information, mister, we've got a fine bunch of brave, young officers in this territorial district. They are doing a good job, and I want you to know I'm proud of them. You bet your bottom dollar that I damned sure am getting value received from them. I'm glad to have them drop by. I enjoy their company."

Inspector Ocean Rider asked permission for himself and Deputy Hutchins to spend the night, so he could pry a little more deeply.

Hutchins knew Uncle Pink agreed to this more for his own sake than for the inspector's. Ocean Rider might as well have talked to a man made of granite, for he could have got about as much out of him as he did Pink Collins.

When they awoke the next morning, a heavy snow was on the ground. The night had been cold; and the morning was growing even colder.

Hutchins fed the team in the stable. He made no effort to hitch up the horses. He guessed that Inspector Rider would sense his stubbornness and ask Pink Collins to harness and hitch them to the buggy. He was also pretty sure that the inspector had ruffled Uncle Pink enough for him to refuse.

Pink Collins stuffed his pipe, Hutchins took out a cigar, and the two of them sat, calmly smoking, while Inspector Rider impatiently walked the floor in front of the big fireplace, anxious to get on with his investigation.

Finally, he stopped in front of Uncle Pink and announced: "Mr. Collins, if you will be kind enough to hitch the team to the buggy, we shall impose on your hospitality no longer."

Uncle Pink held his glance with eagle eyes. "Mr. Rider," he prefaced his remarks politely, "I'm not going anywhere. I'm not travelin' around over the country spendin' a lot of the

214

taxpayers' money to check up on some little items that don't amount to a tinker's damn. You know where the team was put, the harness and the buggy. I reckon they are still there. You are so damned smart, let's see if you can put them all together."

Inspector Rider grinned sheeplishly and his voice mellowed a little. "How much do we owe you?" he asked.

"Six dollars," Uncle Pink shot back at him, promptly and emphatically.

"That's pretty steep," Inspector Rider challenged. "More than you charge the deputies."

"They *work* for a living," Uncle Pink retorted.

Rider paid off, took Pink Collins' signature on a receipt, and from there they went to see Corn Bolling, another old-timer, and an ex-officer.

Corn Bolling charged the inspector seven dollars for all-night accommodations, to which Inspector Rider, of course, objected. Then Bolling told him he considered it quite an imposition to let him stay at all.

They drove several miles to a store, where the deputies had established credit for provisions. Hutchins telephoned Jim Saddler that they would stop at his place for the night. Jim Saddler had been a U.S. Deputy Marshal in the very early days; and Hutchins knew he would be wise to the situation.

When they drove up to Saddler's place, he came out with a rifle and the pretended belligerance of an outlaw and wanted to know what in the name of hell they were doing there.

"Take it easy, Jim," Hutchins said soothingly, playing the act. "This is Mr. Ocean Rider, a government inspector from Washington, who is just doing a little routine checking up on us deputies."

"Hell! With a name like that, he ought to be on the ocean inspectin' ships!" Saddler said rudely. He shook hands indifferently with Rider, then turned to Hutchins and asked, scornfully, "Are these fellers born, created, or appointed?"

"Appointed," Hutchins replied, holding back a laugh.

"You can't prove it to me!" Saddler exclaimed. "I dealt with a few of them, myself, out of Fort Smith court. Old Judge Parker couldn't tolerate them, either. Hutchins, you can stay, but I just haven't got enough beds for both of you. He'll more

215

than likely want to sleep in the widest bed I've got, all by himself!"

"It's fourteen miles to our next stop, Jim," Hutchins interceded. "It's getting dark and colder every minute. Let us both stay, and I'll sleep in the barn."

"All right, Hutch," Saddler relented. "I've got a cot in a side room I guess will be good enough for him. Got too much family for much company."

Inspector Rider slept on a cot in a side room, along with a flock of chickens.

Before they went to bed, Jim Saddler whispered to Hutchins, "This kind of treatment ought to hold him for a while."

The next morning, they left in a drizzling rain. There was a little wooden bridge across a creek just about one hundred yards from Saddler's house, which they had to pass over on their way. Hutchins deliberately drove one wheel of the buggy on to high ground and turned the buggy over.

Jim Saddler came running up, and when he saw nobody was hurt, he laughed loudly. "By gum!" he declared. "That's the first time I ever saw an Ocean in a creek!"

Inspector Rider was climbing up the bank, madder than a wet hen; but when Saddler gave him a hand, he began to laugh, too.

Hutchins never knew if Inspector Ocean Rider believed it was anything but an accident. If he did, he said nothing about it. By the time they got the buggy upright again, ice was freezing on the inspector's heavy overcoat; and they had to turn around and return to Jim Saddler's place for some more hospitality, while Rider dried out and thawed out in front of the big fireplace.

Saddler was very sympathetic to the inspector, but Hutchins knew he was still inwardly laughing about the incident. He brought out his whiskey jug, and they all had a warming drink. It was of local manufacture, but mild and mellow, and Inspector Rider never said a word about its illegality.

They stopped next at J. W. (Windy) Johnson's store at Milo. Windy Johnson was noted for never letting the other fellow say hardly a word in conversation. He began by telling Inspector Rider what the citizens of Indian Territory thought of the deputy marshals, and followed through with how impossible it would be to get along without them, and wound up by telling the inspector straight out he would consider it a special favor for deputy marshals to rob a government that would be so miserly and unappreciative of their services.

"If you are afraid the government will go broke over their little expense accounts," he concluded frankly, "just send me the bill, and if I can't pay it all, I'll get help from some appreciative, respected citizens around Milo who can."

That brought a second laugh out of Rider. Hutchins could tell there was a subtle change coming over Ocean Rider.

Hutchins went around with him for eight days. Some of the other deputies were quite hostile because Hutchins was hauling him all over the Chickasaw Nation, but when they saw the report that Inspector Rider made after he got back to the office, they congratulated Hutchins for doing such a good job.

Now, instead of trying to have all the deputies in the district discharged, he began to question them with civility, and he tried to find out more about their lives, their families and their work.

When he learned just how efficient and underpaid they were, he began to sympathize with them and see their problems and their real and true merits as they were. He and Hutchins had many friendly talks about many subjects.

"Why do you officers carry .45 six-shooters instead of the newer revolvers Uncle Sam issues," he wanted to know.

"Well, you notice I carry the government issue, too, just to go along with the regulations. Some of the boys kid me and call me Two-Gun Hutch sometimes."

He pulled his Colt *thumbuster* from his right holster and handed it to Rider. "Examine it carefully," he suggested. "It has one spring, two or three screws, and the rest is iron. You can throw it into the creek, let it lay there six months, and when you take it out, it will shoot. It may rust a little, but my point is that it is useful in most any kind of weather, can be easily taken apart, cleaned, oiled, and it will stand abuse and wear and tear."

Another question Rider asked Hutchins was what effect breaking whiskey at the depot that came in on the trains from Texas to businessmen, and not to bootleggers, had on the general public.

217

"Just what do you mean?" Hutchins asked.

"Well," he explained, "I saw two businessmen leave my hotel this morning in a somewhat intoxicated condition."

Hutchins knew all the businessmen in Ardmore and other surrounding towns who liked their nips of whiskey, and he happened to know that the two men to whom Inspector Rider referred were a general merchant and a hardware merchant, who were close friends, with stores next door to each other.

They had acquired the habit of alternating every other day in ordering two quarts of whiskey from a liquor dealer at Gainesville, Texas, across Red River. Texas was a "wet" state then, and all along the Red River, people in the Indian Territory ordered their whiskey from liquor dealers in the bordering Texas towns. Hutchins knew the two merchants did not often get drunk, or cause any trouble. He knew they liked their little private nips and did not drink two quarts each day between them. They shared most of it with other friends and some customers who also liked a little nip now and then.

But at this time, all whiskey coming in on trains from Texas was being confiscated by the U.S. Marshal and his deputies, because of Ocean Rider's presence in town. The Marshal wanted to make an impression, and not have any more static stirred up than necessary.

Some of the people who were used to their nips each day had for the past few days drunk alcohol from the drugstore, bitters, Jamaica ginger, or anything else they could locate. Some even got extract from both drugstores and grocery stores.

But the two men to whom Inspector Rider had referred had come from a traveling salesman's room in the hotel. It was customary in those days for some of these men, called drummers, to carry a quart or two of whiskey to treat their good customers.

The merchants had come to his room and had taken the first drink because they felt they needed it, they had taken the second drink in order to be good sports, they had taken the third drink, because their salesman friend had insisted on it. When they were ready to leave, they had taken the fourth drink "because only God knew where and when they could get the next one!"

"That," Hutchins explained in conclusion, "is why they teetered a little as they walked back to their stores. Now as

218

to answering your question about public sentiment; some are against liquor, some are strongly for it, some tolerate it, and others just don't give a damn about it either way." He looked squarely at Inspector Ocean Rider and asked, "Isn't that about the way the public feels anywhere, whether the place is wet or dry?"

"That's about it," Inspector Rider acknowledged. Then he added, "Hutchins, because of the reports from cranks which have been received in the Chief Marshal's Office in Washington, I'll have to admit that I came here with a chip on my shoulder." He grinned warmly. "You've done a very shrewd job of removing that chip. I'm glad to have made your acquaintance, and I wish you and the rest of the boys the best of luck. Hutchins, you are a young man who knows how to get things done. You don't beat the devil around the stump about anything. Just keep the firewater away from the Indians all you can. That's the reason for the dry law, anyhow. That's one of the main promises our government made to the Indian nations. Stay after the outlaws and crooks, and the best of luck to all of you."

He had a long conference with Marshal Hammer before he left. Hutchins took him to the depot in time to catch the northbound Santa Fe train.

Bob Hutchins stood a few moments as the train sped Inspector Ocean Rider back toward Washington. He knew that both he and the inspector were a little wiser about human nature and the ingenuity it sometimes takes for a U.S. deputy marshal to do his job.

Honor Versus
Honest Men

A Santa Fe train was robbed
near Berwyn, Chickasaw Nation,
despite the fact that guards on that train were expecting a hold-up. A lot of shooting was done, but nobody was hurt.

Hutchins received a tip that one of the robbers was a Chicago man, so he took a trip to Chicago and loafed around there for about ten days, getting acquainted. He met a fellow named Chicago Slim in McNary's office in the Masonic building. McNary was chief of the Pinkerton detectives in Chicago. He knew McNary from a previous meeting years before in the Indian Territory.

McNary came to the Indian Territory in 1889, looking for a man named Walker, who was wanted for a boyhood murder in Booneville, Missouri. He had a letter of introduction to Hutchins from the warden of the federal penitentiary at Leavenworth, Kansas. He told Hutchins his business and described the man he wanted.

"There is only one Walker I know that fits that description," Hutchins told him. "He lives at Peterman Crossing on the

Washita River. He has lived there for a number of years. He's married and has raised a fine family."

"This man has been gone from Booneville about twenty years, but we have his description from persons who have kept in touch with him."

"It won't do any harm to drive out and talk to him," Hutchins suggested. "I know him very well."

Hutchins hitched up the team to his buggy and drove out to Peterman Crossing and found Walker plowing and "laying by" his corn crop until harvest. He was using the old reliable double-shovel sweep plow. They waited for him at the end of the rows. After the introduction, McNary said, "Walker, you've been gone a long time, but they still want to see you back in Booneville."

"I guess there is no use denying it," Walker confessed. "I am the man you are looking for, and I'm ready to face the music. It has been a burden to me for twenty years. But since I came here, I've married and reared a family I'm proud of, and I've never changed my name. Let's go to the house, eat supper and talk it over."

After supper, they went into a huddle. Hutchins told McNary how long he had known Walker, never suspecting he was a fugitive from justice. "I'll vouch for him," Hutchins declared. "Let's go back to Ardmore tonight, you set the time when you want to go back, and give Walker some time to get his business in shape to be absent for no telling how long."

"All right," McNary agreed. "If you vouch for Mr. Walker, it's good enough for me."

McNary turned to Walker and asked, "Can you meet us in the marshal's office in Ardmore day after tomorrow by this time?"

"I'll be there," Walker said sincerely; and he was.

But in the meantime, Hutchins took McNary around the country and showed him a good time, and that all the officers he met in the Indian Territory were real men, doing their jobs as they knew how; and that there were also a good many men in the Territory, who were fugitives from justice.

Walker begged Hutchins to go along with them, and he agreed to pay all the expenses. Hutchins went with him and McNary to Booneville, Missouri, advised him, and gave him

221

moral support and confidence. The case was too old to really be a case; a fact which Hutchins suspected, and for lack of witnesses and evidence, Walker was acquitted.

Of course, McNary's only interest was the reward money that had never been withdrawn. He promised Hutchins, before he and Walker boarded a train back to the Indian Territory, that if he ever needed help in Chicago to contact him.

So Hutchins was now in McNary's office in Chicago, asking for that promised help. McNary not only helped him on his train robbery case, but took Hutchins into places such as "dens," underground tunnels, opium joints, and showed him a good many places in the *underworld,* from where if Hutchins had been alone, he would not have ever left alive.

It was an experience Hutchins never forgot. He learned that officers ran gauntlets in Chicago, which were entirely different from problems he met in the Indian nations. Neither officer could have survived alone, if they had suddenly traded places of jurisdiction.

McNary arranged for Hutchins to meet Chicago Slim in McNary's office. Slim was a man McNary trusted and used in his detective work to the best advantage.

Hutchins suspected that the same man for whom he carried a warrant of arrest was Chicago Slim! And by secret contacts, Hutchins learned his hunch was right. He finally declared what was on his mind to Chicago Slim in McNary's presence.

McNary promptly stood good for Slim, as Hutchins had for Walker. He guaranteed that Hutchins would have no trouble getting Slim out of Chicago. They met again in McNary's office, preparatory to his return to the Indian Territory. Hutchins had run short of cash money. He had anticipated having McNary endorse a check for him; but McNary had been called away urgently, and he was out of town.

Chicago Slim was the only other man Hutchins knew in Chicago. He searched his own pockets and discovered he had only one dollar and sixty cents; and it was only two hours until train time.

"I have some money," Slim offered; and he loaned Hutchins the money to take him back to face his own trial.

In Kansas City, a *jackleg* lawyer got on the train, recognized Slim and talked with him. Hutchins learned later the man was the kind of lawyer who made his living by *shyster* work, and that he played around with Chicago Slim's gang. The lawyer telegraphed ahead and had them taken off the train at Topeka. Slim was released and Hutchins was promptly put in jail, and charged with attempted kidnapping. Slim was ordered out of town.

Instead of leaving town, Slim hung around the jail, finally got a constable to take him to Florence. He left word with Hutchins that he would be waiting for him in Florence.

The next day, Hutchins met Slim, as planned, and now they were both broke. They had only about one hour and thirty minutes before train time. Neither of them knew anyone in Florence.

"Slim, you robbed a train," Hutchins joked. "I'll see if I can rob a bank for enough money to get us to Ryan."

They walked into the bank and Hutchins asked a nice-looking young man with a limp if he could see the president.

The young man replied, "The president is not in, but what can I do for you, Mr. Hutchins. I am the vice president."

Surprised, Hutchins looked at the young man and said, "I guess you have me bested. Who are you?"

"I know you very well, Mr. Hutchins, and you can get all the money you need here in this bank, any way you want it."

Hutchins asked for enough money to pay all expenses for him and Slim to reach Ryan. Then he said, "You have my curiosity aroused. Who are you, anyway?"

"When you were working out of Paris, Texas," the young man replied, "I was a crippled newsboy. I went into a saloon there one evening, where you and a group of men were talking. You bought all the papers I had, and you asked me who I was and what I wanted to do in life. I told you I wanted an education. I had finished grade school, and I wanted to go to Texas Business College.

"You said, 'All right, son, we will see that you go.' You told me to meet you back there the next day, which I did. When I met you, you handed me a scholarship in the Texas Business College at Paris, signed by J. A. Baker; and you told me that the men you were with had decided that, instead of drinking up all their money, they would donate part of it to my education. What I am today, Mr. Hutchins, I owe to you and those other officers."

This boy then had had only one leg. But now he seemed to stand on two good ones, for he had an artificial one. He remarked, "Mr. Hutchins, you look just like you did ten years ago. You have on the same suit of clothes, the same pair of boots and the same hat you wore when I was a boy."

"Well, I guess I am dressed very similar," Hutchins confessed later to Slim, "but boots, hat and suits don't last me ten years."

When Hutchins arrived in Ryan with his prisoner, the grand jury was in session. Next, Hutchins rounded up the conductor, brakeman and engineer of the train which had been robbed near Berwyn and brought them all to the U.S. jail in Ardmore to identify Chicago Slim. Every one of them declared Slim was not one of the robbers.

When he was released by the grand jury, Slim laughed about it. He confided in Hutchins that he could very readily identify the conductor, brakeman and engineer. They were all there when he and his friends robbed the train. He also told Hutchins why he had been thrown in jail in Topeka. The officers and the crooks were working together; and the *shyster* lawyer was a *go-between* and a *fixer*. There was a bank in Topeka that handled all the U.S. postage stamps taken from post offices robbed by that particular gang. When paper money was damaged in blowing open safes, this same bank would bundle up the bills and send them to the United States Treasury to exchange for good money.

Bert Casey—As Tough as Any Outlaw

There was a jailbreak in Tecumseh, in Oklahoma Territory. Among the three who got away was Jim Castleberry, charged with murder. Another was "Little Jack" Miller, charged with stealing a whole herd of horses. And the third man was Dad Bruner, sentenced to hang for murder.

This jailbreak had been accomplished by someone slipping into the jail with a key that exactly fitted the lock on the main door. Oddly enough, forty-six prisoners remained secure in jail.

Bill Grace was sheriff of Pottawattomie County, and people were pretty well riled up over the jailbreak of three desperate outlaws. Nobody could understand how they could escape and leave forty-six other prisoners locked up.

Within two hours after the jailbreak, Sheriff Bill Grace and Deputy Marshal Bob Hutchins were driving a hack, hitched to a pair of pestle-tailed ponies, with the three "escaped" outlaws, headed south into the Chickasaw Nation. Their objective was to find and arrest Bert Casey. He had sixteen thousand dollars reward hanging over him. The reward notice read differently from most others. It did not promise the money for Bert Casey's arrest and conviction, but for Casey to be arrested and placed in jail. Any jail!

The three criminals with the officers were members of Bert Casey's gang. The reason Sheriff Grace and Bob Hutchins were taking chances with these three ruthless men was because the three figured Bert Casey had them arrested to save his own skin. They had agreed with Grace and Hutchins to help them capture Bert Casey, and then go back to the Pottawatomie County jail. The officers had agreed to give each of them a share in the reward amounting to one thousand dollars each, and use what influence they could to lighten their sentences.

For three weeks, the five men traveled around the country, trailing Bert Casey, and finally they arrived at Table Mountain, near Desperado Springs, where Hutchins had met Casey before and received a rifle bullet from him just three inches above the heart. Yet he lived to meet Casey again for the third time in combat.

At night, they made their camp and Sheriff Grace would make his pallet on one side of the outlaws and Hutchins would make his on the other. Not nearly enough sleeping was done by either of them, but the officers had made up secret signals between them, and they would take turns about sleeping and watching for spells of two hours at a time. They half expected Bert Casey to come on his own and try to take his former gang members away; for he had undoubtedly heard of their "escape."

Casey was an outlaw who had many of the same characteristics as had Billy the Kid. He was only about twenty-two years old, but he had already killed several men. Like Billy the Kid, he was a killer; but unlike Billy the Kid, he shot more often from ambush and didn't give his victims any chance at all.

Just about every law enforcement officer in both Oklahoma and Indian territories were fairly itching to run across Casey and capture him, if possible, without a fight. Several shootings did take place. Some officers and some of Casey's associates were killed; but Casey always managed to get himself away safely.

At Table Mountain, they stopped near the Widow Greene's place, which they knew to be Bert Casey's hangout at times.

226

They sent Jim Castleberry over to the widow's to see if he could locate Casey. Widow Greene told him that Casey had not been gone over thirty minutes, and that she would see him again that night.

Sheriff Grace and Hutchins planned their strategy. They decided to take a long chance by sending Castleberry with Widow Greene that night to persuade Bert to try to free Jack Miller and Dad Bruner from their captors. He was to tell Casey the jailbreak was real, and that Miller and Bruner had been recaptured, while he, Castleberry, had escaped them.

But, with all his nerve, Bert Casey rejected Castleberry's plan, though he didn't seem to suspect his former henchman.

Grace and Hutchins got in touch with Prince Freeling, now the Attorney General of Oklahoma Territory. By telegram, they told him the situation, and received instructions to get Casey at all costs — he didn't care how — and that he was behind them to the end.

They next released Little Jack Miller to go with Jim Castleberry and talk to Casey. They confessed to him the whole scheme that had been planned, how they came to be out of jail, and promised him that if he would take Dad Bruner away from the lawmen that they would double-cross the officers and help him do the shooting.

Bert Casey listened silently to their story, and then said coldly, "You two have talked too damned much already. If you come back to me with any more of your crooked propositions, I'll gut-shoot you both!"

Grace and Hutchins concluded the "jig was up," and decided to take their three prisoners to Pauls Valley, and then back to jail in Tecumseh.

As they were preparing to leave camp, three horsemen suddenly appeared on Table Mountain. One of them waved a white handkerchief. The officers signaled an answer. They rode to about two hundred yards from the officers and their prisoners, quickly dismounted and started shooting. The fight was short, but furious. Hutchins had taken his weapons off and had advanced to meet Casey for the truce talk. Only Grace returned the fire, as Hutchins wheeled and ran back for his weapons. Two horses of the Casey gang were killed, and Hutchins was shot in the left side, above the hip. Bert Casey got away again, as did his confederates, on foot.

Sheriff Grace and his three prisoners took Hutchins to Woodford where Doctor T. P. Howell discovered the bullet "had banged around a bit and had come out near his backbone."

"Only a pretty bad flesh wound," Doctor Howell assured Hutchins. "I'll patch it up, and if you will take it easy now and avoid infection, you'll be just as good as new in a week." He regarded the deputy now with a grin. "By gad!" he exclaimed. "If I was you, Hutchins, I'd stay away from Table Mountain. Looks to me like you're jinxed around there!"

About four months later, a bank was robbed down at Camden, Arkansas. It was said that Bert Casey had done it. Two men were arrested, and they confessed that Casey was the third man. They also confessed they had been in the Table Mountain shooting scrape with Casey, too.

Sheriff Jim Thompson of Caddo County, Oklahoma Territory, wanted very much to capture Bert Casey, because of a crime Casey and his gang had committed in Caddo County after Thompson's election as sheriff. They had robbed Doctor Beanblossom and his boy and had killed the boy. Two very tough men of his gang at this time were known to be Jim Moran and the shady, illusive man named Simms, who was a slippery character from the Chickasaw Nation.

Jim Thompson was a sort of protégé of Chief Deputy United States Marshal William D. Fossett. He had been a deputy marshal under him. About the time the Comanche and Kiowa lands were opened for settlement to white people, in the year 1901, Thompson appointed Jim Borland as his undersheriff. Fossett knew that Jim Borland had been with Bert Casey's gang in earlier years. He had helped Casey rob the Rock Island train at Round Pond on Pond Creek in 1895, when Fossett had been a special agent for the Rock Island Railway Company.

Fossett didn't like Jim Borland personally, but he knew Jim Thompson had confidence in him. Marshal Fossett also knew Borland had quit the outlaw life right after the train robbery and had lived as a good and peaceable citizen in the Chickasaw Nation ever since. When Sheriff Thompson asked him about Jim Borland, he recommended him, because he considered him to be a man of good basic character and great courage.

In those days, sometimes, there was only a narrow line between some men who were officers and others who were outlaws in that frontier country. Both types of men had a drive for action; and their ambitions urged them to become either famous or notorious. One day, a man might be a good officer, and the next day a dreaded outlaw; good examples of this were Cole Younger, the Daltons and Bill Doolin.

Anyway, officers were fairly itching to get Bert Casey and claim the reward. Following the theory that "it takes a thief to catch a thief," two plots were formed against Bert Casey about the same time, each independent and separate.

Jim Thompson and Jim Borland conspired with officers of the surrounding counties to put a "spotter" on Casey's trail. The spotter they selected was the brother-in-law of Jim Hughes, a notorious outlaw and a close friend of Bert Casey.

The other plot was "hatched" by Chief Marshal William D. Fossett and Prince Freeling, Attorney General of Oklahoma Territory. They picked two young men, being held in federal jail at Guthrie for minor charges, and made a deal with them. They were Fred Hudson and Ed Lockett, and they, too, were set onto Casey's trail as spotters, or informers. Hudson, Lockett and Hughes' brother-in-law all joined up with Bert Casey about the same time.

Somehow, Bert Casey, Jim Hughes and Simms got wise that Hughes' brother-in-law was a traitor. They took him down to the creek bank and hanged him. This nearly caused Ed Lockett to "take his nickel out," but Fred Hudson had enough courage for both of them; and he persuaded Lockett just to be careful what he said and stay put.

Jim Moran, implicated with Bert Casey in the killing of the Beanblossom boy, was to be taken in a few days to the federal court in Lawton and tried.

Hudson, who was secretly in touch with Marshal Fossett, was directed to interest Casey in the idea of raiding the court-house at Lawton to rescue Jim Moran and other members of his gang on trial there. Hudson approached Casey with the idea, and Casey liked the sheer boldness and element of surprise he could detect in it.

"We'll sure have to get to hell and gone when we do," Casey

declared, "because Oklahoma Territory will be hotter than hell for us!"

"We'll need money to travel on," Simms reminded them. "We can go any place we want with money."

Casey came up with the idea that the bank at Cleo Springs would be just the place to get their traveling money.

What had become of Jim Hughes is not known. He had left Casey and the others about the time his brother-in-law was hanged. Jim Hughes was pretty much of a lone wolf, anyway.

The four remaining men moved close to Cleo Springs and pitched their camp under a large, sheltering tree.

Bert Casey and Simms rode into town, patronized the barber shop and carefully inspected the bank and its surroundings. They came directly back to camp and sent Hudson and Lockett to "case" the bank.

When Hudson and Lockett returned, the four of them compared notes and planned the robbery. Casey had the final word. "We'll rob her tomorrow morning at nine o'clock," he said.

Hudson assured Lockett that night that they would not implicate themselves in the hold-up.

"If we don't get killed, Casey might," he declared logically. "And then all chances for the reward money will be shot to hell; for the reward calls for Casey's capture and arrest. It says nothing about his death!"

"What will we do?" asked Lockett, who always depended on Hudson to think for both of them.

"In the morning, while we're cleaning and inspecting our guns, you sit down in front of Simms and I'll park myself in front of Bert. When I give you the nod, I'll make Bert give up, and you kill Simms."

Ed Lockett, already afraid of Casey and Simms, sucked in his breath audibly. Hudson whispered harshly. "Draw fast and shoot first, you damned coward!"

The next morning, after the four men had cheerfully prepared and eaten their morning meal, Hudson and Lockett got out their six-shooters, cleaned them and began twirling them to "limber up their wrists." Casey and Simms cleaned, checked and returned their guns to their holsters, without suspicion of impending doom.

Then in the midst of a quick draw, Hudson nodded to Lockett and exclaimed, "Bert, hands up!"

For a split second, Casey must have thought Hudson was playing, or else he would not have made the foolish grab for his own gun. Hudson's fleeting thought dismissed the reward money in preference to living longer. He blasted Casey, who crumpled over, still clawing at his gun. But Hudson then had to turn his attention to Simms, who was drawing his gun, for Lockett had frozen. Hudson shot Simms dead and whirled as Casey's gun exploded. Casey's shot went wild; and Lockett and Hudson both declared to Marshal Fossett that he must have been dead when he pulled the trigger.

Chief Deputy Marshal Fossett succeeded in having the minor cases against Hudson and Lockett dismissed for their services in ridding the twin territories of two badmen. He revealed to the court that they were possemen, appointed and directed by him; and then he advised Hudson and Lockett to get out of the country.

Where Ed Lockett went is unknown, but Fred Hudson, as the story goes, was living a respectable life in Arkansas when Jim Borland got a warrant against him for murder and went to Arkansas and brought him to Anadarko jail for trial.

Marshal Fosset attended the trial and Hudson was acquitted. This result made Jim Borland very angry.

Knowing that Jim Borland seemed to have a grudge against him from the Round Pond robbery, and that Borland was striking at him through Hudson, Marshal Fossett told Hudson, "Get back to Arkansas as quick as you can, or there will be more trouble. Jim Hughes has been captured, and Borland intends to hold you as a witness against him."

Before Hudson could get out of Lawton, Jim Borland came face to face with him on the street and began to goad and abuse him.

"You are not through yet, Hudson. I'm going to hold you for the Jim Hughes case."

Heated words came fast and furious between them, and a crowd began gathering to watch and listen.

The two men drew their six-shooters and fired about the same instant. Both men fell to the boardwalk. Jim Borland was dead, and Fred Hudson was dying.

231

"How about Jim?" Hudson asked in a hoarse whisper.

"You killed him, Hudson," somebody answered.

"I just wanted to outlive the son-of-a-bitch!" he grated between clenched teeth.

Fred Hudson was able to enjoy that satisfaction for only a few minutes.

Mill Creek Melody

John Poe was the United States Deputy Marshal assigned to duty at Mill Creek, Chickasaw Nation, to discourage bootlegging. For a while, he gave the bootleggers pure "unshirted hell." He kept the little frontier town of Mill Creek as dry as the Gobi Desert.

The nearest "oasis" was Denison, Texas. They ordered their whiskey shipped to them by express from Denison.

John Poe got a pass from the Frisco Railway Company and rode all the trains between Mill Creek and Denison. He confiscated and broke all shipments of liquor from Denison into the Indian Territory.

The bootleggers grew desperate and plotted to rid themselves of their nemesis — John Poe — forever. They boarded an excursion train to Denison, Texas, to a baseball game. That night, a free-for-all fight took place aboard the train. John Poe butted in, as the bootleggers had known he would, and he was "accidentally" killed.

Other federal deputies moved in and made several arrests. A preliminary trial was held, but no direct evidence could be revealed, and all the suspects were released by the court. The bootleggers were back in business stronger than ever.

Henry Sublett, another deputy marshal, was sent to Mill Creek to stop the flow of "firewater." He went after some of them one night and "got his right arm shot off and several other parts of his anatomy pretty well leaded."

Everything went along just as the bootleggers pleased until Deputy Marshal Dero Duncan was sent there to put a stop to it for certain. The bootleggers complained that Dero Duncan held them up going and coming; not just for their whiskey, but *skully* (money) that they derived from the sale of liquors. "When we are overstocked a little," they claimed, "he will lay off arrests for a week and show us how to confiscate the contraband the *funnel route!*"

But Dero Duncan didn't stay in Mill Creek very long; and the "game" went on as usual.

The next deputy marshal sent to Mill Creek was Bob Hutchins, who was transferred there from Ada.

There was a place outside of town on the main traveled road, known as Three Mile, which Hutchins found to be as notorious, tough, murderous and depraved as the Corner Saloon. On his next trip back, he found it going full blast, with no holds barred. Single-handed, he ordered all the gambling equipment piled outside, and he set it on fire. When the equipment was burned, he mounted his horse and rode away.

This brazen, daring deed caused the bootleggers around Mill Creek to regard him with respect, and they made friendly overtures toward him. To their surprise, Hutchins responded warmly and let things ride along for awhile. He found out from what sources their merchandise came, how they got their money, and why whiskey was so much in demand around Mill Creek.

The businessmen of Mill Creek had established a cattle shipping point for cattlemen from both the Chickasaw and Choctaw nations. The news had been spread that they could get whatever they wanted in Mill Creek. The idea among the businessmen was to make Mill Creek a frontier town and stimulate business.

For two weeks, Hutchins played poker with the bootleggers, drank their liquor and got himself known as a *good sport*. Hutchins, in their estimation, became a member of their "fraternity"; he was the best officer on earth. They would keep him in Mill Creek.

At the end of the honeymoon, Hutchins called a meeting of the leading citizens of the town. "Gentlemen," he announced, "I have been sent to Mill Creek to put a stop to bootlegging, and now it's time to do it. We've got to put the lid on!"

The howl of protest at this announcement was prompt and loud, and exactly what Hutchins expected.

"Hutchins, you'll kill this town as dead as a doornail," they argued. "Stop the whiskey here, and all the cattlemen will go elsewhere to ship!"

The meeting was in a turmoil until Hutchins finally got them to listen to a plan he had in mind.

"You all know the grade of whiskey the bootleggers handle in Mill Creek," he declared. "It's rot-gut. There are four trains each day on the Frisco from Texas. You can step to the phone and for thirty-five cents you can order two quarts of the best whiskey for a dollar and a quarter a quart. The express cost will be thirty cents. For only three dollars and fifteen cents, each of you can buy a half-gallon of whiskey. The bootleggers charge you two dollars a quart for poison. If you men will help me break up the nest of bootleggers here in Mill Creek and clean out a bunch of horse and cattle thieves around this part of the territory, we will *not* kill the town. We will boom it!"

Within two weeks, the bootleggers could not even give away their brand of whiskey. Within three hours after a customer telephoned Denison for two quarts of whiskey, it arrived safely in Mill Creek, with no interference from Hutchins. When the cattlemen came to town, they could get liquor through their business friends, who knew their tastes and brands; and the cattle shipping went on undisturbed and Mill Creek prospered.

Deputy Marshal Hutchins made one ruling very plain to all of them: "Order it, have it come in your own name, not over two quarts at a time; be sure never to drink too much at one time. If your wife objects to your ordering it, you should leave it alone."

He told them flatly, "If you don't stick to our plan, I'll sure enough put the lid on!"

The arrangement worked fine until a few church women, urged on by some bootleggers, inspired a widowed circuit preacher to forsake his Bible and begin preaching against Bob Hutchins, until he finally caused a stir that got Hutchins removed from Mill Creek and later, after he had served for a while as United States Constable, assigned the job as circulating deputy marshal.

A young man named Benjamin H. Colbert had been appointed United States Marshal of the Southern District of the Indian Territory, with his office at Ardmore, on January 21, 1902.

Ben Colbert was a very progressive and lucky young man, who was part Chickasaw Indian. He had been the private secretary of Governor Douglas H. Johnston of the Chickasaw Nation. Ben had distinguished himself as a member of the Rough Riders under Teddy Roosevelt in the Spanish-American War. He was Roosevelt's aide in Cuba. At the close of the war, he was mustered out at Montayk Point, New York.

Upon appointing Colbert as United States Marshal, President Theodore Roosevelt said of him: "Ben Colbert is the most versatile man I know. He is capable as a secretary and a good horseshoer. He can do anything."

When Teddy Roosevelt was inaugurated President for his second term, Ben Colbert was one of the forty men selected for a special honor guard. All forty had been Rough Riders. Teddy called them, "My boys."

Ben Colbert led the honor guard in the inaugural parade. He tied his horse to the fence at the White House and had dinner with the President after the inauguration.

Ben Colbert later served as secretary to Congressman U. S. Stone of Oklahoma.

The specific charge brought to U.S. Marshal Ben Colbert was that witnesses had seen Deputy Marshal Hutchins pass a man on the street who was carrying a package of whiskey that had come by express on the train Hutchins boarded to make an official trip, and that he had not arrested him. Hutchins, they claimed, knew what the package contained, since he had been allowing the businessmen of Mill Creek to obtain their whiskey that way for several months.

Hutchins told Marshal Colbert that he not only knew the package contained whiskey, but he had taken a drink of it about a week later. This had happened after the man had helped Hutchins capture Tommy Johnson, the most wanted horse thief at that time. Tommy Johnson was wanted in Texas, Arkansas, Missouri, Kansas, and about twenty places in the Indian Territory. When he pled guilty, he told Judge Hosea Townsend that he had forked as many horses as any other ten men in the territory in the last twelve months.

Johnson received five years in the federal penitentiary at Leavenworth, Kansas, and was glad to get off that light. He went on his way to Leavenworth and remarked to Hutchins, "If they had got me in Texas, and one of them throat-whiskered nester-juries had got hold of me, I would have got life or the rope for sure. I ain't got no kick coming. I can outlive this five years and come again on the green!"

United States Deputy Marshal Millard Burton was assigned to Mill Creek. He played the John Poe game and broke all the whiskey that came by express, even to men who would not sell a drop to anyone, or let it get into the hands of Indians.

Consequently, bootlegging came back into its former glory.

Reel Foot Dick, a noted bootlegger, told Hutchins he came to Mill Creek and found the town pretty dry. He had in his wagon one hundred and twenty quarts of Corner Saloon whiskey, which he wanted to sell quickly. He went to the post office and bought a money order for four dollars, wrote a letter to Mike Sweeny at Denison and told him to ship four quarts of whiskey by express to Mill Creek. Then he hunted up Millard Burton, showed him the letter and told him he had been sick a long time and wanted to get some whiskey to make some "bitters" and he was having it come by express.

Deputy Marshal Burton knew when to expect the train with Reel Foot Dick's whiskey. Burton met the train, confiscated and broke the whiskey; but while he was doing that, Reel Foot Dick drove up main street and called out to everybody who wanted whiskey to hurry, for he had only ten minutes to dispose of his stock. He told the crowd what he had pulled on Burton. The news spread like wildfire, and within twenty minutes, Reel Foot Dick drove away from Mill Creek with an empty wagon and two hundred fifty dollars cash in his pockets.

People of Mill Creek afterward presented a petition to Marshal Ben Colbert, asking him to reinstate Bob Hutchins in Mill Creek district. But Hutchins thanked them very kindly and told them that he had "been punched into the best job he had ever had with the United States government law enforcement service, and he would stay with it."

Hutchins made the people of Mill Creek one promise, that he always carried out. He promised them that if he ever set foot in Mill Creek again, he would be after some criminal who was on his way to the penitentiary. He made two arrests in Mill Creek after that; and they both went to the penitentiary.

The Nickel Hill
Old Settlers Picnic

In 1902, an old settlers picnic was held at Nickel Hill. Down through the ages, communities have often held their picnics to honor their old settlers.

Joel (Red) Thomas, a full-blood Chickasaw Indian, donated the beef for the barbecue. Joel Thomas' one big failure was that he could not let *firewater* alone. He had a young nephew, who idolized him and thought there was nobody else like him.

There were only two stores in Nickel Hill. One was owned by the Brumley Brothers, and the other by the partnership of Barber and Powell. Barber had migrated to the Chickasaw Nation from Louisiana, where he had been a cane broker and top-notch bootlegger. It was rumored that Barber was run out of Louisiana, and he did not look back until he landed at Nickel Hill.

It seemed to fall on Deputy Marshal Dave Booker and Bob Hutchins always to be assigned to chaperone picnics. Of course, they were always invited out to have a good time.

When Booker and Hutchins reached the grounds, they sized

up the situation, for they knew there would be some drinking going on, and they also knew there would be a few little crap and poker games in the brush, and they decided to play deaf, dumb and blind and let them have the "time of their lives."

They separated, stopping here and there, talking socially with this group and that one. Hutchins happened to look toward Barber's house and saw Doug McCalister climbing into his saddle, with a gunny sack in front of him. He rode across the picnic grounds to a group, opened the sack, and the group proceeded to do some hard drinking. It was entirely too plain and flagrant. He didn't like the lack of respect they were showing for law and order here, and he wouldn't tolerate it. He approached the group in such a manner as to place a large oak tree between himself and the drinking party. Before he reached the tree, however, Doug McCalister leisurely mounted his pony and started to ride away.

Just a few feet to Hutchins' right was a long-legged, long-barreled bay horse, owned by Race Horse Campbell. Hutchins hurriedly untied the horse, stepped into the saddle and went after McCalister. He, in turn, dug spurs into the flanks of his pestle-tailed pony and tried to outdistance Hutchins in a dead run, but Doug should have known better than to try to outrun one of Campbell's racehorses with his Chickasaw pony.

When Hutchins closed the gap to within forty yards of him, he yelled to Doug McCalister to stop, or he would shoot. Then Doug really invited trouble by drawing his six-shooter and firing over his shoulder at Hutchins. The bullet missed Hutchins, but killed the racehorse and, as Hutchins went down with the dying horse, he shot Doug McCalister almost through the heart.

As Doug hit the ground and rolled over, Hutchins thumbed back the hammer of his Colt for a second shot. Doug cried out in terror, "Don't shoot me anymore. I'm already killed." And he threw his own six-shooter into the nearby bushes.

As he lay there bleeding in the dust, Hutchins walked up and searched him for other weapons. He saw that Doug McCalister was badly wounded. He asked, "Doug why did you take the long shot chance and kill Campbell's horse?"

"I just shot to scare you off, not to hit the horse or you, at all."

"You made a bad break."

"I know I'm to blame," he admitted. "I'll take my medicine, even if it is bitter."

Hutchins got help, loaded him on an improvised stretcher and they took him to Barber's house, where he had been staying, and put him on a bed. He claimed he had only had two pints of whiskey and had sold them before the "shooting."

"Why did you run then? There was no evidence."

He grinned a faint, pale smile. "I don't know. Habit, I guess."

"Doug," Hutchins told him. "I don't have any evidence against you. What do you want to do?"

"When I get well, I'll plead guilty," he promised, "and take my medicine, like I told you."

In about ten days, Doug McCalister was able to sit up. Hutchins went after him and hauled him in a buggy to Ardmore, where he pled guilty in U.S. court, and went to the penitentiary in Detroit, Michigan, for two years. Doug only served about eight months of his sentence. He died and was buried in the penitentiary graveyard.

Race Horse Campbell charged Hutchins eighty dollars for the dead horse. Before he went to the penitentiary, Douglas McCalister offered to pay it, but Hutchins declined.

Hutchins paid for the horse and filed a claim with the U.S. government for the loss of the horse in his line of duty, and after five years, he finally collected it.

Barber, the real cause of McCalister's tragedy, was a marked man to the marshal after that. So much pressure was brought to bear on him, he lost his head in a deal, murdered his partner and hiked back to his birthplace in Louisiana. Seldom T. Linds, another worthy and fearless U.S. Deputy Marshal, went after Barber with a warrant, and killed him when he resisted arrest.

241

The Keystone
Becomes the Capstone

Bob Hutchins was a loyal and devout Mason. He lived the mandates of the lodge and adhered to its principles. He helped organize several lodges in the Indian Territory, and in Oklahoma after statehood. He wrote and published a number of pamphlets and booklets about Masonic service and its broad application to public welfare and good.

The mysterious *keystone* stands for a noble and glorious cause, but there were many differences in the characters of the men who wore this emblem. It was for some men an evidence of "creed and faith," but to others it was merely an ornament, which revealed that they had become "dues-paying members."

Hugh Myers, city marshal of Davis, and a Royal Arch Mason, was waylaid and murdered on a Saturday night in July, 1901.

Marshal John S. Hammer was concluding his final year as United States Marshal of the Southern District when his office was notified of the murder. Buck Garrett, Bob Hutchins and Thad McCallie were in the marshal's office at nearly midnight, when the telephone message was received.

242

Captain Hammer, who liked to make jokes particularly about Buck Garrett and Bob Hutchins, often referred to them as the "night hawks" and the "twin deputies," because they rode together under him on many assignments. Marshel Hammer said he would have preferred to call them owls, but they didn't have enough *savvy*. All they were fit for was to be shot at, and if they happened to be "bumped off," anybody could take their places!

Hugh Myers was a good friend of the "twin" deputies. He had been killed in the line of duty, and they felt compelled to do something about it. Without leaving a note in the office or notifying Marshal Hammer or anyone else in Ardmore, they hurried down to the depot and caught the caboose of a freight train just going through, as it went slowly across main street. They reached Davis, on the north side of the Arbuckles, just one hour and thirty-seven minutes after they had received the telephone call.

Buck Garrett and posseman Thad McCallie got off the freight train at Davis, but Bob Hutchins remained on the train for another twenty miles to get off at Pauls Valley, where he rounded up Jim Mayes, the U.S. jailer, and his bloodhounds. Together, they rousted out the section foreman and one of his hands, and commandeered a railroad handcar, which they all pumped back to Davis.

The sun was just peeping over a ridge in the Arbuckles as they pulled up to the depot. Buck Garrett and Thad McCallie had already been busy. They had arrested a Negro named "Skeet" and Lyman Hardy, a Chickasaw-Negro freedman. Skeet had given the names of two other half Negroes on Wild Horse Creek, whom he claimed had committed the murder. He said their names were Pink Bruner and Ben Gage.

The residents of Davis were stirred up like hornets, and men and boys were prowling the streets with sticks and stones and enough shooting irons to start a revolution. Pink Bruner, one of the Negro breeds, was shot through the knee by Hugh Myers as Myers fell from his horse.

"Hutch" Hutchins, a blood cousin of Bob, lent him his race mare to ride after the freedman. Buck Garrett got a racehorse from Henry Richardson, and Mayes and McCallie found mounts at the livery stable.

Everybody in Davis seemed to want to join the posse, on any kind of conveyance that could be appropriated, including a few bicycles.

The three deputies and Jim Mayes and his bloodhounds left Davis with a posse of two hundred people, including some women and girls and teen-aged boys. They stopped two miles west of Davis, where they forded the Washita River and the deputies split the posse into squads and appointed leaders for each group. Their intention was to search every foot of the country, clear to Wild Horse Creek.

By the time the search had grown this serious, some of the less zealous members of the posse began dropping out and returning to Davis. Some of them had forgotten to turn out their milk cows and do other urgent chores. Some of the businessmen suddenly remembered they had forgotten to lock their stores and offices; and a few had neglected to tell their wives where they were going.

The posse dwindled to about seventy-five in number. Beyond the Washita, they had no trouble in following the freedmen's trail. They followed the two of them clear to Hennepin, by spots of blood Pink Bruner had shed, for his wound was bleeding profusely. They had traveled to Hennepin before the blood trail played out. They were in Wild Horse country now, where nobody seemed to know anything, except, "Take the lefthand fork of the road and keep straight ahead." It was dry weather, and the bloodhounds now were having trouble with the scents.

Another survey of their posse revealed that nearly all of the seventy-five followers from the Washita had turned back, evidently because the foothills of the Arbuckles were too crooked and rough!

But "Hutch" Hutchins and Henry Richardson were still bringing up the rear in a buggy, even though it was a trail suitable only for good, sure-footed horses. George Burns was still with them, and the rest of the posse now consisted only of Bob Hutchins, Buck Garrett, Jim Mayes with his two bloodhounds, and Thad McCallie.

When they reached the *forks,* they were puzzled which way to go, because one bloodhound took the left road and the other took the right one. They were debating which to follow when old Caesar Franklin rode to meet them. Caesar Franklin was an elderly freedman, who had actually been a Chickasaw slave. He was the boss of all the other Negroes and their offspring with farms along Wild Horse Creek by allotments from the Chickasaws. The deputy marshals knew that his word with the Negroes in that settlement was gospel. Hutchins and Garrett knew him to be a man of his word.

"If old Caesar told one of his niggers to jump into the Washita River or Wild Horse Creek, he jumped, or he attended his own funeral the next day," Hutchins declared.

Buck Garrett rode off to one side and talked to Caesar Franklin. When he came back, he told Hutchins, "That old Negro is looking for information, himself."

"I'll take a fall with him then and see what I get," Hutchins replied, and he rode off to one side for a private conference with Caesar.

"Caesar," Hutchins began, "Hugh Myers, the city marshal of Davis, was shot and killed last night. He wore a keystone exactly like the ones you and I are wearing on our watch chains now. He was a man who loved and lived according to the teachings of the *stone*.

The old Negro listened in stoical silence, then gravely said, "Now, Mr. Hutchins, you understand my position. Kinfolks on one side and fraternal ties on the other. Pink Bruner is my own sister's boy. Here's my proposition. Will you promise me on this *keystone* that you will see that the boys get a fair trial before a court of justice, and not by a lynching mob, if I get up in the collar with you?"

Bob Hutchins answered sincerely, "So be it. It shall be done."

Caesar nudged his little white-faced, skewbald pony into a lope and, saying, "Follow me," he gave out an Indian war whoop. Hutchins followed him, and the others, though somewhat puzzled, followed Hutchins.

Three miles northwest of Hennepin, Caesar Franklin halted his pony on a high point of ground, straightened up in his stirrups, looked at Deputy Hutchins and pointed: "The capstone fits just over yonder!"

The deputies looked and they could hardly restrain their surprise when they saw on another hill about seventy-five saddled horses, with about twice as many men sitting and standing nearby. All were armed and ready for whatever Caesar ordered.

"Wait here," Caesar Franklin warned, "until I go over there and give my boys orders and wave the signal for you to come on."

As he stared unbelievingly at the fast-moving Negro and his pony, Buck Garrett said sarcastically, "Bob, this is where you and your nigger Mason brother get us killed as dead as Hugh Myers!"

"Not on your tintype," Hutchins said. "This is where we get Pink Bruner, without firing a shot."

They watched Caesar Franklin ride up to his clan. He and some of the minor leaders went into a huddle for a few minutes, then the meeting broke up and, returning their rifles to their saddle scabbards, they straddled their horses silently and vanished, quickly and completely.

Caesar then made a sign that Hutchins recognized, and the posse rode down to a desolate log shack in the valley. "Hutch" Hutchins and Henry Richardson could not get their buggy down there, so they remained behind.

In the little hut, Hugh Myers' murderer lay on a suggan. Pink Bruner was badly shot, but Ben Gage had fled.

"There's your man," said Caesar Franklin stoically. "Marshal Hutchins, please tell your men in the presence of Pinky here your promise to me. Have them agree to it, too, and I'll deliver Pinky to you."

Hutchins explained the agreement to his fellow possemen, and all of them readily endorsed it.

Caesar Franklin looked earnestly down at Pink Bruner, as he lay there in pain.

"You are now Marshal Hutchins' prisoner, under his protection and care. Be a good boy and make the best of it from here on out. Don't worry about mob law. You are in safe hands."

George Burns was a big, husky, strong man. He rolled Pink Bruner up in his suggan, threw him across his shoulder and hiked up the steep hill without hesitation.

They reached Davis about seven o'clock that evening, and found everyone prepared for a necktie party.

The crowd kept growing until the deputy marshals from Ardmore saw that they had to do something fast, or they would

246

be overpowered and have their prisoners taken away from them and hanged.

Bob Hutchins hastily called from the crowd such men as old Brother Patterson, John W. McIntosh, W. F. Parker, A. N. Page, Mose Ferguson, Lewis Binswanger, Doctor T. P. Howell and some others, all of whom he knew to be Royal Arch Masons like himself. He told them quickly what he had promised Caesar Franklin on the *keystone*. "And if you men do not rally to our rescue *pronto*," he told them, "blood will run down the streets of Davis. We officers intend to stand on that promise. Now old Caesar and we don't work together in the same lodge, mix and mingle in any way; but when it comes to the spirit, all of us hew to the same line as he does."

They all agreed with Hutchins and spread out among the members of the mob, pausing to talk confidentially with other Masons and friends. In a few moments, the frenzy of the mob was curbed. All grew quiet and the mob dispersed.

The deputy marshals were left alone with their prisoners and just twenty-four hours from the time they had arrived in Davis on the freight train, they took their prisoners aboard the same caboose and, dog-tired, hungry and sleepy, they went on to Pauls Valley to place them in jail.

Lyman Hardy took sick in jail and died a natural death. Pink Bruner was tried before Judge Hosea Townsend and a jury of his peers and was sentenced to life in the penitentiary at Leavenworth. He only lived a short time after being confined there. He left behind five untried cases of the federal court docket against him, and a record of having killed six men — three white and three colored — including City Marshal Hugh Myers.

Sixteen years later, Sheriff Buck Garrett got a lead on Ben Gage. He traced him through Colorado, Missouri, Kansas and Texas before losing him for a while. Then he cropped up in the Creek Nation. Gage had changed his name, after making his getaway the night Hugh Myers had been killed. When Sheriff Garrett finally located this Negro, who had escaped him that night of the crime and he was a U.S. Deputy Marshal, he notified Sheriff Walter Alexander of Murray County, who soon had Gage in his own jail at Sulphur. Buck Garrett identified the Negro as Ben Gage. He, too, was sentenced to a long term in the penitentiary.

Novel Schemes
and Schemers

Two Soiled Doves

Ardmore, Chickasaw Nation, Indian Territory — and now Oklahoma — has always been known as a place that a person could get a drink of just about anything he called for by giving the right sign; a wink, a slang expression, a certain question, or some other method of recognition.

Even today — on weekends, holidays and after ten o'clock at night, when the legal liquor stores are closed — Ardmore still maintains that "dignity."

Grosvenor A. Porter was appointed United States Marshal of the Southern District of Indian Territory by President Theodore Roosevelt on February 6, 1906, to succeed Ben Colbert. Marshal Porter was a distant relative of President Roosevelt, and he decided to show folks how things were done in Montana. One of his resolutions was to dry up the liquor oasis.

Marshal Porter and his deputies kept on preventing infractions until things got to where it was hard to find anything. Then a couple of loose ladies who lived east of the Santa Fe tracks hit upon a scheme to get rich; and it worked successfully for a long time, until Deputy Marshal J. P. Irby got wise to their game.

This deputy marshal happened to notice that the two ladies visited Gainesville, Texas, about two or three times each week. The queerest thing about them was they were both slender and petite when they went down to Gainesville on the train, but they were plump and fat when they returned.

To anyone else except a man of Irby's calibre, this might never have been noticed. But Irby couldn't quite figure out just how two innocent little beauties could gain and lose so much weight in so few hours. So he took them before United States Commissioner Thomas N. Robnett, who had them examined by a matron to find what was causing all their bloat. She found hot water bags filled with some of Haley and Russell's best conversation water.

They would wear tightly fitting waist-belts and fill up several hot water bags with cheap "Red Horse" whiskey, tie them to their belts, put their petticoats and dresses back on, and come back to the Indian Territory to alleviate the thirst in Ardmore.

The Zinc Vest

Use of wagon hounds was one of the oldest methods of transporting hidden liquor around the Indian Territory. They did this by fastening tin containers of whiskey to the hounds where they could ride inconspicuously under the wagon bed.

But the zinc vest was a novel device for carrying *firewater* in the Indian Territory. It was constructed like an ordinary vest worn by any man, except that it was worn under other clothing. The zinc vest usually held about two gallons of whiskey that, occasionally, was pretty good. It was hollow, of course, and it narrowed to feather edges at the sides. The main part of the bulge was fitted up under the armpits. The length came down to the waistband of a man's pants. It had a hole at the top, with a tight-fitting screw-cap where, to use the bootleggers' term, "you loaded the animal." At the bottom in front was a small opening with a stopcock or faucet.

A bootlegger could walk around at a picnic or camp meet-

249

ing, looking prosperous and wise. If a fellow wanted a drink, he and the customer would go behind a wagon, bush or tree and squat down in earnest conversation. The bootlegger would take out a folding drinking cup, or some other container, fill it and charge the customer just twenty-five cents for a drink. Sometimes, the man with the vest would be so busy, he looked like a candidate running for office, or some buyer and trader.

Bob Hutchins found a zinc vest on Whiskey Bill Watson at Ada, after the second or third search. It was a brand new trick to him. He was used to patting their pockets and looking into their boots for bottles. Watson sold out his first vest-full after Hutchins had searched him. Then he got on his horse and rode away. When he came back in thirty minutes and started business all over again, Hutchins finally got wise. He took Watson down into a dry branch, made him take off his top clothes and found the vest.

Watson set up a howl, not so much for getting caught, but for having to give up the "vest to his winter suit."

"Hutch, I paid a tinner in Gainesville, Texas, twenty-five dollars to make that contraption for me. That's my meal ticket, and I don't want it to go to a deputy marshal."

Hutchins merely laughed at his remarks.

"I think very little of a man who would deprive another of his living."

Hutchins took him before United States Commissioner B. F. Talbot, who didn't think it was funny. He set Bill Watson's bond at five hundred dollars and sent him to the federal jail in Ardmore. Watson explained the reason he couldn't place a bond was because nobody wanted a good work hand, unless he had tools with which to work and deliver the goods.

Marshal Porter became the proud owner of the vest. He took it to Washington, D.C., and presented it to President Teddy Roosevelt for his collection of curios and novelties.

Mr. Bootlegger John

Bob Hutchins had an odd experience in connection with a life-size portrait of Teddy Roosevelt, which hung on the wall of a bootlegger's den in Madill. The bootlegger had a room in one of the most prominent hotels in town, and was never known to be "whiskey-broke."

A number of deputy marshals had searched his room many times, but found nothing. While in Madill one day, Hutchins decided to unearth Mr. Bootlegger John. He rented a room across the hall and took up his vigil. He didn't have long to wait until Bootlegger John went into his room. Hutchins gave him time to get a bottle out of his plant, then he walked into the room. In his hand, John held an empty pint flask, but no whiskey.

Now Hutchins began the search in dead earnest, and he knew he should not look for bottled whiskey, but *bulk* whiskey. If he had waited three or four minutes longer, he knew he would have caught John filling the empty flask. He looked every place imaginable and found nothing. He had almost given up when he stopped in front of Teddy Roosevelt's big picture, life-size, hanging there on the wall. Hutchins teased the bootlegger about the President.

"Are you two any way related?" he quipped. "Or just good friends?"

"I was a Rough Rider with Teddy in the Spanish-American War," he maintained.

Most rough riders Hutchins had heard make the remark had always said, "in Cuba," or "at San Juan Hill." So Hutchins knew he was lying. He also recollected he had known about Mr. Bootlegger John and his activities at least as far back as 1898, when the battle of San Juan Hill was being fought in Cuba. He didn't argue, however. He went right ahead gazing at Teddy's grinning visage. Bob knew the only way to get bootleggers was to outwit them by acting gullible.

An art critic would not have more carefully surveyed Teddy's portrait than Hutchins was doing. He had already detected that his scrutiny of the portrait made the bootlegger nervous. He got up in the chair for an even closer inspection; all the time watching John out of the corner of his eye, to see when he was on the right track. Finally, he took the picture down from the wall and found a twenty penny nail head protruding from behind the portrait. He took hold of the nail and it came loose. He pulled it out of the wall and, along with it, came a slender rubber tube, tied with a string. He untied the string and the whiskey began to flow.

Hutchins looked the whole setup over carefully, got some answers to two or three questions and learned about the entire operation. Bootlegger John would take his wagon to Denison, Texas, buy a barrel of whiskey, smuggle it into Madill after dark, unload it before daylight, take it to his room and put it into a false wall he had built. He attached the rubber hose, brought it through the wall and tied it to the big nail. He employed a close-mouthed man who helped him do the lifting. What better front could he have than the President of the United States?

Hutchins took John before Judge Alexander Gullett, United States Commissioner at Tishomingo, for a hearing. Judge Gullett bound him over to await action of the grand jury, and set his bond at five hundred dollars. Bootlegger John promptly paid, and went back to Madill that evening.

Mr. Bootlegger John went back to Denison that very night and was back in Madill ready for business.

Hutchins received word that he was again going full blast. He decided to put the man out of business permanently, if it took all summer. He met John on the street in Madill.

"Are you after me again?" John asked testily.

Hutchins feigned surprise. "Certainly not! When I catch a bootlegger like you, he either reforms, or I lay off and let him go."

"That so?" he asked dubiously.

"John, just how much whiskey have you got on hand now?"

"With careful dispensing, I have enough to last about a month."

"You must have another barrel hid around somewhere."

"You said a mouthful when you said *hid*. It's put away this time where Roosevelt won't snitch on me."

"The President did sort of let you down," Hutchins admitted, "but maybe that was because you lied about being one of his Rough Riders."

Hutchins stood around town most of the day, watching Bootlegger John's maneuverings. He decided it was no longer upstairs. John had someone else watching Hutchins constantly, too. He was not asleep, by any means. Finally, Hutchins concluded that it had to be in the stairway. He got a hammer and a nail bar and went after the stairway. It was simple, and an old scheme, too. Four steps in the lower section had been made to revolve by taking out a wooden key, which held them in place. It was a good trick, but Ada bootleggers had worn out that one long before.

Bad luck had overtaken poor old Bootlegger John again. Judge Gullett was not quite so merciful this time. John's bond was set for one thousand dollars. John put up the money again and went back to Madill.

He laid off the racket for about six months, then proved the old adage that "once a bootlegger, always a bootlegger" was true.

Mr. Bootlegger John embarked upon John Barleycorn's credit once more; and this scheme was somewhat short-lived, too.

John had a few busybody neighbors who couldn't stand seeing him do well and prosper. They wrote Deputy Marshal Bob Hutchins a letter to come over and attend to John, for he was cutting up again, and Hutchins seemed to be the only officer who ever had any luck with him. Bootlegger John was the first man he met when he got off the Frisco train.

"Well, who are you after now?" he asked indignantly. "Me again? If you're after me, you had just as well go back. You've made a Christian out of me. I have quit for good."

"John," Hutchins declared, "I'll tell you what I'll do."

"What?" he asked suspiciously.

"I'll bet you a new hat that when I go back to Tishomingo, you'll go with me. I don't have a warrant for you now, either. How long has it been since you sold a pint of whiskey? And who did you sell it to?"

"I tell you I have quit for sure!" was the irritable reply.

Hutchins left him abruptly and asked a few questions around town, such as: "Who is John running with now?" and "Where does he do his loafing?"

He learned John had stopped living in the hotel and was now rooming with the man who operated the coal yard.

Going through a coal yard looking for booze will make any man dirty and tired, Hutchins discovered. He gave that coal yard a going over just short of moving every lump of coal, and found nothing.

Hutchins went to the hotel, rented a room, cleaned up, ate supper at a restaurant and, tired as he was, he did considerable studying, trying to outguess John. He was sure John's plant was somewhere in that coal yard, for it is second nature for a law violator always to watch his "hole card," and Bootlegger John did most all his loafing around that coal yard.

The next morning, Hutchins just happened to saunter into a hardware store to say hello to a friend. His friend, the hardware merchant, guessed his business in town. He did not want to be a witness, but he remarked, "Hutchins, what do you suppose old John wanted with a coal oil pump? He bought one from me several days ago!"

Hutchins knew instantly what John wanted with the pump. He remembered similar plants he and other deputies had unearthed in Chickasha a long time ago. His only problem now was to locate the pump.

He hunted up two little boys and gave them a silver dollar apiece to go play marbles all day in the coal yard, and then come and tell him what John did.

The boys went in a run to the coal yard to play marbles, each clutching his silver dollar in glee. Hutchins went back to the hotel, lit a cigar and awaited the outcome of the marble game. Soon one of the boys came to him and said, "John came out into the yard with a great long thing, moved a big coal scuttle they use for loading coal on the wagons. He took up a plank and put the long thing down in a hole and filled a jug with something."

"Good boy!" Hutchins exclaimed. "Let's go!"

When they reached the coal yard, Bootlegger John was sitting out in front of the house. "Come on, John," Hutchins said curtly. "Let's go over to your plant."

"Hell!" he blurted. "I might have known when them boys was playin' marbles there in the yard you had something to do with it."

Hutchins had him move the scuttle and raise the plank to reveal another barrel of whiskey.

"Now ain't that hell!" John wailed. "Three barrels of booze lost and three cases in federal court!"

"For the first time, I think you're telling the truth," Hutchins told him. "You will lose all three of those cases, too!"

254

He tried his best to persuade Hutchins to take him to Ardmore to be arraigned, rather than appear before Judge Gullett again.

"John, you are hard to convince," Judge Gullet declared harshly. "Madill is not as healthy as it used to be. Your bond this time for the third offense will be five thousand dollars — and she's going to be a dandy, gilt-edged schedule, too."

This time, poor John drew a bobtail flush and failed to catch the right card, so he went to jail in Ardmore. He remained in jail about three months. When court convened at Tishomingo, he pleaded guilty to one case, and the U.S. Attorney dismissed the other two. He received a sentence of six months in jail and a fine of five hundred dollars. He served out the jail sentence, but he had used up his savings on attorney fees and other expenses. He sold a home he owned in Madill and left town.

Mr. Bootlegger John next moved down on Red River, bought out a ferry service and began a brand new scheme.

All a person had to do who wanted a little *firewater* was to go down to Red River, walk out on John's ferryboat and say:

"Hello, John. "How's fishing today?"

He would answer, "All right."

"Got any bait?"

"Plenty."

"Give me a long pole. I think I'll try my luck."

John would take three dollars from the "fisherman" and then he would walk leisurely up and down the river bank, looking for a good place to fish. Presently, he would come to a very convenient pole, set in the bank, with bait and line already in the water. When the "fisherman" took up the pole and lifted the line out of the water, he would find a *fish* already on the hook. But the *fish* was shaped like a quart bottle, and predictably it held *firewater*.

The *fisherman* would take his catch and return to camp. He had caught his limit; according to John's "game laws."

No matter how many *fishermen* were waiting, only one could go fishing at a time, for John had to guide each one separately to catch the kind of *fish* he wanted. If the *fisherman* was looking for a *short fish,* such as a *perch,* he would have to ask for a short pole and shell out only one dollar and a half. Then John

255

would lead him to a pole on the bank, where he would find on the end of the line a *pint fish*.

The grand jury became interested in John's fishing trade. They sent Deputy Marshal Hutchins, an old familiar side-kick of John's to look into it. Then they sent out deputies with subpoenas to bring in some *fishermen* witnesses. But the *fishermen* were a very ignorant lot who couldn't remember anything. The grand jury failed to indict John, but it did put the fear of God into him. John moved to the Texas side of Red River and thought up another good scheme. And this one was a dilly! It was so good that it bore the qualities of permanence.

If a customer lived in the Indian Territory, John would row him to the Texas side and sell him whiskey. If he lived on the Texas side, John would row that customer to the Indian Territory to sell him whiskey. Consequently, a witness would not testify against Mr. Bootlegger John without incriminating himself. For the customer, who would always be the only witness, would violate the law even more than John. The witness from the Indian Territory had done worse by *introducing* whiskey into the Indian Territory. The witness from the Texas side had broken the law for *possession* of liquor in the Indian Territory. Thus John had his bets coppered going and coming back. Mr. Bootlegger John had at last found a way "to do business on the square," as he explained it.

The Horse Collar King

Among Hutchins' memories was one of the Horse Collar King, a title humorously bestowed on George Hancock, who lived at Thackerville, Chickasaw Nation, in an area near Red River, known now as Love County, Oklahoma. George did considerable horse collar traffic between Gainesville, Texas, across the river, and Thackerville. The most peculiar thing about it was the large size of the collars he bought in Gainesville. Everyone around Thackerville knew he owned only a team of pestle-tailed Indian ponies.

One night, coming up from Gainesville on the Santa Fe passenger train, Hutchins noticed George Hancock had a large horse collar slung over one arm, but nobody else seemed to notice. George seemed just an old honest farmer, who didn't seem to know enough to violate the law. Hutchins watched him get off the train at Thackerville to go home.

Number Six passenger train was known to the marshal's force as "the booze special." The marshal regularly assigned one or more of his deputies to ride it, from time to time.

A few nights after he first saw George Hancock with his big horse collar, Hutchins was on Number Six again, and so was Horse Collar George.

"You seem to be going pretty stout on horse collars, George," Hutchins remarked innocently.

"I'm gettin' things ready for my boys to make another crop," he explained easily.

George had a perfect right to buy his horse collars in Gainesville. Hutchins didn't know then about the standard joke among the local folks, about the number of teams George Hancock had, and the size of the collars they wore.

Still later one night, Hutchins happened to be on Number Six, and so was George. He decided the horse collar business was getting out of hand. Either the old man's boys were careless, or they were breaking some wild horses to harness for farming.

Another point that aroused Hutchins' curiosity was the fact that the horse collar George Hancock was holding now was remarkably like the other two he had seen. He casually sat down by George, and he noticed this made him a little nervous. George held tightly to the huge horse collar and squirmed in his seat.

"George," Hutchins began questioning him quietly, "why do you go to Gainesville after all your horse collars? Why don't you buy them in Thackerville and save train fare? It makes them come pretty high, doesn't it?"

"No, sir! I more than save my fare by going to Gainesville. Thackerville is just a little jerk-water town. The hardware owners there don't carry big enough collars for my horses."

"How many big teams do you have?"

He began stammering an answer, when Hutchins reached for the horse collar. "Let me see that collar, George."

"Oh, hell!" Hancock exploded. "Who put you next?"

Hutchins took poor George Hancock on to Ardmore, where he had a hard time trying to explain to Judge S. B. Bradford

257

how many teams he had, and how he needed size nineteen horse collars for a pair of pestle-tailed ponies. His explanation was very unsatisfactory; and the worse yet for poor George, Commissioner Bradford happened to be a prohibitionist from Kansas. Judge Bradford didn't know how to set a bootlegger's bond under one thousand dollars, and the bondsmen had to be good ones, too, if the bootlegger didn't have the cash, himself.

George Hancock had nearly-grown children. When he finally did make bond, Judge Bradford delivered him a lecture about the immoral example he was setting for his children; and George seemed to love his children. He cried and promised the commissioner he would never sell another drop as long as he lived. This was a promise the old man never broke, but he did attempt to drink the territory dry a few times after that. A few years later, he was killed in Marietta by a kid whose father George had killed in earlier days.

The Punch in Judy

Doc Ellington was a ventriloquist who owned a Punch and Judy show. Between performances, he sold a very popular brand of medicine. Many who attended the show went away with their spirits highly elevated.

All of Doc Ellington's dolls had unusually large legs. The reason for this, it became known, was that each leg was hollow and held about a gallon of whiskey.

Arrested, Doc insisted that the concoction he sold was medicine, which he had a perfect right to sell. He filed suit to get back his confiscated dolls. Before the U.S. Judge got through with him, Doc Ellington changed his mind. He withdrew the suit and drew with it thirty days in jail and fifty dollars fine. He served one and paid the other. But he refused to pay his attorney, and when the lawyer insisted on his fee, Doc Ellington hurried back to the sunflower state of Kansas, where people knew a good thing, and they didn't go about "shooting their mouths off" to deputy marshals.

Very few bootleggers were ever really as ignorant as they pretended to be in the parts they played; and as time and inventions progressed, they kept pace with their schemes and practices. While riding passenger trains, some of them became

258

knowledgeable about the function of air brakes on trains. Then they began placing planks across the rods under box cars, to make a place to ride and carry a grip or suitcase of booze, too. They never rode the rods into town. Just outside the city limits, they pulled the air brakes, stopped the train and fled into the nearby woods. Then they trudged on into town on foot. When a train was stopped this way on a grade with a heavy load, it sometimes took an hour to get rolling again, and this threw the train off schedule. A few even managed to bribe the conductor or brakeman, and rode in the caboose on cushions, or concealed themselves in a closed, empty boxcar, with certain security of a ride.

The Painter's Paint

An old painter in Ada used to carry around a couple of paint buckets that caused no suspicion. Then one day, Hutchins saw him talking to a man named Jess Reed. He began to look around for some places the painter had painted, but could find none. The next morning, Hutchins inspected the buckets and invoiced four half pints and three whole pints of whiskey, and one bottle of gin — but no paint.

The painter was sentenced to thirty days in jail and fifty dollars fine. When he got out of jail, the poor fellow stuck an old rusty nail in his foot, so he said. He had to go around on crutches. His leg swelled to an enormous size and looked as if it might have to be amputated.

That same, unfeeling Deputy Marshal Hutchins who had ruined his paint business, met him on the street, hauled out his six-shooter and whacked his swollen leg a hard blow. Red liquid flowed freely through the bandage; but it wasn't quite red and thick enough for blood, and it certainly didn't smell like blood. Hutchins didn't arrest him again. He was punished enough by losing his booze, but the boys fairly hooted him out of town.

The Widows' Mites

While searching for liquor and other violations, Hutchins ran across some quite clever schemes of women, mostly widows.

He found five pints of whiskey in one widow's sewing machine. The cabinet held one of those drop-type Singer heads which, when removed, left a trap for hiding whiskey under the table lid that usually closed down on the sewing head.

Another had a piece of two-by-four lumber nailed under the window sill. The bottles were pushed back near the center, so they would not show. When she wanted to get out a bottle, she would take a broom handle and shove it through.

Another widow had a false back on the enlarged, framed picture of her dead husband, which she kept locked. When she wanted to take out a bottle for sale, she would take down her husband, lay him face down on the bed, unlock his false back and take out the booze.

Dealers: Past
and Present

Here are a few of the peculiarly interesting nicknames by which bootleggers were known during the years that Bob Hutchins was a United States Deputy Marshal, a United States Constable, Special Agent for Governor Charles N. Haskell and Chief of Police of Ardmore, in the Indian Territory and Oklahoma.

Ace High	Hell Roaring Jake	Rough House
Alkali Ike	High Ball Johnnie	Murphy
Arkansas	Horse Collar	Rufus Rastus
Baggie	Human	Scar Faced Jim
Baggy Pants	Disappointment	Scar Faced Pete
Bandy Shanks	Ikey	Sheeny Mike
Big Bill	Jamaica Ginger Bill	Six-shooter Babe
Big Nell	Jingle Bells	Skeet
Big Nose Kate	Just A Little	Skeeter
Big Shot	Knox	Skey Kate
Big Tit	Leck	Slew Foot
Bitter Creek	Lucky Lou	Slick Tongue
Blue Nose	Missin' Minnie	Smiling Nine

Boll Weevil	Missy Mousey	Snow Ball
Booze Bill	Moving Picture	Spanish Jack
Bowlegged Ira	Odd Ball	Speak Easy Otery
Bullet Head	Odd Money	Speck
Cat Fish Kid	One Wing Dock	Squirrel
Chocolate	Peg Leg Joe	T-Mike
Chocolate Drop	Penny Ante	The Key
Chuck-A-Luck Mike	Percolator	Dispensatory
Coon Can	Peruna	Top Hat
Cotton Eyed Joe	Pinky Perfume	Tow Head
Count Zeke	Polite George	Up-stairs Shoog
Dago Fritz	Quick Change	Weeping Charley
Dam-A-Mule Walter	Charlie	White Mule Shorty
Doll Face	Read The Bones	Whizzing Willie
Dopey	Red	Worty Wonder
Even Money	Red Bird	Whippoorwill
Fat Head	Red Hoss Joe	Wee Weempy
Good Intention Jim	Red Shirt Bill	Zooney Zike
Hard Scramble Ed		

Bob Hutchins swore he could go on for weeks listing such names of liquor peddlers. He reflected that reading off these names to some of the surviving pioneers today would seem like getting a letter from their old home. It might remind a few of them of many a dollar that had spilled away so easily in the good old days that it didn't create any suspicion at the time.

Some of the names used for all liquors — government inspected and that run off in the woods uninspected — both then and now, are: firewater, booze, red-eye, hooch, rot-gut, hog wash, joy juice, conversation water, eye-opener, and dreamwater. Illegal whiskey, made in the mountains of Oklahoma and Arkansas, is still plentiful, despite Federal Alcohol Tax Unit men and state and county officers. It is still referred to as: moonshine, firewater, wild-cat, Kickapoo joy juice, mountain dew, dripping visions, nux varmint, hooch, rot-gut, hog wash, dew poison, and still others. There are some people in Southeastern Oklahoma who will turn down bonded whiskey every time in preference to mountain-made, local stuff. The old-timers who leisurely made good whiskey that was good enough to pass government inspection are all gone. Today, very little good whiskey is distilled in the Kiamichi Mountains, because the "moonshiners" run it off scared, and many do not use copper outfits. They use propane bottles and propane to avoid betraying smoke from wood fires, but the federal officers offset this by sending up small airplanes to spot them.

The illegal traffic of liquors in the Indian Territory and the state of Oklahoma has always been a serious problem. It was one of the constant duties of federal officers to keep it to a minimum in the Indian Nations, because of the evil effects it had upon the Indians.

Many bootleggers in those days committed other crimes, too. Any kind of weapon one carried was generally called a "side kicker"; but some other terms applied to weapons were: pistol, revolver, six-shooter, smoke-gun, six-gun, smoke-pole, hog leg, bloody wagon, Old Betsy, side-line, Old Pard, the difference, a forty-some-odd, my convincer, a gentle persuader, a pistologer, pistoleer, glycerine wagon, dynamite, main stay, a friend-who-wouldn't-be-bribed, shooting iron, and yet others.

Every time a bootlegger was arrested, the officer first frisked him for his weapon, then his liquor. Quite frequently, a bootlegger would elect to "shoot it out" with an officer before he would submit to capture or search.

Bootleggers can rightfully be divided into several classes.

There was one type who rode around from place to place and stopped at stomp dances, home firesides, camp meetings and places of religious worship. This type usually didn't care whose horse he rode, where he sold his stuff, or where the shooting took place.

There was another class that was too lazy to work, would just as soon be in jail as out, never had enough money to buy a new batch of whiskey, white mule, bitters or Jamaica ginger. He relied on the "king pin" of each locality to stake him to a list to sell on commission basis. Outside of the stuff they sold, there was no harm in them at all. They seldom if ever carried a gun; and if they did, they would "hock it at the first *three-ball* shop in sight."

Next was the lonely widow class — with a cow-pen full of almost starving children. Some "king pin" would stake them to a tow-sack full of booze. The desperate widow would take the stuff, put on a bold front and wade into the liquor traffic. A widow with a house full of hungry mouths was up against a cold world. Often her only friend was a bootlegger; and he wouldn't have been, if it had not meant money in his own pocket. In those days, there were no welfare workers, except now and then a circuit rider preacher or a missionary worker. They were very far between, and they usually had only spiritual comfort to offer; nothing to comfort the gnawing pains of hunger in children's stomachs.

Hutchins often "went blind" when searching a widow's home, and usually failed to find any evidence in the official discharge of his duties. Only when ordered to do so did he search such widows' homes. But if some of them became involved in other crimes besides selling a little whiskey, it was then a different matter.

Finally, there was the druggist in larger towns who handled a little liquor to accommodate special customers. The druggist belonged to the church, usually, and was often the leading light of religious circles. He just could not afford to be seen in a bootlegging joint, or even in a bootlegger's company; but he could drink it, and slyly sell it to his friends.

The clientele were usually men and women prominent in society, who went to bed with the grippe, or some other ailment, and would send down to their friendly druggist and have him send out a little more "medicine" to help them through their illness.

The Little Blue Goose

For several days now, Bob Hutchins had lived a dull life in Sulphur, Murray County, with nothing more exciting in his official business than drawing his salary.

Then he received a telegram from "Chief" Marshal Samuel G. Victor, summoning him, without explanation, to appear in the United States Marshal's office in Muskogee, which had been the capital of the Creek Nation. Victor had just been appointed U.S. Marshal of the newly created Eastern District of Oklahoma, on March 31, 1908. From that time forward, there has been only two districts in Oklahoma, Eastern and Western, and only two "Chief" Marshals.

While packing for the trip, Hutchins wondered if he would soon be looking for another job. But when he arrived in Marshal Victor's office in Muskogee, he was greeted cheerfully and courteously by Marshal Victor, whose smile soon faded as he said very grimly, "Bob, they killed one of our deputies and two other men in Tulsa last week. Do you think you can get along with those bootleggers there and not get killed?"

"Yes, Marshal, I believe I can." Hutchins breathed easier now.

265

"Then it's Tulsa for you. Get going!"

Hutchins arrived at Tulsa, took charge of the U.S. Marshal's office there, and was a total stranger in town.

The next day after his arrival, he had a visitor, who bore himself with importance. He told Hutchins he had just returned from Muskogee, where he went before a grand jury and indicted a criminal. When Hutchins received the warrant for the man's arrest, he would consider it a favor if he were allowed to go along and help make the identification and arrest.

Hutchins decided to go along with him and play dumb to find out what he had in his mind. He took his name and telephone number and told him he would let him know when the warrant arrived.

On the third day after his arrival in Tulsa, Hutchins went to the post office about five o'clock in the evening and received a large envelope, which he knew from past experience contained warrants. He stuck them into his inside coat pocket and went back to the office, locked the door and sat down to ponder how to serve the warrants. At nine o'clock, he had not yet made up his mind, but he opened the envelope and found that the first warrant was for the arrest of a W. J. Creekmore. He turned to the telephone directory and found the name, address and telephone number. Then he looked up each of the other warrants in the telephone directory with similar results for most of them.

He picked up the telephone and gave the operator the number of Mr. Creekmore. A lady answered the telephone, who he later learned was Creekmore's wife. He politely informed her that he was the new deputy marshal for the Tulsa district, and that he had a warrant for the arrest of Mr. Creekmore, and that his bond was set at five thousand dollars. He requested that she tell him to appear at the U.S. Marshal's office promptly at nine o'clock the next morning with his bondsman.

He delivered the same message to the others and then sat back and waited.

About eight-thirty the next morning, a big, broad-shouldered man appeared in the office and announced: "Creekmore is my name, sir. I wanted to see what the damned human looked like that has got the nerve to call my home and tell my wife he has a warrant for me, when it is thoroughly understood by all the officers of the Eastern District that there is a thousand dollars of good, lawful money forfeit to any officer who can put me in jail."

"Well now, I'm new in this district. I didn't know that. I regret I have missed the opportunity to earn a thousand dollars by making arrangement for your bond. I should have arrested you without going to the trouble to be polite."

Creekmore let that one pass. "Hutchins," he said, "I want to tell you that if you succeed in keeping up the record you have started here, you will get along."

In the meantime, those busybodies who wanted to help make the arrests found out that the warrants had been delivered to him at five o'clock the day before; and Hutchins had not been seen on the streets since then. They telegraphed Marshal Victor at Muskogee this information, and that it was their opinion that Hutchins had been thrown into the Arkansas River.

Ernest Hubbard, chief deputy marshal, had been an old-timer at Fort Smith. "There's nothing to get alarmed about," he told Marshal Victor. "Hutch can take care of himself."

Marshal Victor was worried, however, and he ordered Hubbard and Deputy Marshal "Dad" Davis to go to Tulsa on the first train.

Bob Hutchins, in the meantime, had telephoned United States Commissioner Ben Conner to bring his court docket over to the marshal's office to take the bond money. Mr. Creekmore assured Hutchins that the entire eighteen wanted men would be there.

Ernest Hubbard and Dad Davis arrived just as Hutchins and Conner began processing the eighteen men as they filed by. Hubbard had a sense of humor, and he began humming an old melody about a bootleggers' reunion and the gang's all here! They all made bond.

After it was over, Creekmore told Hutchins in private, "Now, Mr. Hutchins, whenever you get a warrant for a man who sells whiskey, or introduces it into Tulsa, or anything at all about liquor, just call the Big Four. Tell what you have got, who he is and the amount of the bond. If he is one of us, we will tell you what day we will make his bond, and you can pigeon-hole the warrant until he shows up. He'll show up without delay, then you can make your return to the court." Here Creekmore grinned. "If he does not belong to our bunch, we will tell you

267

when and where you can find him. It is our aim to get rid of all the small fry. The man who does not buy his whiskey at the right place has no standing in Tulsa, in our estimation. If you will just keep up the pace you have started here, you will certainly get along."

Hutchins stayed at Tulsa seven months that tour of duty. During that short time, he and his deputies made five hundred and ninety arrests; and at least three hundred of them were men he had never seen.

One day, he called up the Big Four. Mr. Creekmore, himself, answered the telephone. "Creekmore," he said, "I have a warrant for Jimmie, your private secretary."

"Jimmie has gone to Joplin, Missouri, in our Little Blue Goose," Creekmore readily replied.

The Little Blue Goose was the name of the seventy-five horsepower Mitchell touring car, which had been cut down to a racer for hauling quick loads of whiskey for special occasions. This time, it was for a supper for oil men to be held in Hotel Tulsa, he frankly said. He added in a joking manner, "Hutchins, if you should happen to catch him, you would have some mighty good whiskey for your own use. That blue label stuff is rare and mild and really heart-warming!"

Hutchins thanked him calmly and went out to intercept the Little Blue Goose. Jim evaded him and gave him the merry laugh. The next morning, Hutchins warned him, "Jimmie, the time-limit is on, and I will get your combinaton within twenty days."

Hutchins considered that group of Tulsa bootleggers good sports. When one got caught, he admitted the joke was on himself; and if he got by, it was on the officer.

About fifteen days after his prediction, Hutchins was cruising and watching in his own automobile. He noticed tracks going across a vacant pasture, which looked remarkably fresh and suspicious to him. He opened the gate and drove through, and six hundred yards farther, he came across the confident Jimmie and the Little Blue Goose stuck in a mud hole. All the Little Blue Goose's *eggs* were there. It was loaded with special Joplin, Missouri booze.

Jimmie looked up at Hutchins with a wry face. "Ain't it

hell!" he declared. "A man can't even do a little private business without someone interfering!"

"Why, Jimmie!" Hutchins chided him. "I just figured you needed help to get on into Tulsa. I just came by to unload you and help you along!"

Creekmore met them when they came into town. "Have you and Jimmie formed a partnership?" he joked. "I see you two are running around together a lot lately."

Creekmore made Jimmie's bond, and Hutchins confiscated the Little Blue Goose. After that, he gave the bootleggers plenty of trouble, for he had the fastest automobile on the line.

Close to the Limit

On a fine, sunny Sunday morning in Tulsa, a mysterious telegram came to the United States Marshal's office from Joplin, Missouri, announcing that a Red Ball freight train would arrive there with a carload of booze. Even though the sender was anonymous, the reason for the telegram was very clear, for Bob Hutchins knew that certain elements in Tulsa and Joplin were at war with each other for control of the Tulsa liquor market. If a bootlegger in Tulsa wanted to prosper, he had to know when and where to buy his stock.

Hutchins was alone in the office at the time, so he locked up and went down to the depot to see what was going and coming in the rail yards. The Red Ball freight was already there.

It was a violation of the law for the railway companies to bring liquor into the state, the same as it had been for bringing it into the Indian Territory; but the cattle car in question was labeled "Livestock," and was scheduled to be switched to the Tulsa Race Track. Hutchins climbed on top of the car and waited for the switch engine to get busy.

While sitting there, the vice president of a bank in Tulsa

appeared on the scene with a cheerful, "Good morning, Mr. Hutchins!"

Hutchins acknowledged the greeting and the banker said, "Come down, Mr. Hutchins, I'd like to talk to you a few minutes."

When he reached the ground, the banker said, "Mr. Hutchins, that switch engine will hit that car pretty hard, and if you are knocked off, you will be taken to the hospital, all your expenses paid, and a thousand dollars placed to your credit in my bank."

"All right," Hutchins replied, and climbed back upon the car.

The engine did hit the car hard, but it didn't jar Hutchins off. He investigated the car, found it stocked with liquor, impounded the car and confiscated the contents.

The next morning, Hutchins was invited to come over to the bank and talk to the vice-president again.

"Hutchins," he said jovially, "I was never so proud of anything in my life as I was when you didn't fall for the bribe. Those fellows play rough. They came to me and told me that you didn't have sense enough to take good money and get off their backs. They have something like $110,000 on deposit in this bank, and they threatened to withdraw and deposit it in another bank where someone could oblige them. That's why I just had to come to you yesterday and make that offer."

Hutchins grinned: "You may say I am a darned fool for not taking their money and just keep on taking it." He paused and looked the banker in the eyes. "Maybe I am, but I can live with my conscience. If you think about it, you can possibly recall some instance where an officer took money, and they got the record on him, and he afterward tried to hold his job and go after them. If you cannot recall such an incident, go to some of our cemeteries and read the epitaphs; or ask about certain convicts in the state prison at McAlester."

The banker agreed with him, patted him on the back, gave him a cigar and said, "Keep after them! When you need money, your credit is good here!"

About three weeks later, Marshal Victor paid Hutchins a

271

visit from Muskogee, and inquired, "Hutch, how are you and the hijackers making it?"

"Okay to date, Marshal," he replied, "but they're shooting at my limit pretty stout."

Marshal Victor laughed. "All right, Hutch! Any time they hit the bull's eye, just wire me your resignation!"

Hutchins Takes a Tip

The liquor racket worsened with the discovery and development of oil in Oklahoma at Bartlesville, in the Osage Nation, in April of 1897. The Osages who held the oil and mineral rights to their land during the *twenties* became the richest tribe of people in the world. The oil fever spread with the coming of statehood; and Tulsa, being located where it was, in the center of the greatest oil fields in the nation, drew five railroads into it: two branches of the Saint Louis and San Francisco; one from the southwest corner of the state into Missouri, at the northeast corner; the other from a junction with the Santa Fe at Avard in the northwest corner that joined the main line in West Tulsa. It was also intersected by the Missouri Valley Railroad and the Missouri, Kansas and Texas (Katy) Railroad. And a branch of the line of the Atchison, Topeka and Santa Fe Railroad began at Tulsa and went north into Kansas to join the main line of the Santa Fe at Topeka.

Tulsa just naturally became the Oil Capital of the World. The railroads were the main arteries of transportation and provided the means of shipping out oil, as the inventions of various motors improved and the demands for refined oil in-

273

creased. This all brought more wealth and more industry. All this created positions and jobs, which in turn attracted job hunters. And all this just naturally attracted the bootleggers to Tulsa in huge numbers, because of the influx of the population, which demanded recreation.

Tulsa and all the rest of the growing young giant of a state — known originally in Choctaw as *Okla homa* (home of the red men) — thrived and prospered with the rest of the nation, through the first world war, into the *Roaring Twenties,* and the catastrophic crash of the stock market in 1929.

Those were the good old days, which sometimes got out of bounds in certain places like Tulsa. Marshal Samuel G. Victor picked United States Deputy Marshal Bob Hutchins to handle the situation; and he sat Hutchins down in the middle of it all!

Sitting in his office on an August afternoon, a few days after he and his enforcement officers had captured and destroyed a freight carload of liquor, a certain bootlegger came to Hutchins with a sad story.

"That carload of booze you busted down at Purgatory Siding yesterday was mine," he confessed, "and I'm a blowed up sucker!"

Hutchins doubted his statement, but he was curious about his angle, so he was ready to listen.

"How's that?" he asked.

"I mortgaged my home for the money to buy that liquor."

"Bootlegger's luck!" Hutchins remarked crisply. "Don't you think you had it coming to you for breaking the law?" And he added, "You know you're laying yourself wide open for arrest, don't you? There may be other ears listening."

The man glanced around apprehensively, then grinned. "Now don't pull any tricks on me. I saw there was nobody here but you. Try to use what I say against me, and I'll deny every damned word in court!"

"All right," Hutchins agreed. "I'll listen to your tale of woe and act accordingly."

My wife is an invalid in the worst stage of consumption," the man complained. "The doctors say she can't live in this climate. I know it's not right to bootleg. Even my wife declares it is the will of God to get me out of the racket. But my note is due at the bank in two months, and my home will be taken away from me. My wife is helpless in bed, and I'm plumb broke and desperate! Put yourself in my shoes, Marshal, and tell me what you would do."

While Hutchins pondered the man's problem, the bootlegger, himself, offered a solution.

"Some of my competitors are bound to have tipped off my cargo to you," he asserted, "and I'm going to give you a hot tip, if you'll promise to keep mum and not haul me into court as a witness! If that bunch of cutthroats find out I told you anything, they'll kill us both! Do you promise not to tell, Marshal?"

"I promise."

"Nine o'clock tonight at Bruner Crossing, a man on horseback will ride up onto the roadbed, with two six-shooters on, and a rifle in his saddle scabbard. He will be the guide for three wagonloads of mixed booze, with three armed drivers. You've got a dodger over there on the wall about the guide. The reward is one thousand dollars. In the name of human mercy, Marshal, I want half the reward money to take my wife to Arizona!"

Hutchins studied the face of the bootlegger closely. Previous experience had taught him to be wary of traps. He decided the man was telling the truth. His story tied in pretty well with other bits of information that deputies had picked up here and there. A penniless, harrassed man will do lots of things under pressure that he wouldn't do or even consider under better circumstances.

"It's a deal!" Hutchins told him. "I reckon I'll take a chance."

"Now don't you go out there and get yourself shot up," the bootlegger cautioned, promptly assuming the air of a confederate. "This is a bad bunch you're fooling with, and they will come a-shootin' if you don't get the drop on them!"

Hutchins knew he was right about that, if it was the ones he had in mind. By midnight, he and two other officers had captured the three wagonloads of liquor and their escorts. By four o'clock in the morning, the officers had left behind a shambles of broken glass and puddles of liquor. They went back to Tulsa with the four prisoners, three shotguns, five six-shooters, a rifle and enough liquor for evidence.

About seven o'clock, Hutchins settled himself wearily in his swivel chair to make out his government report. Looking across the street, he saw his ally, the bootlegger, calmly smoking a cigar and looking in his direction with an air of good will.

Uneasiness came over Hutchins as he watched him cross the street with springing steps. Forcing himself to his feet, Marshal Hutchins met him, smile for smile.

"You sure got them okay! Didn't you, Marshal?"

"We did a land office business. You didn't miss a bet on what you told me."

"Well, thanks to you, I did pretty good last night, myself!"

With roosterlike importance, the man perched himself upon a chair. "My wife says to tell you she feels much better already. Fortune has changed our minds about the Lord's will."

Happy as a new father, he extended a cigar. Hutchins took it mechanically, amused at this change from humbleness to grand confidence. His bootlegger confederate was acting like a different man.

"What's this about good fortune and the Lord's will?" Hutchins asked, smiling.

The bootlegger arose and swaggered. "While you and your men were out of town chasing down these two-by-four white line dispensers, I got in three Red Ball freight carloads; and my men and I got all the stuff unloaded and stored away in safe places!"

The bootlegger grinned from ear to ear and swelled to his full height. Puffing generously on his cigar, he remarked, "The drouth in good old Tulsa is now broken for a spell, Marshal! I'm glad I could be of service to you. Come around and see me sometime."

"Just a minute!" Hutchins voice cracked like a whip. The fine mannered bootlegger stopped dead-still.

"Yes?"

"You're under arrest!" Marshal Hutchins announced in the same steel-trap voice.

The bootlegger's face froze in surprise. Then he relaxed and began laughing halfheartedly.

"Come now, Marshal," he said. "All you've got is my own statement. You know you can't prove anything in court I say. A man don't have to testify against himself in court!"

"That is dead certain right," Hutchins agreed. "You don't have to."

"Ah!" exclaimed the bootlegger, smirking. "What's the delay?"

Hutchins let him have it unmercifully. "While you were playing your clever little game of hide-and-seek with me, I had some of my men watching you."

The bootlegger groaned and Hutchins grinned as he played his trump card. "While you were unloading and hiding, they were watching and checking. When I got back from Bruner Crossing, my men had all the information, including names of the parties to whom you distributed your liquor. They are all out now making the arrests. I waited here for you, pal, because you are the king bee of them all!"

State Seal Larceny

Guthrie was the capital of Oklahoma Territory before it united with Indian Territory to become Oklahoma, the forty-sixth state in the United States. The majority of people in Oklahoma Territory intended to keep it there. The "Enabling Act," passed by Congress and signed by President Theodore Roosevelt on June 16, 1906, provided for the qualified voters in both Oklahoma and Indian territories to vote on the question of their becoming one state on November 6, 1906. They voted and approved the proposition, and the state of Oklahoma was born on November 16, 1907.

Charles N. Haskell, the first governor of the state of Oklahoma, declared that the provision to keep the capital at Guthrie until 1913 was invalid and an encroachment on state sovereignty. He agreed with the citizens who wanted the capital to be in Oklahoma City. Three cities were in the running for the permanent location of the capitol site; Guthrie, Oklahoma City, and Shawnee.

Governor Haskell issued a proclamation calling for a special election to be held on the capital question on Tuesday, June 14, 1910; but on second thought, he struck through the typewritten date with his pen and changed the voting day from Tuesday to June 11, which was a Saturday.

A few days before the election, he was in Tulsa with his wife, on their way to Muskogee to vote. Tate Brady was a good friend of the governor; and he and his wife always stayed at Brady's hotel. Governor Haskell knew that Bob Hutchins was the United States Marshal's office deputy marshal in Tulsa then. He telephoned Hutchins to meet him in the Brady hotel on an important matter. But the governor met him halfway between the hotel and the marshal's office. Haskell was nearly six feet tall and weighed 175 pounds. His blue eyes were glowing and he was smiling as they gripped hands. Hutchins knew him well enough to suspect that the governor had something in mind.

"Hutchins," Governor Haskell declared, "you have been on my mind with your backbone, guts, gall, and political pull for some time!"

He knew Haskell was the type of man who would let you know if he liked you; and if he didn't, you'd know that, too. Hutchins grinned at the governor's introductory remark. He knew Haskell was referring to his own activities in helping him get elected to office. It had always seemed humorously odd to Governor Haskell, because Hutchins was a Republican, and Haskell a Democrat.

"You're my governor, Charlie," Hutchins remarked. "I wanted it the way it is. With your special referendum election coming up on the capital issue, what are you hatching now?"

"Just this," he declared, coming to the point. "I'm looking no farther for an officer I can trust. I'm giving you instructions now."

He handed Deputy Marshal Hutchins a book of blank checks on a Tulsa bank. "Use expenses freely," he said. "The money will be in the bank in your name. Catch the next train for Oklahoma City. Go to the Lee Huckins Hotel and register as Office Deputy United States Marshal, Tulsa. Don't use your name. Go to your room. Don't talk with anyone. Just wait."

Governor Haskell paused, knowing Hutchins was curious. "I can't explain now, Bob, but I will later. This is a job of trust." His blue eyes sharpened as he warned, "There may be certain

279

risks. That's why I've chosen you. I'll take care of you, whatever happens."

That was all. Being an officer, accustomed to accepting orders without question, Hutchins asked none now.

In Oklahoma City, Hutchins waited in his hotel room, except for going out for meals, until about four o'clock in the afternoon of the election day. Then there was a light knock on his door. Hutchins opened it and saw his old friend, James Bourland, a state officer. He knew Bourland was a brave and dependable man.

"The gov'nor said you'd be waitin' here," Bourland drawled, with a grin. "Danged if you ain't!"

Hutchins grinned back at him. "Now what do we do?"

"My friend," Bourland announced pompously, "we're going to take a little historical ride over to Guthrie. It has something to do with this special election being held today. The results are nearly a foregone conclusion."

"Suits me," Hutchins agreed. "Anything to break the monotony."

He buckled on his bone-handled six-shooters and followed James Bourland out of the hotel. At the curb, Bill Light, another officer, was waiting for them in a brand-new automobile. Bourland and Hutchins climbed into the jalopy and they chugged away.

Neither James Bourland nor Bill Light briefed him about their mission. The distance to Guthrie was only about thirty miles, but it was a rough road, and they drove into Guthrie before the middle of the night in a hard, downpouring rain. They stopped in front of the capitol.

James Bourland left the automobile, saying, "I'll be back in a few minutes." He disappeared in the rain and darkness. In five or ten minutes, he returned with three men. When they came close enough to the vehicle, Hutchins recognized W. B. Anthony, Governor Haskell's private secretary, Bill Cross, the state secretary, and the capitol porter, a Negro who was called Crow.

Crow thrust a package about twice the size of a cigar box into Hutchins' hands. "Heah 'tis, Mistah Hutch!" he said.

As Hutchins clutched the package, he felt that it was tied and sealed.

"What goes on here?" Hutchins wondered, but nobody explained anything; and he decided to stifle his curiosity and play along with the rest of them.

Then James Bourland spoke up formally: "As an Oklahoma State officer, I place this instrument into your hands for safe-keeping, Marshal Hutchins. You, a federal officer, are charged with its safe delivery into the hands of Governor Charles N. Haskell."

He was ceremonious, but brief. Then he, Anthony and Cross got into the automobile, and Bill Light drove them away, leaving Crow alone in the rain and the dark.

The return journey was as silent as the first, but even slower. The rain came down in torrents and threatened to drown out their motor. Several times, they almost got struck as they slogged and slid along cautiously over the dirt highway.

They found Governor Haskell and a large group of friends in the Lee Huckins lobby. They had come from Tulsa by special train after midnight on the day of the election. Tate Brady had already heard unofficially by telephone that Oklahoma City had been voted by the sovereign people of Oklahoma as the site for the capitol. The unofficial, but still reliable, count before the final tally was over 98,000 votes for Oklahoma City, over 24,000 for Guthrie, and over 7,000 for Shawnee.

There was a jubilant crowd milling around in the hotel lobby. The officers found Governor Haskell, and Hutchins said, "Here's your package, Governor," as he thrust it into the governor's hands.

"Thanks a million, Bob," Haskell said. "Just wait here a few minutes."

Governor Haskell took the package over to the clerk's desk, where he and Bill Cross, Secretary of State, and W. B. Anthony were busy for a few minutes. Then Governor Haskell returned and handed the package back to Hutchins, saying, "Bob, we don't have a capitol yet, and there's no official place for this. You guard it with your life. Wait for my next orders. Don't fail me, Hutch. I'm betting my shirt on you."

Hutchins noticed the package had been opened, for the seal was broken, but the package was retied.

After breakfast, Hutchins, James Bourland and Bill Light went to D. Wolfe's wholesale and retail store and saloon. They figured they could stand a drink after their all-night trip in the mud and rain. They were standing at the bar when Deputy Marshals Heck Thomas and Bill Tilghman appeared on the scene.

"Mind if we join your party, Hutch?" Heck Thomas asked.

"Not at all!" Hutchins laughed. "You're plenty welcome. Looks as if the situation is building up to where it will be a matter of the more the merrier."

For Hutchins, the case was beginning to take on sinister overtones. This was no accidental meeting, he knew. Like himself, Bourland, and Light, the two new arrivals were wearing two six-shooters each. When Heck Thomas and Bill Tilghman hung two six-shooters on their belts, they expected trouble.

"What will it be, gents?" he invited.

"Same as yours," said Thomas. A bartender set out straight whiskey.

"Hutchins," said Tilghman, "we're with you in this deal all the way. You call the play."

"We're glad to have you men with us," Hutchins declared with feeling.

"Hutch, suppose you have the manager put that package over there in the safe," James Bourland suggested quietly, "and tell him that no other hands are to touch it."

Hutchins called the manager, handed him the package with instructions, and asked for a telegram blank. If this was to be a waiting game for action, he had a few more staunch friends to invite to the party. He sent the following telegram:

JUNE 12, 1910

BUCK GARRETT
CHIEF OF POLICE
ARDMORE, OKLAHOMA

COME FIRST TRAIN. BRING BANKS KING, PLENTY AMMUNITION AND NERVE.

HUTCHINS

That afternoon, Buck Garrett showed up alone.

"Where's Banks King?" Hutchins asked.

Buck grinned. "I left him in charge of the office."

282

Hutchins must have shown his disappointment, for Buck Garrett slapped him on the back and laughed heartily. "Don't worry, Hutch, I'll make two. How about a drink?"

They joined the others in D. Wolfe's place. There they all stood again at the bar, talking and joking, when the sheriff of Logan County, from Guthrie, walked in, with eighteen deputies.

The silence that came over the place was as rigid as death. When the Logan County Sheriff spoke, Hutchins was more surprised at what he said than at his sudden appearance.

"Hutchins," the sheriff demanded softly. "I'm asking you for the Great Seal of the State of Oklahoma. It belongs in Guthrie, despite the election, until nineteen hundred thirteen."

Hutchins flashed a quick glance at James Bourland and saw him grinning thinly. Heck Thomas and Bill Tilghman were tight-lipped and grimly alert. Bill Light and Buck Garrett were poised and expectant.

So that was it! Hutchins' first impulse was to laugh in the Logan County Sheriff's face. He had helped steal the state seal and the capital, in a way, and he hadn't even known it. Charlie Haskell had really pulled a fast one!

Hutchins was acting under orders of the highest state authority. Governor Haskell had told him he was protected against any eventuality. He had no intention of shirking his duty now. He looked the sheriff and his crowd over carefully. He was really stalling for just a few more moments of precious time. The five officers who were with him were counted among the most fearless in Oklahoma.

In a gunfight like this, anybody could get killed. Hutchins gambled that the sheriff was thinking the same thing. He decided to be calm and patient.

"What will you boys have to drink, Sheriff?" Hutchins drawled in friendly tones.

The sheriff's eyes held Hutchins' smiling face for a long moment. Yielding cautiously, he said, "Whiskey straight."

Every man turned to the bar, and a wave of relief went through the room. The bartenders sprang to their duties.

Raising his glass, Hutchins proposed a grim, blunt toast. "Here's to the few men left standing when the smoke clears away!" He looked that grim line of men full in their faces.

"Drink hearty, men," he invited evenly, "for this may be your last."

Hutchins dashed down his shot, set his glass on the bar and then spoke again. "Mister Sheriff," he drawled, boldly, "what you say is the state seal is in a package in yonder safe. The contents, until you declared your business here, were unknown to me. But I have orders — and so do these federal and state officers with me — direct from the governor of Oklahoma to defend that seal with our lives. If anyone touches that package, the shooting starts."

The tension was almost explosive. The sheriff studied him for a long moment. He was obviously a man of cold nerve and sound judgment. His eyes roved over his opponents and saw that all of them were ready to back Hutchins all the way. Hutchins read his thoughts, saw him making his decision. His voice was husky as he relaxed and smiled. "This time, the drinks are on me." His smile broadened. "After all," he added, "what's a little state capital between friends?"

Again the bartenders got busy and served them. When they drained their glasses, the sheriff turned to his posse and said, "Let's go back to Guthrie, men. We can't buck the governor."

There have been so many versions told about the removal of the state seal and the capital from Guthrie to Oklahoma City that no incident in Oklahoma history is more clouded by legend. In 1932, Charles N. Haskell was asked to tell his own true story of the removal, and he said, "I never spoil a good story anyone wants to tell, especially in the middle of it, whether it is fact or just romance."

But referring to the night of the election, he recalled: "I had asked Tate Brady to get the results of the election as soon as possible. When my wife and I returned to Tulsa from Muskogee that night, Brady had telephoned around over the state and he had received reports significant enough for us to know that Oklahoma City had been voted the permanent capitol site. I said to Brady, 'When can we get a train to Oklahoma City?' He said, 'Not until tomorrow, as the midnight train has already gone.' Then I told him, 'Call the division office on the telephone,' and I asked the agent to send a locomotive and a coach to Tulsa at once to make an Oklahoma City trip. In

284

about thirty or forty minutes, the special engine and a sleeping car was ready for us.

"I looked around and invited every Oklahoman in sight to make the trip, and a number of them went with us straight to Oklahoma City. We all took this special train and reached the Lee Huckins Hotel about six o'clock the morning of the twelfth.

"One thing I did before leaving Tulsa was to telephone my then private secretary, W. B. Anthony, at Guthrie to get the Secretary of State with his official seal and meet us at the Lee Huckins Hotel in Oklahoma City early in the morning.

"We really had been visiting all night and had not been asleep, and everybody was hungry. They found a place to eat our breakfast; and somebody said, 'Well, let's go in and get our breakfast.' I said, 'Just a minute.' I stepped up to the clerk's desk in the hotel, got a sheet of paper — a hotel letterhead — a pen and ink, and I wrote the official proclamation based on the returns, which I thought were plainly adequate, declaring Oklahoma City the capital of the state of Oklahoma.

"I signed it as governor, Bill Cross put the official signature and seal on this proclamation and, complying with the law which said such proclamation should be posted in a public place, I posted it on the wall of the Lee Huckins Hotel, adjoining the clerk's desk.

"Then I said, 'Very well, now I am ready to have breakfast in the state capitol.'"

On the night of June 15, just four nights after the election, Governor Haskell told a cheering crowd of fifteen thousand, in Oklahoma City:

"It has never been the policy of your present governor of Oklahoma to let another man get to first base before he gets there himself. If there are to be any injunction suits, he proposes to let those suits find him where he wants to be, rather than at the place from which he is trying to get, and that is why the official seat of government for the state of Oklahoma today is in Oklahoma City."

Guthrie citizens, headed by Judge Frank Dale, obtained a district court injunction against the move, but Governor Haskell ignored the summons. Frank Greer, editor of the *Oklahoma State Capitol*, a bitter foe of Haskell's, denounced the governor for his removal proclamation with blazing headlines: "CZAR CHARLES HASKELL ISSUES HIS IMPERIAL UKASE AT NEW STATE 'CAPITOL.'"

Most secondary state officers and the supreme court chose to stay in Guthrie, while the Oklahoma City Chamber of Commerce, called upon to furnish quarters for state offices, issued an apology for the sudden change. Referring to the Enabling Act for statehood, which had designated Guthrie as the capital until 1913, Sidney L. Brock, the Chamber president, issued this statement:

"Oklahoma City's Chamber of Commerce, businessmen and citizens in general, were greatly surprised at the sudden call of Governor Haskell for state quarters, and by the announcement that the seat of government is now transferred to Oklahoma City. We had no intimation or thought that the capitol would be removed until 1913, and we were quite sincere in our campaign statements that there would be no effort by the Chamber of Commerce or citizens of Oklahoma City to remove the state capitol until 1913."

Lee Cruce, an Ardmore banker, was elected the second governor of Oklahoma on November 8, 1910. When the supreme court, a week later, held the initiative petition for the capitol removal to be legally defective, Haskell bided his time. Terms of the old legislature would expire fifteen days after the election. On Saturday, November 19, 1910, he drove over to Guthrie by automobile to have lunch with his daughter and son-in-law, the Leslie Niblacks.

After lunch, Governor Haskell strolled down to the courthouse — the interim capitol — and issued a proclamation convoking the new legislature in special session in Oklahoma City on November 28.

When the legislature met, the senate balked on the idea of Putnam City as the site for the state capitol, which had been selected by Governor Haskell's capitol commission. With civic leaders urging a more central location, the capitol site committee finally chose a location astride the Lincoln Boulevard at Northeast 22nd Street.

Although Oklahoma City had doubled in population in three years since statehood, this young metropolis had been hard pressed to meet the state demands for the capitol site. Now

Governor Haskell demanded an additional $71,200 to wind up the Putnam City matter before signing the bill.

By 6:30 on the evening of December 29, 1910, the citizens' committee had raised $66,000, which they reported to the governor; and to make good the remainder, the members organized a capitol expense company. The governor accepted their pledge, and boarded a train for Guthrie at 7:10.

The northbound Santa Fe would meet the southbound train at Guthrie. Governor Haskell and W. A. Ledbetter, his legal advisor, got off the northbound train at Guthrie, went into the Harvey House for a cup of coffee, and there at 8:40 the same evening, Governor Haskell signed the three bills, which finally removed the capitol.

As the train bearing Haskell and Ledbetter reached Oklahoma City at 10:30 that night, "whistles screeched, bells rang, and automobile horns tooted," the *Oklahoma City Times* newspaper reported. Governor Haskell was met by a reception committee and paraded to the Lee Huckins Hotel. After twenty years of struggle, Oklahoma City was definitely and permanently the capital city of Oklahoma.

Hell in Ardmore

Bob Hutchins had been an enforcement officer under Governor Charles N. Haskell, the first governor of Oklahoma, and a holdover officer while Lee Cruce, the second governor of Oklahoma, elected in 1910, was in office. In that year, he was authorized to conduct the United States census in Southern Oklahoma. Then he became an associate deputy sheriff of the Sheriffs' Association of Oklahoma, to help enforce the law and order of oil field towns.

At this time, oil fields were being discovered throughout the new state and, like all boom towns, conditions soon grew so hectic that the sheriffs of the entire state had banded together to cope with the unlawful conditions. Hutchins was a close friend of the nationally famous Sheriff Buck Garrett. They had ridden together as deputy marshals, split accounts, cooked and eaten at the same campfires, taken turns guarding each other and watching prisoners while they alternately slept, and had even shared hot lead meant for both of them.

In 1915, Bob Hutchins "threw his hat into the political ring" for chief of police of Ardmore. Many looked upon his act with dismay and were sure he had committed political suicide, because he filed on the Republican ticket. He had dared do this in an election in Southern Oklahoma, even then so strongly Democratic it was called "Little Dixie"; where the Democratic Primary election results very definitely settled any contests for all public offices.

Talk went around in Ardmore that Bob Hutchins didn't have a ghost of a chance to become the chief; and this talk persisted even on the day of the general election, April 30, 1915. But the forward-looking people, who wanted to be certain that Ardmore would be rid of many of its nefarious vices, remembered Hutchins' reputation as the nemesis of bootleggers and as a fearless, honest and hard-riding officer, who had already come up against all classes of criminals. These good citizens kept their mouths shut and voiced their sentiments on the ballots. Hutchins was given a popular vote at the polls that left no doubt in anybody's mind. They had discarded politics to vote for a man of action.

Hutchins took his election seriously. He knew he had a job to do; not a soft, swivel chair to sit in while shady characters plied their trades in the same tradition.

There is a street in Ardmore named Caddo. In the Indian Territory days, where this street ended at the north edge of town, a dirt road ran out to Caddo Creek, about five miles away. From that time, when many old-style western gunfights took place on the board sidewalks and in Caddo Street, blood flowed profusely enough for this roughest street in town to become known later nationally as notorious *Bloody Caddo* — one of the toughest streets in the entire world.

When Bob Hutchins became chief of police in Ardmore in 1915, Caddo was a roaring lion, still craving human blood, day and night, as men's tempers exploded in dispute, grudge, or vengeance. That was about the time Captain Maggie Hobbs of the Salvation Army came to Ardmore and found her way into the hearts of thousands of Ardmoreites and dedicated her life to the cause of God and humanity. With his eyes moist with memories that faded the steel glint in them, Hutchins told this biographer: "I've seen the time when Captain Maggie stood on one corner of Bloody Caddo and Broadway with a Bible in her hands and religion in her soul; and I stood on the opposite corner with my old six-shooter in my hand and a

289

firm determination in my mind! What Maggie and I did to that Caddo bunch of renegades was a miracle!"

Bob Hutchins' election left a bad taste in the mouths of the grafting political clique which had opposed him fiercely. They filed impeachment proceedings against him before he was even sworn into office. But Hutchins hired Judge Stillwell H. Russell as his attorney, and his opposition got no farther against him in the court room than it had in the election. Nevertheless, the clique, which he called the sobriquet, "Upper Ten," continued to hound, harass and criticize his administration as long as he was police chief.

Indian Summer had arrived with the first day of autumn. Hutchins had been in his office all day wrestling with the problems caused by the Upper Ten political ring to thwart his successful administration, when he decided to go home for a good rest. His mind wearily reviewed the trials of the long day, even after he had gone to bed.

He soon found himself rolling and tossing from one side of the bed to the other, studying rebuttals to the accusations of his political enemies. In the hour just before dawn, he arose, put on his clothes, made breakfast and decided he was sufficiently fortified for the day's turmoils.

He walked down G Street to East Main and then headed west for another day's scrapping with the Upper Ten. He had no way of knowing that the worst catastrophe in Ardmore's history was eminent. It would require all his ingenuity and resources and dwarf all other problems such as the Upper Ten's connivings.

When he reached East Main Street and turned west, he noticed a Negro bootblack across the street just in time to see him take a bottle of rot-gut booze out of his pocket and set it down on a box on the sidewalk before sneaking away.

Hutchins crossed the street to pick up the bottle and heard angry words around the corner. There, he saw two colored bootleggers, with drawn pistols, arguing that each had the right to make the sale by right of discovery. Hutchins knew they were working themselves up to a heat and the nerve to kill each other.

In a stern voice, he said, "If you boys have any business to

290

attend to, high-tail it. Skeedaddle and get busy, or I will put you both in jail."

Surprised, they both sprinted away.

It was then that Hutchins noticed a strong odor of gasoline in the air. As he crossed the railroad tracks, he saw the tank car of gasoline in the freight yard to his left, just east of the freight depot, making a screeching noise with escaping gas. A closer examination sent a shock of fear through him. He realized the awful fate of Ardmore, if the car exploded.

He met Ebb Evans, the Santa Fe freight agent, coming out of his office. "Ebb," he said, addressing the agent with alarm, "that leaking tank car over there is dangerous. As chief of police, I demand that it be taken outside of Ardmore before it explodes and kills half the people in this town. That tank car contains 250 barrels of high-test gasoline!"

"Listen, Mr. Hutchins," Evans replied, "I'm just the freight agent here, and you still carry a card as special agent under the chief of detectives for the Santa Fe. Try your luck with him and see how far you get."

Hutchins saw a group of railroad men on the depot platform. He walked over to them and asked if they were the switch crew. A big Irishman he had known in Ragtown answered, "Yes, we are."

"I just notified Ebb Evans to move that tank car that's leaking gas to outside the corporation limits."

"If you and Ebb Evans want that car moved, you and him can move it. We wouldn't touch it with a ten-foot pole!"

Hutchins went to the police station. When he arrived, both telephones were ringing. He picked up a receiver and a voice demanded the removal of the tank car of gasoline outside the city and ordered him to get busy.

Hutchins answered, "I just came from the freight depot, and Ebb Evans refused me. You are a resident and a taxpayer, I presume. You tell Ebb Evans, the Santa Fe freight agent, about your troubles."

The telephones kept ringing, and Hutchins took down the receivers and then walked over to a real estate agent's office, used his telephone and notified the acting mayor, J. M. Hoard, and the three city commissioners — Joe M. London, H. T. Hunt and W. C. DeWitt — to come at once to his office and help him

291

get rid of the tank car before it exploded and blew up the town. Val Mullens, the mayor, was out of town on business.

In just a few minutes, they were all in his office.

Chief Hutchins explained what he had already tried to do. Joe London, police and fire commissioner, wrote out a notice to remove the tank car outside the corporate limits immediately, and all four men signed it.

Hutchins took the notice to Ebb Evans for him to execute the order. He merely read it, wrote one word, "Impossible," on the bottom of the order, courteously signed it and handed it back. Hutchins was apprehensive and worried. The instrument he placed in his inside pocket absolved him of all blame about the situation, but it did not remove the danger. He walked back toward the police station, ate his lunch at the American restaurant, saw a few friends and told them about the danger in the freight yards he couldn't get moved, and returned to his office.

The city marshal from Gainesville was there, having come after a thief and a stolen automobile, which Hutchins' policemen had captured. While they were talking, the tank car of gasoline exploded.

The police station shook and vibrated, windows crashed and the ground quaked. In the twinkling of an eye, the eastern half of the Ardmore business district had been completely destroyed. Damage done over the rest of the town was also quite extensive. Not many windowpanes were left unsmashed in Ardmore; and windowpanes were shattered miles away. The force of the blast had radiated outward from Ardmore like rings on a calm lake when a rock has been tossed into it.

In the instant of the explosion, forty-one persons were killed. Many more people were left bleeding and dying, and the toll finally reached the half-hundred mark. Worse yet, many more were trapped under the caved-in buildings, and would suffocate, if not rescued soon. It seemed that the blast had instantly consumed all oxygen where the pockets of gasoline vapors had been collecting, thus forming vacuums, causing the walls of many buildings to collapse inward.

On October 6, just nine days later, the total dead reached forty-three, with more dying. The explosion had taken place at 2:27 P.M., on September 27, 1915.

Ardmore had for years been the largest inland cotton market

292

in the world. Ginning season had begun. As usual, the intersection of Washington and Main Streets was jammed with wagons of farmers' cotton for many miles around, who had been to the gins in Ardmore. They had driven their wagons to the market center, with the bales of cotton they wanted to sell. Some of the teams panicked and ran away; but alert farmers, and those who had their brakes set securely, managed to avert runaways.

There were many flimsy, wooden buildings in Ardmore at that time. Most all of these from Washington Street down East Main Street and across the railroad tracks were flattened or burning. The fire department, consisting of a few regular firemen and many volunteers, did an excellent job to bring all fires under control, and they helped with the rescue tasks.

Chief Hutchins had notified Governor Robert L. Williams, who declared martial law in Ardmore, and sent state troops within a few hours.

Never before in the petroleum industry history had there been such a tragedy; but in 1915, the industry was still young. The blast at Ardmore was counted as one of the greatest explosions in history. *Bloody* Caddo Street, for a couple of blocks both north and south off of Main Street, was a holocaust of fire; and the same was true a block east and a block west on Main Street, and around the passenger and freight depots.

The fire department was taxed beyond its capabilities, mostly because of lack of proper equipment and improper water pressure, caused by broken water lines.

The next morning, a committee of Santa Fe officials, headed by E. P. Ripley, president of the Atchison, Topeka and Santa Fe Railway Company, met in Ardmore with the city commissioners, the acting mayor and some of the prominent businessmen to hold an investigation.

Chief Hutchins was sent for and questioned carefully. Chief Attorney S. T. Bledsoe, for the Santa Fe Railroad, had already talked to Ebb Evans before the meeting. Now he fixed Bob Hutchins with an impassive stare and asked, "Mr. Hutchins, did you officially notify our agent, Mr. Ebb Evans, to remove that tank car outside the limits of the city of Ardmore?"

"Yes, sir, I did."

"How?"

"Verbally as chief of police, and later by written notice, signed by all the city commissioners and the mayor."

"What was Mr. Evans' reaction to the notice?"

"He first rejected my verbal request, saying he had no authority in the matter. Then he very courteously wrote his reply, 'Impossible,' beneath the order, signed it and handed it back to me."

"Do you still have that notice?"

"I do," Hutchins replied, and handed it to him.

Bledsoe read the note carefully with a faint smile of chagrin. He turned to his assistant, P. M. Jackson, the Santa Fe attorney for Ardmore, and said, "Jack, we are stuck!"

The two attorneys went into a huddle with President E. P. Ripley and the Santa Fe committee. Then Bledsoe came back to Chief Hutchins and asked, "Mr. Hutchins, will you lend us six of your most trusted policemen?"

Without asking why, Hutchins replied, "Gladly, sir."

He assigned to Bledsoe: C. G. Sims, Lee McCoy, Dow Brazil, Dan Blackburn, Ed Leach and Will Fraser. Bledsoe instructed them to select twenty-two businessmen, who had made a success with their respective businesses, who represented a good cross section of intelligent thinking in Ardmore. Bledsoe appointed a Board of Arbitration from the list to settle all claims against the Santa Fe Railway Company. Then he appointed ex-governor Lee Cruce as chairman of the board; and the difficult, but well executed, task of the board began.

In the meantime, the rescue work and the general cleaning up of the debris continued. Precarious walls, left dangerously tottering, were pulled down by the workers, headed by the fire chief and his men.

It was discovered that the spark which touched off the explosion had been created by a railroad mechanic. The Santa Fe yard superintendent, Mr. Cox, took the mechanic to the tank car to try to stop the escaping gasoline and vapor. Cox had expected the mechanic to use wrenches to tighten the control nut and thus stop the leak; but instead, he started hammering on the big nut with the heavy pipe wrench.

"No! No!" Mr. Cox warned. "Don't do that!" His warning was loud enough for railroad workers to hear it across the railroad yard; but the mechanic had not heard it over the noise he was making. When Cox saw he did not hear him and kept hammering, he started running away. He was only about fifty yards away when the spark he feared ignited the high-test vapors. Mr. Cox lived less than a week, swathed in bandages soaked in linseed oil. Only remnants of the mechanic were ever found. One was a finger with a gold ring on it. Another was his pocket watch, stopped at 2:27 P.M.

The Santa Fe paid out millions of dollars in claims, ranging from just a few dollars to many thousands, for both lives and property, without a single lawsuit. The Board of Arbitration, composed of leading citizens, did a fine job of justice for the unfortunate people of Ardmore.

When the rebuilding of Ardmore began, the town's commissioners passed a zoning ordinance, which prevented the business section from being reconstructed with wood. Some of the wooden buildings had been built back out of lumber after the fire of April 18, 1895, which had destroyed much of the business district then. On the wreckage of old Ardmore, a more permanent and modern city was built.

Chief of Police Bob Hutchins, during the tenure in office, started a movement to clean up vice and corruption that succeeded to a remarkable degree. Dope addicts and *pushers* began to disappear. Liquor flowed regularly down the gutters of Ardmore instead of down some gullets.

The Three Sleuths

When Bob Hutchins took office as chief of police in Ardmore, Oklahoma, his first official act was a secret one in which he appointed two men as anonymous policemen. They were J. G. Spreckelmeyer and H. G. Stong.

They never wore badges and they never made a single arrest, but they probably caused more arrests than any known man on the force, especially during Hutchins' first year. They did not appear on the regular police roll. They went about their usual occupations around town, but their eyes and ears were open; and they reported privately every bit of information they thought Hutchins should know about the vice rackets and other violations of the law.

J. G. Spreckelmeyer sold advertising for *The Daily Ardmoreite,* the city's daily newspaper. He went all over the business district and associated with people at all levels.

H. G. Stong was a cabinet builder, and such a good one that he was in demand most of the time. When a bootlegger or dope pusher employed him to build a secret cabinet, wall safe, or some other type of clandestine cache, Stong made drawings of the construction and its location and turned it over to Chief

296

Hutchins. When it was time to make a raid on one of these locations, Chief Hutchins sent a couple of his policemen, or more when necessary. If they returned empty-handed, he went alone and brought back the goods and the bootlegger or dope pusher. Of course, it was an easy task for him, but to his policemen, it seemed uncanny.

Spreckelmeyer and Stong were paid out of funds of his expense account, which he explained to the city commissioners as "endeavoring expenses." This covered many little necessary expenses that were recognized by them.

Another "ace in the hole" Chief Hutchins had for his third sleuth was a little Negro, known about town as Snowball. Hutchins would fix Snowball a bunk in the jail sometimes at night, hand him a dollar and a half and send him out to buy a pint of whiskey from some suspicious source. He instructed Snowball to pay attention to where the bootlegger got the whiskey. When Snowball returned with the whiskey, he would give Chief Hutchins the information, and go on to his bunk and guest cell. Then Hutchins would usually wait until later in the night, or the next morning, before sending his men to raid the place.

But poor Snowball decidedly developed a thirst for liquor, which proved to be his own doom.

Chief Hutchins' tip about one of his biggest confiscations in Ardmore came about in the same way that he had been informed by telegram of a carload shipment from Joplin, Missouri, in Tulsa a few years before.

This tip-off, too, was telegraphed from Joplin.

JOPLIN, MISSOURI
NOVEMBER 22, 1916

J. R. HUTCHINS
CHIEF OF POLICE
ARDMORE, OKLAHOMA

SANTA FE CAR NUMBER 6282 STOLEN RACE HORSES BILLED STOCK YARDS ARDMORE. INVESTIGATE.

JOHNNY SURESHOT

When the freight train rolled into Ardmore, Chief Hutchins and a coterie of his men and federal officers were there to ride herd on the stolen racehorses. They opened the stock car and found barrels of whiskey.

They hauled the fifty and sixty gallon barrels of whiskey up Main Street, turned left down A Street, and unloaded the illegal spirits behind the old Dunlap Building. There they rolled out the barrels without polka music, opened up the bungholes and let the gutters fill.

The incident attracted much attention. A crowd gathered around and watched with mixed emotions. Some laughed, while others deplored the loss of so much whiskey.

The Daily Ardmoreite gave the event much favorable notice. Jack Snyder, a seasoned, witty veteran reporter, who knew good whiskey when he found it, had this to say in the issue of *The Daily Ardmoreite* that came out that evening, November 23, 1916:

TELL ME, BIG CHIEF ROBERT!
Oh, tell me, Big Chief Hutchins,
    And tell me quick and true,
Why is it you're always grouchin'
    'Gainst booze so truly blue?
Why, honest Big Chief Robert,
    In this town of Old Ardmore,
We hate to see you, Robert,
    Shut out our booze galore!

We've always had our *mornin's*
    And then a wee drop more;
Why strain your mind thus scorin'
    And close this good town's door
'Gainst nimble, booted-legger,
    Who's plied his subtle callin'
And eased both white and nigger
    From eve to early mornin'?

Who had sold men of ev'ry nation —
    The paleface and the Choc —
That joy-made creation —
    Now why seekest thou to block
The flowing of the dollars

From out of the hole-patched jeans;
The gentle, nimble dollars we
    Exchange for nightmare dreams?

We've always had our tipplin',
    Since the days now old in story,
When the buffler chased the Injun
    In all his pristine glory,
'Cross plains where snowdrops bobble
    And sand fleas hop and bite,
Since then we've had our noddles,
    And our inwards, day and night, —

Filled with the good red likker;
    Now, Bob, please be a sport,
Just say you'll let 'er flicker;
    And we'll forgive your erring
And the way you've acted up.
    We're dry as sun-dried herring
Since you closed the wet spots up!

While the other officers were busy emptying a dozen barrels of whiskey at once, Snowball sidled up to Chief Hutchins and whispered, "Chief, how about my gettin' down the street a little way and gettin' me a sip or two ob dat good likker 'fore it all go to waste?"

Hutchins pretended not to hear the little Negro, and moved over to another barrel just being opened. He promptly forgot about the little Negro; and when the work was finished, one of his policemen called his attention to Snowball, who was limber drunk beside the building. They took him up and carried him to his usual bunk in the jail, thinking he would sleep it off by morning.

But the next morning, they discovered that Snowball had overloaded his stomach and his physical system with so much of the poisonous stuff that his heart had pumped so hard it had broken down under the load. Snowball was dead.

Thus ended the life and career of poor Snowball; an un-recognized, uncommissioned member of Chief Hutchins' police force. All Hutchins could do now for his little old friend was to see that he received decent burial.

Six-Shooter Man

The Clara Smith Hamon case in Ardmore, Oklahoma, attracted widespread national attention; but few people today know the events that led to the unfortunate shooting of Jake L. Hamon, one of the greatest oil promoters in the world. He was a multimillionaire at the time of his death.

Some two years before the tragedy, Bob Hutchins had been hired by Jake L. Hamon to protect his oil field interests, and to be a kind of bodyguard for him.

Jake L. Hamon had graduated from law school at Kansas State University in 1898. Then he decided to seek his fortune in the Oklahoma Territory. He clerked in a store at Newkirk, in Kay County. When the Kiowa-Comanche-Apache country was opened to settlement by land lottery in 1901, he went with the crowd to Lawton, where he became the first city attorney and helped organize the city's government.

Jake Hamond conceived the idea of promoting a railroad from Lawton to Ardmore, over in the Chickasaw Nation, and one from Wichita Falls, Texas, to Oklahoma City. This project brought him to Ardmore. He could not get proper backing and float enough bonds to finance his dream of a railroad empire, so he dropped the plan in despair. But he did not give up all his railroading ideas. He shuttled back and forth between Lawton, Wichita Falls and Ardmore. He practiced law and worked at other positions and, as the oil boom sentiment went southwestward across the twin territories from Bartlesville and Tulsa, he became interested in that aspect of possible wealth. He acquired extensive leases and royalties in Western Carter County, which became known as the Healdton-Ragtown Oil Fields.

After statehood, Jake L. Hamon settled permanently in Ardmore. By this time, he had reaped a substantial fortune. In Lawton, he met the attractive Clara Smith; a girl of nineteen, with blue eyes and brown hair with a reddish glint, that looked golden in direct sunlight. Hamon persuaded her to come with him to Ardmore as his personal secretary. In that capacity, she was proficient, proving to have an alert and perceptive mind where making money was concerned.

They maintained a suite in the Randol Hotel on West Main Street, north side. Hamon arranged for Clara to marry his nephew, Frank Hamon. It was a marriage of convenience, which gave Clara the Hamon name. Jake paid Frank off and sent him to San Francisco. Clara was now known as Clara Smith Hamon.

Jake Hamon and his wife naturally became estranged to each other; and Mrs. Hamon lived most of the time in Chicago with the children.

The Ragtown oil field boom began in earnest in 1913. For the first three years, it attracted all types of people that flock to boom towns. Bob Hutchins was in the thick of it, sometimes alone, sometimes with Bud Ballew and Frank Jones and other officers.

During two of the best years in the oil fields of Western Carter County, Jake L. Hamon was said to have acquired three million dollars. But as the oil fields settled down to regular production, and the days of wildcat speculation ended, life in this area ceased to be much of a challenge to him.

Jake Hamon was torn between loyalty to two women whom he loved very dearly. In his last days, he seemed to realize, however, that his real love was his true wife and family.

He began drinking more frequently. Clara carried on, managed the business skillfully, and successfully discharged her duties as private secretary, business manager, chauffeur and mistress.

Hutchins claimed it was Clara's influence, more than Jake's, which caused John Ringling of Ringling Brothers Circus to accept Hamon's proposition to build thirty-one miles of railroad from Ardmore into the oil fields in 1913 and 1914.

Jake Hamon told Hutchins the story of how he came to meet John Ringling, while he and Clara were stopping at the Waldorf Astoria in New York City. Hamon was in the lobby one day when a well-dressed gentleman walked in. He asked the desk clerk to introduce him to the stranger, but the clerk declined. "That is John Ringling, circus owner," he said. "Just forget about my introducing you to him. He's too high-toned even to talk to."

"All right," Hamon declared, "I'll just make the introduction myself."

He walked across the lobby to Ringling and said, "I'm Jake L. Hamon. I used to work for your circus. I was a tent-sticker, swung a maul and drove stakes and stretched your tents; and you still owe me three dollars and fifty cents. Have you got that much in your pocket, Mr. Ringling?"

Ringling was a game man like Hamon. Just for the sport of it, he nibbled the bait. "I've been a circus owner all my life," he said, with a smile, "and I know all your phrases. Just come out of the bushes, Mr. Hamon, and I'll play along with you."

"All right," Hamon conceded. "I am an oil man from Oklahoma, a chief politician in the state, and I'm going to build a railroad through the oil fields from Ardmore, Oklahoma, and name it and the terminal Ringling. I want you to come up to my room and meet my financial secretary. You'll like her, for she is a good sport to go my gait."

"You can show her to me, too," John Ringling replied. "I want to gaze upon the female with enough nerve to go your pace."

"Come on then," Hamon urged. They went up to his luxurious suite, where John Ringling met Clara Smith Hamon.

John Ringling confessed afterward, "I met a brainy, jam-up secretary. The first one I had seen in all my masquerading."

An amusing story Hutchins told about one of the antics Jake Hamon pulled was this:

He was sitting in Hamon's office one morning, with his boots

302

propped on Hamon's desk and smoking one of his choice dollar cigars, when the telephone rang. Clara picked up the receiver in the outer office, but Hutchins listened on the extension telephone and recognized Hamon's voice.

"Get in touch with Hutch, Clara," he told her urgently, "and you and him go to the bank to talk to P. C. Dings, my banker. Tell him it is very urgent and imperative for him to put thirty thousand dollars in a grip and give it to you to bring to my office in Healdton the quickest way. You must make it here by three o'clock this afternoon, or the deal is lost. Now don't you two slip an inch. I've got on a hot deal."

Jake Hamon was always making oil deals, and they considered that he had now found one requiring cash on the barrelhead. They went to the Guaranty State Bank and told Mr. Dings, the president, about Jake's request. He hesitated a few moments, then asked, "What brand of liquor is Jake going up against now? Thirty thousand dollars right off the reel is a big undertaking for my bank in a town the size of Ardmore, but here goes for a trial. Have you two had your dinner yet?"

"No," Clara said, "but it's about that time, isn't it?"

"You and Hutchins go eat your dinners, and when you get back I'll have the money ready for you."

Dings had the money in a little black grip when they returned, which he handed to Hutchins with a key. They stepped into Clara's new automobile and headed for Healdton. Clara had the throttle open and she was hitting the high spots, but Hutchins wasn't uneasy. She was a good driver, and sober, and there were enough rough places to slow her down from time to time, anyway.

As they neared Bayou Creek, they saw four parked automobiles along the road.

"Hutch, this is a hold-up!" she exclaimed. "What shall we do?" She slowed down almost to a stop.

"You can turn around and head back to Ardmore and let Jake miss his oil deal," he replied, "or you can stiffen your backbone, tighten your guts and blaze on through. I've got a six-shooter here."

Clara stepped on the gas peddle as she said, "Get ready for the showdown then, Bob, for we're blazing through."

As they passed the automobiles and some men standing by

303

the road, all they got from them was a wave of hands. They left them in a cloud of dust. It was only a party of men from Ardmore discussing an oil deal, Hutchins learned later.

It was twenty minutes before three o'clock when Hutchins set the little black grip of money on Jake Hamon's desk in Healdton. Then he took the key, unlocked the grip and dumped onto the desk more cash money than most people ever got to see at once in a lifetime.

J. P. Hollingsworth, who was with Hamon, took a piece of paper and wrote a note to his banker there in Healdton: "He wins. Give Jake the money." Then he signed it.

Hamon handed the slip to Hutchins and said, "Go get that money, Hutch, and bring it to my Ardmore bank along with what you brought."

Then he turned to Hollingsworth and said, "Old hoss, the next time you get bullheaded and think it can't be done, notify me and I'll loan you my sweet little brains and my six-shooter man. Then look at your bank roll when the smoke blows away."

Now Hutchins and Clara knew for the first time that Jake Hamon had simply made a bet with J. P. Hollingsworth that he could have thirty thousand dollars in cash brought to him by three o'clock that day, and Jake had won a thousand dollars.

Clara Barton Smith Hamon grew disillusioned at the way her life with Jake Hamon was progressing. She began drinking even harder than her employer. From that time forward, there were periods in her life when she was no longer the sweet, demure woman she had been.

Bob Hutchins watched her change, in spite of his warnings. He knew the whole affair would wind up in a squabble, but he never could reconcile himself to the realization that a woman of Clara's intellect could degenerate that way. Clara became reckless and extravagant in her spending; whereas before, she had always used good taste and good sense in her buying.

Clara had been urging Jake Hamon to divorce his wife and marry her; but Mrs. Georgia Perkins Hamon, struggling to maintain respectability, had refused to allow it.

Clara's wine-fogged brain decided she wanted a certain dress. She could have taken it while shopping and charged it to an account, but she liked to make cash transactions. She came back to the office and requested Hamon's bookkeeper to issue her a check for five hundred dollars to buy the dress. He told her that he had no authority to sign Mr. Hamon's name to such a check.

"Take the authority," she demanded, "and I will square it with Jake."

"But I don't have the authority now," the bookkeeper insisted. "Just wait until Mr. Hamon returns and gives it to me. I don't intend to jeopardize myself in that way."

Clara stamped her foot and threatened, "I'll have you fired, if you don't have that check ready for me in twenty minutes." With those words, she pranced out of the office.

Hutchins was sitting in Hamon's private office, with his boots resting on the corner of Jake's desk and a cigar in his mouth. Hamon was in Chicago with his family. The little bookkeeper came into the office and asked, "Mr. Hutchins, what shall I do?"

"Use your own pleasure," Hutchins replied. "You are fired either way. If you don't give her the check, she'll make Jake fire you. If you do, Jake will fire you of his own accord. So it looks to me like it's just hoss and hoss. Do what you please."

The little bookkeeper sat down and cried. Hutchins sympathized with him, for he knew the young man was married and had a son only two months old. His home's security was being threatened.

Soon Clara tripped in again and said, "Hand over the check, or your time is up when Jake returns."

Hutchins had heard enough from Clara. He, in his own words, humorously exaggerated, of course, "seized her by the neck and skirt and kicked her aurora borealis down the stairs, then used her anatomy a few moments for a piano keyboard and never missed a note."

"That was one little thrashing that little bunch of innocence will remember to the end of her life's trail," he remarked later. "She was a spoiled brat and needed that spanking."

Jake Hamon returned to Ardmore that night. When Hutchins and the little bookkeeper reported for duty the next morning, they were unemployed.

A little later that morning, Hutchins was walking down Main Street, wondering where to get a job, when a friend who was an insurance and real estate broker, accosted him. They exchanged greetings and talked casually until the businessman

305

asked Hutchins if he knew where he could find a good office man and bookkeeper.

Hutchins thought of his miserable friend with a family to care for. "I think I know the very man you need. He's efficient, honorable and trustworthy. I don't think you can beat him. In fact, he was fired from a job this morning because of his fine qualities." He laughed at the look of astonishment that came over the broker's face. Then he explained to him what had happened.

They went into the broker's office and Hutchins telephoned the bookkeeper. They waited only twenty minutes for him to appear. At ten o'clock the same morning he had been discharged, he had a new job.

Bob Hutchins was elated because he had helped his friend get squared away with a new job. He, himself, was yet young, active and still liked excitement. He went to El Paso, Texas, where he took jobs as a special officer for the E. P. and S. W. and the G. H. and S. A. railroads, to guard against smuggling and sabotage. For a while, he was a deputy sheriff of El Paso County, Texas, then deputy sheriff in succession of Hidalgo County, New Mexico and Lordsburg; Grant County at Silver City; Santa Fe County at Santa Fe; and Maricopa County, Arizona, at Phoenix. Then he became a general prohibition agent in Division No. 15, circulating around El Paso, Santa Fe, Phoenix, and even out in West Texas and over in Eastern California.

It was about this time that he accepted a commission from President Venustiano Carranza as a special narcotics agent for the Mexican government, and later became a deputy sheriff in Val Verde County, Texas. (The specific dates and periods of times he worked at these different jobs are not recorded in his memoirs.)

Hutchins returned to Ardmore in November of 1920 for a visit with relatives and friends. Jake L. Hamon heard he was in town, sent for him and apologized for discharging him from his services. He asked Hutchins to "just let bygones be bygones."

"I've always liked you, Hutch," he stated. "I guess I just let Clara stir me up and prod me a little too far that morning. I'll consider it a favor if you will make my office your headquarters while you are here on your vacation. Just hang around for old time's sake."

Clara was friendly with him, too, but Hutchins saw a great change in her. She had developed a rebellious spirit, and he was not long in discovering the reason for it. Clara's secret bitterness happened to be Jake's elation. He had played a major role in the very recent election of Warren G. Harding as President of the United States. He had put a lot of money into the campaign, and had been the National Republican Committeeman from Oklahoma. It was rumored that the reason for his sudden political activities was prompted by his closeness to Harding, since their wives were cousins. Jake L. Hamon was slated to get some kind of cabinet position, or the ambassadorship to England.

Jake Hamon had renewed a proper relationship with his family. It was rumored that Mrs. Hamon had prevailed upon her cousin, Mrs. Harding, to make sure the life that Jake L. Hamon would lead in Washington, D.C., would be a respectable one with his family. Harding had, therefore, informed Jake Hamon to bring his own legitimate family with him to Washington, and leave his *secretary* behind in Ardmore to look after his oil interests.

Some time during Bob Hutchins' association with Jake L. Hamon, Lillie Langtry played the old Robinson Opera House in Ardmore, under the auspices of the Dubinsky brothers, theatrical producers. One of them was with her at this appearance, and Lillie Langtry quarreled with him over some difference of opinions that arose. She grew very angry and intended to "pot-shoot" him. Dubinsky slipped around and told Bob Hutchins that she was carrying an attractive, but deadly, little .25 calibre Colt automatic with pearl handle. He declared she had it safely hidden between her breasts, and that she was waiting at Ramsey's drug store on the corner of Washington and Main streets for him to come along.

Hutchins sauntered into the drug store and began a casual conversation with the actress. She was quite pretty, sweet, charming and deadly, he decided. He reached deftly into her bosom and brought out the little automatic, with a smile. She gasped at his bold action.

"Now let me give you some advice," he told her. "Your train is due in a few minutes. You catch it, take a seat by yourself, and if you have to talk, just talk to yourself."

Flustered at first, but on second thought relieved when she learned he only meant to disarm her and not arrest her for carrying a deadly, concealed weapon with intent to kill, she smiled and thanked him for preventing her from committing murder.

It was such a pretty little weapon that Bob Hutchins showed it to Jake Hamon. Jake, after examining it, thrust it into his coat pocket and remarked, "You misplaced that gun somewhere. Just forget about it."

Jake Hamon often carried the little weapon on his long trips. Later on, when Hutchins learned he had given the little weapon to Clara, he said, "Jake, you should not have done it. You have signed your death warrant."

On the night of Jake Hamon's fatal injury, politicians from Washington, D.C., and others had come and gone all day. Some of the visitors to Jake's suite Hutchins didn't like; especially those who spoke privately to Clara. It looked as if some double-crossing were going on. Clara was "hitting the bottle" heavily, and he feared she was being baited by political opponents of Jake L. Hamon.

A politician from Washington, D.C., came there to interview Jake about the part he was to play in the administration of Warren G. Harding. Jake and he had been conferring off and on all day.

W. B. Nichols, former chief of police of Oklahoma City, and Kelly Roach, an insurance agent from Oklahoma City, had checked into the hotel. They were planning to go to Texas with Jake Hamon the next morning in connection with his interests in the Hamon-Kell Railroad.

That Sunday night, Jake Hamon was planning a special supper for the envoy from Washington and his business friends. He asked Bob Hutchins to bring him two large, wild ducks for the occasion. Ducks were plentiful around Ardmore, and the assignment was an easy one. He brought two big, wild mallards and gave them to the cooks at the Randol Hotel. Jake and his friends were out of town looking over an oil lease. When they returned, the wild duck supper was served.

Hamon had not included Clara in the dinner party, because of her drunkeness; but she came into the dining room, drew up

308

a chair from another table and proceeded to tell Jake what she thought of him for leaving her out of the affair.

Jake Hamon immediately told her to go back upstairs, or he would have the police arrest her for disorderly conduct. She seized one of the ducks and hurled it into his face. Hutchins appeared and escorted her to her room, where she fell across the bed in a tantrum, but soon fell asleep.

When he went back downstairs, Hamon told him he would slip up to her room later and console her. "I've been mean to her," he admitted, "by not telling her earlier today to be ready to dine with us."

"Jake," Hutchins warned him, "don't you go up there at all. I have been watching what has been going on here today. Your political enemies are striking at you through her. She is all torn up because you are going to Washington without her. She thinks you are giving her the brush-off. If you go up there now, you will come down on a death wagon."

"Oh, no!" Jake belittled the warning. "Clara hasn't got enough nerve to shoot me!"

Hutchins walked away, and Jake Hamon went upstairs.

It seemed hardly more than ten minutes to Hutchins before Jake Hamon staggered back down the stairs, holding his hands to his right side. Hutchins went after him as he went through the dining room door. By the time he reached Hamon, he had staggered over to the table where Doctor A. G. Cowles, the house surgeon for Dr. Walter Hardy's Sanitarium and Hospital, was awaiting his dinner order.

Doctor Cowles and Bob Hutchins walked him to the hospital, two blocks away. Hamon reported he had accidentally shot himself while cleaning the little .25 calibre automatic to take with him on his trip the following morning.

Doctor Cowles and Doctor Walter Hardy held a hasty consultation and decided to operate immediately to recover the bullet. The small, steel missile had entered his body to the right of center, passed through the upper lobe of his liver and lodged in the muscle of his back, near his spinal column.

Within one hour, the wound had been probed, the bullet removed from his back, the damage repaired as much as possible, and Hamon was placed in a room in the hospital to recuperate.

The wound was painful, but not considered too serious by his physicians. The anesthetic had made him very sick all through the night, but he was resting better the next morning. He rallied a little and sent for Bob Hutchins.

When the nurse ushered Hutchins into his room, the first thing Jake asked was, "Have you seen Clara?"

"Yes," Hutchins answered.

"What did she say?"

"She's speechless and hurt as bad as you are."

"Hutch, stay with her. She didn't murder me, even if she did fire the fatal shot."

His voice trailed off and he lapsed into a brief coma. In about five minutes, his eyes opened and his speech became clearer. He said, "Hutch, take Clara home with you and send her to Mexico till this trouble comes to light — and — and see that she comes clear in court."

Hutchins lived in El Paso, Texas, at the time, just across the border from Juarez, Mexico; and he knew his way around over there.

Jake Hamon asked for a piece of paper and his pen. "How much money will it take, Hutch?" he asked hoarsely.

"About two hundred," Hutchins replied.

Jake Hamon gave him an order to his bookkeeper to issue him a check for three hundred dollars. Hutchins presumed that was the last time Jake Hamon ever signed his name, though he lingered on nearly a week after that.

During his fleeting moments of consciousness, he would whisper hoarsely to Doctor Walter Hardy and Doctor A. G. Cowles and the nurses, "Clara didn't do it! It was an accident!"

Hutchins never again saw Jake L. Hamon. He carried out the last order from his old boss, however, and he did an excellent job, too.

The Bold Evasion

Hutchins went straight back to the Randol Hotel and told Clara to pack her trunks *with things she would not need.*

"I'll call John Gernand and have him come and get them and ship them to Kansas City on the next train," he told her.

Clara asked no questions. She knew that Hutchins was a resourceful man. He did tell her that he had talked to Jake Hamon, however, and Jake had asked him to see that she came clear of the mess he had brought upon her.

"He holds no blame against you, Clara. He is a real man and true blue. He's telling the doctors, the nurses and everybody allowed to see him that you didn't do it, that it was an accident."

"It was," she sobbed. "Honest, Hutch, I didn't mean to shoot him. *The gun went off accidentally!*"

"He understands that, Clara," he told her gently. "Calm yourself, and let's do as he wishes."

"I want to see him," she wailed.

"That would never do, Clara. You might get arrested. If not, you would hurt his chances of getting well! He wants you to go now!"

311

John Gernand, the drayman, and Hutchins had known each other for several years. In the past, Hutchins had turned a lot of business his way.

Hutchins handed John Gernand the money to ship the trunks, and then gave him an extra five dollar bill. Then he told him to ask several friends if they thought the Law could bother him for helping Clara escape by sending her trunks to Kansas City, where she had gone.

Next, Hutchins took Clara and her suitcase down the back stairs to her automobile and took her to the home of Buck Garrett, the county sheriff. Then he went down to Westheimer and Daube's department store and bought a good suit of clothes for a small man; and they caught the first Santa Fe passenger train going south that night. They looked like a deputy marshal and his posseman on some official duty. They changed trains at Fort Worth and caught the Texas Pacific train to El Paso, where Hutchins took her across the border to Juarez. He arranged for her to stay with the family of an old friend of Hutchins, who was the alcalde of Chihuahua City.

None of the family except the well-educated alcalde could speak any English, and he was away most of the time. Clara could not speak a word of Spanish, but they got along pretty well with gestures.

If Jake L. Hamon suffered much before he died, Hutchins considered that Clara suffered morally and spiritually much worse. In a few days, he went over into Mexico to see how she was faring. In a few more days, he received a letter from Jake Hamon's office. It was typewritten and unsigned. With it was a check for two hundred dollars. The message simply read, "Come first train. Talk to nobody but Jimmie Mathers and Russell Brown, County Attorney."

Jimmie Mathers had been a friend to Jake Hamon and Clara a long time. He had resigned his office as county attorney in order to defend Clara. Russell Brown had been appointed county attorney to succeed him.

Hutchins secretly brought Clara back to Ardmore, where they learned that eveything was set for Clara's acquittal, except one witness, who was Clara's close friend; but she was an unreliable alcoholic. They returned to El Paso — this time taking with them Elizabeth Mayes, with whom Clara stayed at Sheriff

Buck Garrett's home. This time, Clara had with her an English-speaking companion in Mexico.

An impressive coterie of lawyers had been employed to defend Clara Barton Smith Hamon. *The Daily Ardmoreite* carried all the details of the case, beginning with the day after Jake L. Hamon was shot: Monday, November 22, 1920. The newspaper was in sympathy with both Jake Hamon and Clara Smith Hamon. It was also deferential toward the Hamon family; though the metropolitan newspapers across the nation played up the story sensationally.

The Ardmoreite reported that Jake L. Hamon, prominent oil man and national Republican political figure, was in the Hardy hospital, suffering from a pistol wound, accidentally self-inflicted. The explanation was that he had been cleaning the weapon to take with him on a business trip the next day. He had held the muzzle of the pistol against his body, while slipping the magazine into place when it discharged. The report explained that the wound was painful but, unless complications arose, it would not be serious.

A telegram had been sent to Mrs. Jake L. Hamon in Chicago, informing her of the accident, and stating that it was not serious. Assurances had been given out to his friends that Hamon would soon recover. He had lost about a pint of blood during the operation to remove the bullet.

November 23, 1920

The Daily Ardmoreite's front page headlines announced further assurance by the local hospital doctors that chances for Hamon's recovery were considered fair.

November 24, 1920

The front page headlines announced, "Hamon may have passed the crisis and will soon recover from his wounding."

November 26, 1920

The top front page headlines announced Jake L. Hamon's death as follows: "Holding the hand of his loving wife, he

313

drifted forth upon that Unknown Sea, which rolls around all the world.

"Death closed the eyes of Jake L. Hamon, Oklahoma Oil and Railroad Magnate, and the National Republican Politician passed to the Silent Land of Eternal Shadow.

"His wife was at his bedside when the Grim Reaper beckoned her husband to join the ranks of that innumerable caravan. The body will lie in state at the Convention Hall."

The Ardmoreite ran a large picture of Hamon, beneath which was revealed he was a man whose life story reads like a page torn from a vivid romance.

"From a poor clerk to a briefless lawyer; from the courts to promotion circles; from promotion development of oil properties and railway building, from successful business to successful politics, has been the history of this man who carved success from the most adverse circumstances and won the crown of achievement.

"He died at 8:15 o'clock Friday morning, November 26, 1920."

A great crowd attended the funeral at the Convention Hall; and many of those followed the casket to Rose Hill Cemetery in south Ardmore, where he was entombed in a vault on a hill.

There was no doubt that Ardmore had lost its greatest booster; the man who would have definitely done more than any other in promoting Ardmore's growth to the great metropolis that the city should be today.

Clara Smith Hamon's final return to Ardmore to stand trial for the murder of Jake L. Hamon can best be followed again through the pages of *The Daily Ardmoreite*:

Thursday, December 23, 1920

Clara Smith will arrive in Ardmore Friday afternoon, on Christmas Eve. Woman whose life story reads like a page from a melodramatic novel is returning here.

Sheriff Garrett met fugitive at Juarez.

Bond in sum of $10,000 alleged has been provided and will be made following arraignment.

El Paso, Texas, Dec. 23. "Clara Barton Smith left El Paso at 6:00 o'clock this morning, bound for Ardmore,

314

Oklahoma, by way of Fort Worth. She was accompanied by her lawyers and Sheriff Garrett.

El Paso, Texas, Dec. 23. "Clara Barton Smith slept under her parents' roof last night. Ending a search which began November 22, Miss Smith came to Juarez, Mexico, opposite here, last night, surrendered to Sheriff Buck Garrett of Ardmore, Oklahoma, and was taken to the home of her father, James L. Smith, in El Paso, where she spent the night. Early today, if permitted, she was to be taken aboard a train for Ardmore. She is to plead to a murder charge in connection with the death of Jake L. Hamon in that city on November 26.

"Little of her story of her disappearance following the shooting of Hamon on November 21, was made public by the young woman. She was met at the train in Juarez by Sheriff Garrett, her Uncle Ben H. Harrison, and attorneys who had been engaged as her counsel. There was a short greeting and consultation on the station platform, and then the party was whisked back over the international bridge and into El Paso.

"Miss Smith's father supplied the only information given out regarding the woman's flight from Juarez to Chihuahua City, Mexico.

"A man she met on the train from Juarez to Chihuahua City must have been Heaven sent," he said. "She had never seen him before. They did not even speak the same language. He approached her, knowing she was in trouble, and volunteered to shield her. And Clara reposed her trust in him. He guarded her as carefully as though she were his own child. I believe that's a miracle. I believe God guided that friend to her in her hour of need."

"Her friend was a Chihuahua official," her father said, "who took Clara to his home, and his wife became Clara's companion. The official policed his estate with private detectives to keep her safe, and not even her brother, Jimmie, aged 19, could approach until he had thoroughly established his identity. . . ."

Sheriff Buck Garrett made good his promise to allow her freedom with her family. Sheriff Orndorff of El Paso deputized a taxi driver and stationed him in front of the Smith home;

not so much as a guard, he said, but to keep newsmen and curious people from approaching the house.

"The sympathy of the people of Carter County, Oklahoma, is with Miss Smith," Sheriff Garrett said.

The County Attorney first swore out a warrant for assault with intent to kill, which he later changed to murder.

Sheriff Garrett said he would telephone Kansas City to have Miss Smith's trunks, which were opened there some weeks ago, sent back to Ardmore.

"I have nothing to wear except this," pointing to her blue serge dress, the girl is reported to have told Sheriff Garrett, after the two had entered her father's home.

According to a friend of the family who was present, the greeting at the house was dramatic.

"Dad, good old dad!" the returning daughter shouted as her father came to meet her. They embraced, while tears of pity from the father's eyes mingled with the tears of heart-penitence from the eyes of the daughter. Mrs. Smith came from another room, and Clara flung herself into her arms.

"Clara! Clara!" was all the girl's mother said.

Miss Smith said nothing, but clung to her mother, bitterly weeping.

"Would you have run away from Ardmore, if you had seen me in my window?" the sheriff is said to have asked the girl.

"Run away?" repeated Miss Smith, as she shot a side-long glance and smiled. "I didn't run away. I drove up and down the street for a long time after the shooting, you know. If I had seen you, I would have gone to you. You are the very one I wanted to see!"

The Ardmore Sheriff continued, "If I had been passing by your house in Chihuahua, would you have called to me?"

"You bet I would," the woman is said to have replied. "But you could never have taken me from my home in Chihuahua, unless I were willing to go. You could never get me out of here against my will. But if I had seen you in Ardmore, I'd have gone to you, even though people might say you were making love to me, or I was making love to you!" Miss Smith added, laughingly.

316

Sunday, December 26, 1920

Clara arrived in Ardmore at noon Saturday. Her bail was set at $12,000. She is now with relatives near Wilson. Case is to come to trial early next month. Special counsel may be named to aid the prosecution.

Justice of the Peace Hal M. Cannon was summoned from his Christmas dinner to hear Clara's plea. Crowd gathered at Courthouse.

Edith C. Johnson, feature writer for The Daily Oklahoman newspaper, met train.

The Ardmoreite published Edith Johnson's feature story about Clara on page two, on Christmas Day.

Clara took a chair proferred to her, admitting she was ill, but she stood up while County Attorney Russell Brown read the charge against her.

Judge Tom Champion signed the bond. "Now, Mrs. Hamon, you are free to go wherever you like," he said.

She smiled. Judge Champion added, "We have just one intention — to be fair with you and be fair with ourselves."

"Oh, you are just the little boys, and I am an old, old woman!" she exclaimed to the officials.

Then Clara expressed her gratitude for the kindness that had been shown her by people everywhere — in Mexico, Texas and Oklahoma. . . .

Tuesday, March 1, 1921

Clara Smith enters plea of "Not guilty" to charge of murder of Jake L. Hamon. H. H. Brown appointed by Judge Tom Champion as special prosecutor.

Trial set for March 10. Clara said, "I know I will be all right. God has been too good to me to fail me on that day. I will be here."

Thursday, March 10, 1921

The case of the State of Oklahoma versus Clara Smith Hamon is under way. Attorneys for the prosecution and the defense are at work and making rapid progress in selection of the jury.

Most sensational homicide trial known to criminal annals of Oklahoma began this morning. Accused woman calmly greets friends with nods and smiles as lawyers spar

317

over legal technicalities. Multitude of morbidly curious present.

Attorney General Prince Freeling is the leading counsel for the State.

Under Clara's big picture appeared this caption:

Divorced wife of the nephew of the multi-millionaire oil man, railway king, president maker and Republican politician, Jake L. Hamon, whom she is alleged in the State's information with having fatally shot last November. While but 27 years of age, the defendant's life story reads like pages torn from the sordid romance of the regime of Louis XV.

J. B. Champion, a defense attorney, tilts with Freeling over his presence at the trial; criticizes Governor J. B. A. Robertson for sending him.

James C. (Red Necktie) O'Brien, noted Chicago criminal lawyer, present as observer, representing Mrs. Jake L. Hamon as her personal lawyer. Mrs. Hamon not present.

Jake L. Hamon's picture and that of his wife appeared on page two. The pictures of County Prosecutor Rusell Brown and his brother, Assistant Prosecutor, appeared also on page two.

Friday, March 11, 1921

Jury made up of men of mature years, fathers of families.

J. B. Champion, for the defense, twin brother of judge.

Champion's picture and Buck Garrett's were on the front page.

The list of the jury selected from the panel was published as follows:

B. F. C. Loughridge, Ardmore, 73 years old, retired; father of one child.

D. E. Allen, Ardmore, 70 years old, retired; father of one child.

Gabe Newman, Ardmore, 33 years old, merchant; father of two children.

318

G. M. Haney, Nelda, farmer, 60 years old; father of one child.

W. A. Jolly, Ardmore, 55 years old, groceryman; father of nine children.

T. H. Roberts, Ardmore, 65 years old, barber shop proprietor; father of four children.

A. D. Davis, Fox, 43 years old, merchant; bachelor.

R. R. Callaway, Ardmore, 45 years old, dairyman; father of five children.

Tom Deen, Ardmore, 42 years old, banker; father of four children.

D. D. Sellar, Springer, merchant; married.

Tom L. Wilkes, Ardmore, 37 years old, tailor; father of one child.

O. D. Thomas, Berwyn, 42 years old, merchant, two children.

Attorney General Freeling ruthlessly rends the veil and exposes sickening details of her life's story, while Clara sheds bitter tears.

Jury and Clara, accompanied by Buck Garrett, visited fatal room in hotel.

Dr. Walter Hardy and Dr. A. G. Cowles, house surgeon, were pictured on page two.

Reverend T. J. Irvin, pastor of the Presbyterian Church at Lawton, who delivered Hamon's funeral oration, testified: "This was a frame-up by others." The dying man told him, "Three times, I have paid her off, but this is the last time."

Defense counsel interrupted the statement. Dr. Irvin didn't get to say any more. Both defense and prosecution let that angle drop. He didn't say Hamon told him direct she shot him.

W. B. Nichols, former chief of police of Oklahoma City, testified that Hamon told him, "Bill, she got me." He stated Hamon was lying down when Clara came to him, placed her left hand on his head and fired a bullet into his body.

Frank Ketch (Hamon's business manager) advised Clara to leave town to save further disgrace of the Hamon family, since Mrs. Hamon was coming to Ardmore from Chicago to be with her wounded husband.

Monday, March 14, 1921

The picture of the jury appeared on the front page.

Mrs. Hamon testified on one occasion she brought her daughter, Olive Belle, age 11, to Ardmore from Chicago to play her violin at an entertainment. She testified she later talked with her husband and went to his rooms in the Randol Hotel, which he and Clara occupied. Clara came in, threw her hat and gloves on the bed and ran out of the room. Mrs. Hamon took a pistol from Clara's room on that occasion.

She also testified she saw her husband in Chicago from time to time. He took her and Olive Belle and put them on the train at the depot in Ardmore on that occasion.

The State claimed Clara was 29 years old and was 19 when her association with Hamon began.

Tuesday, March 15, 1921

Clara told how she met a debonair young attorney and loved "not too wisely, but too well." She admitted she was 29 years old. Had known Mr. Hamon since a girl in Lawton.

Sheriff Garrett testified Hamon told him he did not want Clara prosecuted, that he wounded himself accidentally.

Thursday, March 17, 1921

[A better picture of Clara appeared on the front page. Also, a picture of Alfredo S. Garcia, a spiritualist from Chihuahua, his native city.]

Señor Garcia is in Ardmore attending the trial of Clara Smith Hamon. He claims to have held communication with the spirit of the late Jake L. Hamon, and says that the vital spark of the dead politician expressed the hope that Clara should escape punishment lash of the law.

Women sobbed; men unabashed wiped tears from their eyes as James Mathers pleaded with the jurors and appealed to Oklahoma mothers for the acquittal of Clara Smith, "A woman more sinned against than sinning." He demanded in impassioned tones for "justice against gold."

Friday, March 18, 1921

[This final issue about the trial carried a big spread, with banner headlines, on the front page.]

SMITH TRIAL ENDS IN ACQUITTAL

[The front page contained a big picture of Clara Barton Smith Hamon, wearing a sailor hat, in the center of the page, smiling.]

"I am the happiest woman alive," she said. "I knew you would free me!" she said to the jurors when, late yesterday afternoon, after deliberating 39 minutes, the verdict of "Not guilty as charged in the information" was returned.

When the jury filed back into the courtroom, Judge Tom Champion asked, "Gentlemen, have you reached a verdict?"

"We have, your Honor," responded B. F. C. Loughridge, foreman of the jury, as he advanced a step and handed the folded document to the judge, who after glancing at it, passed it on to the deputy clerk, instructing him to read it out loud.

A silence second only to the silence in the dark and solemn tomb in which today reposes all that is mortal of the late Jake L. Hamon, pervaded the courtroom.

"NOT GUILTY!" read the clerk.

Then there was a demonstration in which Clara's friends and well-wishers rushed upon her and besieged her with hand-shakings and words of congratulations. The trial had a happy ending, in accordance with the public sentiment. Clara Barton Smith Hamon, who had borne the heartaches and emotional tensions day and night through it all, was a free woman again.

But with the woman and the family that had been wronged, perhaps a bitterness of regret will always linger.

321

Guard on the Border

While yet commissioned as a United States Deputy Marshal and employed by the railroad companies on both sides of the border, Hutchins was away from home a lot. Running down international smugglers and dope pushers kept him busy. It was after World War One, when the rackets of all kinds grew worse all over the United States and across the border in Mexico.

The same revolt of morality was taking place in all other nations; particularly those most deeply involved in the first world war. Morals became lax. The young women raised their skirts over their knees and were called "Flappers." Young men greased and slicked back their hair and wore sporty clothes and were called "Jelly Beans."

The corruption in the United States ranged from top-level government officials to the grass roots of society. In August of the year 1923, President and Mrs. Warren G. Harding were returning from a trip to Alaska, when Harding suddenly took ill of ptomaine poisoning and died in San Francisco. It was hinted by newspapers across the nation that Mrs. Harding had poisoned the President to spare him the disgrace and suffering from the Teapot Dome oil scandal. That and other scandals caused Harding's administration to be stigmatized as the most corrupt in American history.

The stock market tickers ran day and night on Wall Street in New York City. Stock promotors, brokers and buyers went wild. Stocks and bonds were floated and burst like bubbles. Something happened in the stock market business that had never happened before. Ordinary American people became interested in stock market investments. *Everyone* was going to get rich. This was the super climax of an industrial get-rich-quick revolution that finally came to an explosive end on September 29, 1929. People of all walks of life lost money. Many banks went bankrupt, and others lost heavily.

Congress gave J. Edgar Hoover some authority "with teeth in it" for the Federal Bureau of Crime Investigation, organized by him in 1924. He hired and trained more agents, who waded into the gangsters all over the nation.

Franklin Delano Roosevelt was elected President over one-term Herbert Hoover in 1932, and he remained President until his death in April, 1945, during World War Two. He declared a "bank holiday" to prevent more banks from going bankrupt, induced Congress to pass laws insuring bank deposits, and adopted silver for the standard of money exchange in America, instead of gold. The "Blue Eagle" National Relief Act provided soup lines, and then public work for the downtrodden common people.

These conditions affected Bob Hutchins, as well as all other peace officers, *nationwide*, of his time. Strangely enough, Hutchins wrote very little in his memoirs about the last twenty years of his career on the border, but this biographer talked with him about his activities in interviews, and I still preserve letters that I received from him there.

He would not disclose how many men he had to kill or wound in his dangerous duties while dealing with the smuggling rackets between the United States and Mexico; but one day he admitted, "The border patrol started a veritable graveyard with those hardheaded, nondescript characters who persisted in violating the laws of Mexico and the United States. I shot

323

some — like shooting turtles — and watched them drift down the Pecos and Rio Grande with the currents."

He once told about a horse he named Smuggler, who was engaged in international traffic of crime. Smuggler traveled a secret trail alone through a wilderness on both sides of the Rio Grande. He forded the river at a shallow spot and got by with his international contraband for a long time before he was discovered. His bases of operations were two corrals — both in out-of-the-way places on each side of the border. The men who handled him at both corrals treated him royally. He was fed, groomed, petted and pampered; and dispatched day and night on his errands. Any casual observer would think some rider's horse had gotten away from him and that he was going home. That was what the mounted border patrolmen thought, too, until it seemed to them that Smuggler was straying off too often. That was when they intercepted him and found saddle bags stuffed with marijuana and opium. On his return trips to Mexico, he carried mostly firearms and ammunition.

The U.S. government sold the horse at public auction, and Bob Hutchins liked him so well that he bought him and rode him several years.

But Hutchins had only been on the border a short time before he resigned his commission temporarily as United States Deputy Marshal, went to Mexico City and accepted a commission from President Venustiano Carranza as a special narcotics agent for the Mexican Government. As had always been his habit with other responsible trusts in his life, Hutchins realized he was working for the good of his own country, also.

When intriguing friends discovered he was held in high esteem in Mexico, they prevailed upon him for favors and requests. The identity of some of them shook his faith in human nature; to learn that their love of money surpassed all respect for good government and decent society. This troubled him so much that he resigned his commission with Carranza and returned to El Paso. His thirty years as an officer had led him to believe there were few people he could trust. During the past years, he had seen selfishness and greed among men that led them into crime for both luxury and dictatorial power; from not only the heads of governments, but to the lowest form of *rackets.* This realization made him hate himself and despise erstwhile friends at times.

He drifted to Del Rio again, and became a deputy sheriff in Val Verde County. It was there that he learned about the job that would lead him into retirement. The Southern Pacific Railroad Company wanted a guard to protect the high bridge across the Pecos River Gorge. He applied for the job and got it.

It was the first day of April, 1924, that he and Mrs. Frances Hutchins moved into the little cottage that nestled on the banks of the Pecos, in the shadow of the bridge.

The old Pecos high bridge that spanned the gorge was strictly a railroad bridge, 321 feet high, 1516 feet long, and weighing 5,252,775 pounds. It was the fourth highest bridge in the entire world. Built by the Southern Pacific in 1892, it was a Southwest Texas landmark of the era of Judge Roy Bean, who had witnessed its construction.

On September 6, 1907, Miss Ada Upshaw, of Langtry, and B. J. McDowell, of Del Rio, were married on the center of the bridge by Judge C. K. McDowell, brother of the groom.

Perry Brotherton — at the time the new bridge was built — was leasing forty thousand acres of land for sheep grazing from Mrs. E. T. Bell, of Del Rio. This acreage is bisected by the Southern Pacific right-of-way on the east side of the gorge. Brotherton drove a Model T Ford across the old bridge many times.

"The old bridge was a shortcut that saved me one hundred fifty miles in going from my old ranch near Shumla to the county seat at Del Rio," he explained. "One time I had a flat tire right in the center of the bridge, three hundred twenty-one feet above the Pecos."

Mrs. E. T. Bell claimed to be the first person to walk across the structure when it was completed. Afterward, she frequently rode her horse across the bridge to Shumla, three miles away, to get the mail.

In 1921, Jimmy Doolittle flew an open cockpit airplane beneath the old bridge, by tipping the plane's wings.

Compared with his Indian Territory days, Bob Hutchins had found a quiet career of semi-retirement. He and Nellie were happy and contented in their neat little cottage, where his mother sometimes came and spent a few days with them.

They raised gardens, chickens and for a few years had a dog and Smuggler, the horse. Hutchins never neglected his duties. He inspected the old bridge regularly for defects and weakening structure and kept a watchful lookout for smugglers — and sabotage after World War Two began in Europe.

He and Nellie often took quiet walks in the evening together over the hills. He always carried his rifle and packed his old Belle Starr six-shooter.

"We were not troubled with the petrified heat of summer, nor the wintry blasts of winter," he mused. "We had the best and the purest water in the whole country, all the fresh air our lungs could hold, fished right at our door, plenty of arguments to keep us from getting lonesome." Here he smiled, as he said, "Nellie was my constant, temperamental side-kick; ninety percent temper and ten percent mental."

He confided that he had grown tired of shooting his fellow-men, or seeing them punished for crimes. He grew sick of the double-crossing, seeing men's souls bartered for selfish gains, and leading intriguing existences. "When I saw I could not achieve my simple wishes, and I was offered that job in a little Garden of Eden by the Pecos — even though far removed and much inferior than that one in the valley between the Tigris and Euphrates rivers, occupied an aeon ago by Father Adam and Mother Eve — I took it," he disclosed with satisfaction.

There beneath the great bridge and with the Pecos almost at their door, they settled down for seventeen years.

After the second world war broke out in Europe, Hutchins had to sharpen his wits and be alert again. But, when the United States became involved in the war, Bob Hutchins was relieved of his guard duty. That was the third war in which the old Southern Pacific Pecos Gorge Bridge was put under military protection. This same precaution had been taken during the Spanish-American War and World War One.

Mr. and Mrs. James Robert Hutchins came north again to Ardmore, Oklahoma. With a gleam in his steel-grey eyes and a wide grin on his mustached face, he declared:

"It took a whole damned company of soldiers to replace me!"

Trail's End

When Bob Hutchins returned to Ardmore, Oklahoma, he was happy as he went about town, hobnobbing with the surviving old-timers.

He was limping much more noticeably from the old Lou Bowers bullet in his pelvis bone for so long. It caused him to walk a sort of angling, shuffling gait. He walked the streets of Ardmore no longer tall and Indian straight.

He visited with my father, but my mother was dead; and he could no longer talk with her about her father, who guarded the "Bull Pen" federal jail, and her two brothers, with whom he had ridden for awhile under Marshal John S. Hammer.

I had recently taken up my duties in the county superintendent's office in the court house, and I was pretty busy. Hutchins came into my office one morning and bluntly wanted to know when we were going to get started on his biography.

"When things simmer down, I guess," I told him.

He still held an honorary commission as a U.S. Deputy Marshal, and he was packing in his old, worn holster the bone-handled, .45 calibre, single action, "thumb-buster" six-shooter.

327

I admired the antique, which was still quite serviceable. He hauled it out of his holster and handed it to me. It was loaded, except for the empty chamber on which the hammer rested. "No use carrying an *empty* gun," he remarked.

"Where did you tell me you got this gun?" I asked, grinning at him.

"That was Belle Starr's gun," he told me proudly. "She was carrying that six-shooter when Jim Jully killed her. See where one of the buckshot clipped a corner off the handle on the outer side? Bob Stacy took that gun off of her before her body was hauled home in a wagon.

It was true. Bob Stacy was still alive then, living out north and east of town at Chigger Hill. I later appointed him to the school board. He came to my office from time to time to transact school business and we also talked about old times. He told me about taking the six-shooter and belt from around Belle's waist and giving it later to Jim July Starr, from whom Hutchins took it after shooting him for resisting arrest.

I looked the gun over casually and, with a smile on my face, I mused out loud, "I wonder how many Belle Starr guns there are across this nation, like those that were supposed to belong to Jesse James, Cole Younger, Bill Doolin, Bob Dalton and the rest of those old bad characters. Do you reckon there would be a train load of them, if they were all thrown together?"

I knew this would get a rise out of my old friend.

"Have you got some time you can spare from your most important official duties?" he asked.

"When?"

"Hell! Right now! There is no time like the present to *educate* an educated man like you!"

"What are we going to do?" I asked.

"I'm going to prove something to you once and forever. Bring one of your secretaries. One that can write."

I asked Mrs. Selma Brown to come with us and bring her shorthand machine. We got into my automobile, and he directed me to drive out to the outer edge of what had been both Hutchins' and my own neighborhood. We stopped next door to the old home of Tom Ellis, a former county commissioner.

We walked onto the porch and Hutchins rapped sharply on the door. It opened and we saw a little, old, slender, slightly

328

stooped man, with clear blue eyes and thin, grey hair. He and Hutchins greeted each other like long lost cousins. After Hutchins had made the introductions — without former warning — he hauled out the six-shooter and laid it in the hands of our host.

"Old scout," Hutchins inquired bluntly, " did you ever see that six-shooter before?"

I noticed the flush of excitement that came into his eyes and face. "I know exactly where that gun came from," he said. "That was Belle Starr's gun. I was there when our gang leader gave it to her. We robbed a train and rode to Belle's cabin in Younger's Bend. She counted our loot and divided it among us, share for share. When she had finished, our leader asked, 'Now, Belle, what do we owe you?'

" 'Not a thing,' she said with a smile. 'I'm glad to have been able to help you.' Then she saw his six-shooter, and she remarked, 'That *is* a nice looking gun you carry there.'

" 'It's yours,' announced our leader. He unbuckled the gun belt and handed it over to her. Gun, cartridges and all."

Hutchins turned to me with an "I told you so" grin.

"Are you willing to sign what you have just told us in a statement under oath?" I asked the former outlaw.

"Yes, sir!" he replied, unhesitatingly. "That's all behind me now. My wrong-doings have been paid for. I'm a free man."

Never again did I doubt anything Bob Hutchins seriously told me; but I did question him enough at times and made comparison with other reliable sources on some points to help him get his facts straight.

As the former outlaw gave me the detailed facts, Mrs. Brown took it all down in shorthand. We returned to my office, where she wrote up the statement I dictated to her from her notes. We took it back to the little man. He signed it under oath and notary seal.

Bob Hutchins suffered a slight paralytic stroke after that, which impaired his ability to walk even more. While he lay confined in his bed for a few days at the home of his son-in-law and daughter, Will and Pearl Eaves, on West Main Street, I visited him and we talked about some of the sections of this manuscript. Then I was inducted into the United States Navy.

I corresponded with Bob and told him as much about what was going on around Saipan, Guam, Tinian, Kerama Rhetto and Okinawa as the naval censors would allow. He wrote back in words of humor and encouragement and told me in his old idiomatic way, "Stay right with them till hell freezes over."

Another time, he wrote, "I've got a pretty good idea of what things are like out there from the newspapers, radio and what little I can grasp from your letters, which look like a slice of cheese after the mice get through playing hide-and-seek through it."

At the close of World War Two, I returned to the United States and was dismissed from naval service at the south base in Norman, Oklahoma, on November 9, 1945. I hurried home and went to see my old peace officer friend again. He had suffered a second stroke the year before on Main Street, while showing some friends an acrobatic stunt he had pulled in his years of health and vigor. They picked him up in an ambulance and hauled him to the old Confederate Home in South Ardmore.

"I wouldn't have given a plugged nickel for my life," he told me cheerfully, "but good old Doc Jackson pulled me through." He still looked forward to getting out of bed and walking again, but he never made it any farther than a wheel chair.

He showed me newspaper clippings his youngest daughter, Ruth, had mailed to him from Pecos, Texas. They told about the tearing down of the old high bridge he had guarded so long. It had been shipped to Guatemala to be erected again. The new bridge had been constructed during the war, and it opened to heavy military traffic on December 21, 1944. The new bridge was much better and stronger. It was one inch shorter than the old one, and was then the fourth highest bridge in the world.

Much later, I started to work on Bob Hutchins' biography, while I was attending Oklahoma University, and I made many trips to Ardmore to confer with my old friend. We discussed different aspects of his manuscript, and I began writing some of his experiences into short stories and succeeded in having a few of them published.

"You've made me feel like something important on the other end of the stick!" he exclaimed to me one day, with a grin. But it wasn't enough. He longed for the book. We

330

planned it, outlined it, and I started writing it. Other authors came to his bedside and asked him for his manuscripts, but were refused. We had a notarized agreement by then, and that was the way he kept it. Some enterprising reporters, however, did interview him and write about his career for newspapers.

When I graduated from Oklahoma University in 1949, with two degrees, including a number of courses in creative writing, my wife and I were as poor as Job's turkey when it came to money.

I accepted the position as Superintendent of the American Legion Home School (orphanage) at Ponca City, Oklahoma, where I was steadily and exhaustively employed — and my wife, too, part of the time — for twenty-six months. Bob Hutchins and I corresponded, as usual, and I visited him from time to time, but less frequently.

My position did not allow me time to write anymore on the book; and the psychological problems I dealt with in some of those frustrated orphans were making harmful effects upon my health. Then, one day, I picked up a newspaper and was stunned by the glaring news that my dear old friend, Bob Hutchins, was dead and buried!

I hurried back to Ardmore and visited his daughter, Pearl. She told me sorrowfully what had caused his sudden death. Then she gave me some more of his writings, which she had found among his personal things.

"Everybody, it seems, wanted them," she said. "They have almost worn out my doorsteps and my door bell asking for them. I have saved them for you. I knew you would want them. You are entitled to them." The she added, "Some day, I hope, you can use them." Her words gave me a feeling of indictment, which, in a way, I knew I deserved.

I gazed wistfully at the old Belle Starr six-shooter, hanging on the wall in its worn holster, symbolic of a way of life now relegated to the historical ages.

"That goes to a grandson of his," she said. "Essa's son. Papa promised it to him when he was a boy."

"I know," I said. "He made that clear to me, himself, when we were planning the book.

I drove out to the Rose Hill Cemetery to Bob Hutchins' grave, in the Eaves Plot, farther over to the southeast of my family's plot. The grave was still fresh. The flowers were just beginning to wither and fade. No tombstone had yet been put up. Just the undertaker's marker. There had not been time for the stone.

I stood there silently with my head bared, and I thought of many questions I wanted to ask my old friend. I hadn't asked them while it was easy to get answers. Now I had to dig them out through research and interviews with a few remaining old friends who might know; *for dead men tell no tales.*

The doctors explained that "lead poison from the bullets embedded in his body, and uremia, accumulated and saturated his system. His paralytic condition kept his kidneys from throwing off the poison as waste from his body."

At long last, Bob Hutchins had reached the end of his life on earth. A long line of relatives and friends — and a few enemies — were waiting for him. He was the youngest of all the old frontier officers who rode out of "Hanging" Judge Isaac Charles Parker's court — and he had survived them all.

He was cheerful and conscious right up to the end. His brother, Sam, and son-in-law, Will Eaves — both now deceased — Reverend Roy Heron, Jim Pike and other friends were there with him in the old Hardy Hospital. About the last statement any of them could remember him making was, "I am the same old buck."

Death closed the steel-grey eyes and stilled the deep voice of James Robert Hutchins just a quarter hour before midnight, on April 29, 1951.

The funeral services were held in the Bettes Chapel at four o'clock in the afternoon on Wednesday, May 2. Reverend Leslie Shaffer, pastor of the Christian Advent Church in Ardmore, assisted by the Reverend Roy Heron, a Freewill Baptist minister, presided at the services.

The chapel was filled to overflowing by those who came to pay their respects and to mourn at his casket, and those who wanted only to see a once strong, active, virile and fearless man now stilled by death. Among his mourners were a few peace officers who had known him and worked with him during his last career days around Ardmore: court officials, lawyers — and a younger breed of officers, who had known and admired him as boys.

His pallbearers were all Masons; members of the Order he loved so much, and about which he had written and published numerous little books and pamphlets. Masonic rites were performed at his graveside.

His greatest tribute can best be phrased in the words of his oldest daughter, Pearl Hutchins-Eaves:

"Papa loved everybody. He always tried to help everyone. Even the outlaws he had arrested liked him. One called to him once and said, 'Bob, go back! I don't want to shoot you, but I don't mean to go with you.' Papa kept coming, and the outlaw shot him in the flesh below the knee."

The Fifty Years
Record

Here, just about as chronological as possible, is the list of positions James Robert Hutchins held during his career as a peace officer.

Most of these years were spent as a Deputy United States Marshal, which commission he carried during most of his entire career. The number of years he spent in all other official capacities is not exactly known.

United States Posseman and Deputy Marshal under "Chief" Marshal John Carroll, United States Court of the Western District of Arkansas; Fort Smith, Arkansas.

United States Marshal under Jacob Yoes, "Chief" Marshal of the United States Court of the Western District of Arkansas; Fort Smith.

United States Deputy Marshal under J. J. Dickerson, "Chief" Marshal of the United States Court of the Eastern District of Texas; Paris, Texas.

United States Deputy Marshal under J. S. (Sheb) Williams,

"Chief" Marshal of the United States Court of the Eastern District of Texas; Paris.

United States Deputy Marshal under Marshal John S. Hammer of the United States Court of the Southern District of Indian Territory; Ardmore, I. T.

United States Deputy Marshal under Marshal Benjamin H. Colbert of the United States Court of the Southern District of Indian Territory; Ardmore, I. T.

United States Constable under Hosea Townsend, United States Judge of the Southern U.S. Judicial District of Indian Territory; Ardmore, I. T.

United States Deputy Marshal under Marshal Grosvenor A. Porter of the United States Court of the Southern District of Indian Territory; Ardmore, I. T.

United States Circulating Deputy Marshal under "Chief" Marshal Samuel G. Victor, All United States Courts of the Indian Territory; Ardmore, Muskogee, Sulphur, Pauls Valley, Purcell, McAlester and Tulsa.

Enforcement Officer and State Ranger under Governor Charles N. Haskell; Oklahoma City, Oklahoma.

Associate Deputy Sheriff, Sheriffs' Association of Oklahoma Oil Field Enforcement; Healdton, Ragtown and Ringling.

Chief of Police of Ardmore, Oklahoma (1915-1917); elected by popular vote in Ardmore, Oklahoma, city election.

Six-Shooter Guard for Jake L. Hamon and the Hamon Oil Company; Ardmore, Healdton and Wilson, Oklahoma.

Special Officer for E. P. & S. W. and G. H. & S. A. Railroads under government control; El Paso, Texas.

Special Narcotics Agent for Mexico by appointment by President Venustiano Carranza.

Deputy Sheriff of Hidalgo County; Lordsburg, New Mexico.

Deputy Sheriff of Grant County; Silver City, New Mexico.

Deputy Sheriff of Santa Fe County; Santa Fe, New Mexico.

Deputy Sheriff of Maricopa County; Phoenix, Arizona.

General Prohibition Agent, Division No. 15; El Paso, Texas; Santa Fe, New Mexico; Phoenix, Arizona; West Texas and Eastern California.

Deputy Sheriff of Val Verde County; Del Rio, Texas.

Inspector in Charge of Pecos High Bridge for Southern Pacific Railway Co. and U.S. government; 1924 to 1941.

Bibliography

Acknowledging the following list of references, which in some way touch upon the characters, incidents and other subjects in this career biography of James Robert Hutchins, this author does so in order to inform the reader of the sources, that the reader may read them, if he desires.

This list of various sources is not intended to corroborate and prove this biography necessarily, but to admit that this author is aware that they do exist, and that they have been read and considered.

In some cases, for logical reasons, the information contained in some of the bibliography that varies or disagrees with Mr. Hutchins' memoirs and this author's extensive research, is rejected. Careful deliberation has caused this author to conclude the conflicting sources erroneous; or the variance is too slight or too minor to the main point in question to give more than casual attention.

Books

Breihan, Carl W. *Younger Brothers*. San Antonio, Texas: The Naylor Company, 1961.

Clark, Joseph L. *A History of Texas, Land of Promise*. Dallas, Texas: D. C. Heath Company, 1939.

Croy, Homer. *He Hanged Them High*. New York, New York: Duell, Sloan and Pearce, 1952.

Croy, Homer. *The Last of the Great Outlaws*. New York, New York: Duell, Sloan and Pearce, 1956.

Dale, Edward Edverett and James B. Morrison. *Pioneer Judge, The Life of Robert L. Williams*. Cedar Rapids, Iowa: The Torch Press, 1958.

Dalton, Emmet and Jack Jungmeyer. *When the Daltons Rode*. Garden City, New York: The Sun Dial Press, Inc., 1931 and 1937.

Debo, Angie. *The Rise and Fall of the Choctaw Republic*. Norman, Oklahoma: University of Oklahoma Press, 1934.

Dewitz, Paul W. H., ed. *Noble Men of Indian Territory at the Beginning of the Twentieth Century — 1901 and 1905*. Muskogee, I. T.: Southwestern Historical Co., 1905.

Doublas, C. L. *Cattle Kings of Texas*. Dallas, Texas: The Book Craft — Published by Cecil Baugh, 1939.

Eaton, Frank and Eva Gillhouse. *Pistol Pete*. Boston, Massachusetts: Little, Brown and Company, 1952.

Fleischer, Nat and Sam Andre. *A Pictorial History of Boxing*. New York, New York: The Citadel Press, 1959.

Foster-Harris. *The Look of the Old West*. New York, New York: Bonanza Books, 1960.

Haley, J. Evetts. *Charles Goodnight, Cowman and Plainsman*. Norman, Oklahoma: University of Oklahoma Press, 1949.

Harkey, Dee. *Mean as Hell*. New York, New York: Signet Books, The American Library of World Literature, Inc., 1951 and 1955.

Horan, James D. *The Great American West*. New York, New York: Crown Publishers, Inc., 1959.

Horan, James D. and Paul Sann. *History of the Wild West*. New York, New York: Crown Publishers, Inc., 1954.

Horman, S. W., ed. by Frank L. Van Eaton. *Hell on the Border*. Fort Smith, Arkansas: Hell on the Border Publishing Co., 1953.

Houts, Marshall and James Mathers of Oklahoma. *From Gun to Gavel*. New York, New York: William Morrow and Company, Inc., 1954.

337

Lloyd Everett. *The Law West of the Pecos. The Story of Judge Roy Bean.* San Antonio, Texas: The Naylor Company, 1936; Eighth Printing, 1960.

Morris, Lerona Rosamond, ed. *Oklahoma Yesterday-Today-Tomorrow.* Guthrie, Oklahoma: Co-Operative Publishing Company, 1930.

Morrison, William Brown. *Military Camps and Posts of Oklahoma.* Oklahoma City, Oklahoma: Harlow Publishing Company, 1936.

O'Conner, Richard. *Pat Garrett.* New York, New York: Ace Books, Inc., by arrangement with Doubleday and Company, Inc., 1960.

Pruitt, Moman. *Moman Pruitt, Criminal Lawyer. Autobiography.* Oklahoma City, Oklahoma: Harlow Publishing Company.

Rascoe, Burton. *Belle Starr, The Bandit Queen.* New York, New York: Random House, 1941.

Roosevelt, Theodore. *The Rough Riders.* New York, New York: Signet Classic, The New York American Library of World Literature, Inc., 1961.

Shackleford, William Yancey. *Belle Starr, The Bandit Queen.* Girard, Kansas: Haldeman-Julius Publications, 1943.

Shirley, Glenn. *Heck Thomas — Frontier Marshal.* Philadelphia and New York: Chilton Company, Publishers, 1962.

Shirley, Glenn. *Six-Gun and Silver Star.* Albuquerque, New Mexico: University of New Mexico Press, 1955.

Sonnichaen, C. L. *Cowboys and Cattle Kings.* Norman, Oklahoma: University of Oklahoma Press, 1950.

Wellman, Paul I. *A Dynasty of Western Outlaws.* Garden City, New York: Doubleday and Company, Inc., 1961.

Williams, Thomas Benton. *The Soul of the Red Man.* Oklahoma City, Oklahoma: Privately Printed, 1937.

Magazines

The *American Legion Magazine,* May Issue, 1929.
Southern Pacific Bulletin, September Issue, 1936.

Sunday News Supplement Magazines

The *American Weekly,* May 25, 1947.
The *American Weekly,* June 29, 1947.
The *American Weekly,* August 8, 1948.

Newspapers

The files of *The Daily Ardmoreite;* Ardmore, Oklahoma, 1893-
1962.
The *Dallas Morning News;* Dallas, Texas, August 16, 1912.
The *Daily Oklahoman;* Oklahoma City, Oklahoma, August 18,
1912.
The *Wichita Falls Record News;* Wichita Falls, Texas, May 6,
1922.
The *St. Louis Post Dispatch;* St. Louis, Missouri, May 14, 1922.
The *El Paso Times;* El Paso, Texas, November 1, 1925.
The *Tulsa World;* Tulsa, Oklahoma, March 7, 1937.
The *Val Verde County Herald;* Del Rio, Texas, December 3,
1937.
The *Tulsa Daily World;* Tulsa, Oklahoma, January 23, 1946.
The *Daily Oklahoman;* Oklahoma City, Oklahoma, June 9, 1957.

Miscellaneous

Numerous letters and newspaper clippings — from newspapers unidentified — Mr. Hutchins had collected in connection
with his memoirs.

Government Sources

The National Archives and Records Service; Washington, D.C.
The Library of Congress; Washington, D.C.
The Oklahoma Historical Society; Oklahoma City, Oklahoma.